After my first reading of *A Concise Guide to Catholic Church Management*, I am more anxious to return to this very helpful book. Because of my many years in parish, organizational, and diocesan management, I am certain that the insights offered here will be helpful at every level of the Catholic Church. The book is practical and much more than a self-help guide. I highly recommend this new resource for Church managers.

Most Reverend Nicholas DiMarzio
Bishop of Brooklyn

The Vincentian Center for Church and Society at St. John's University has produced a book that is refreshingly reader-friendly; rooted in Gospel principles; and eminently practical for any priest, deacon, or lay minister entrusted with parochial leadership. Its pastoral/scriptural perspective makes it more than just another generic management manual about skills and techniques, but a guide specifically intended for Catholic leadership. Concepts are presented clearly, and chapters conclude with relevant reflection questions and activities, designed to develop and apply the ideas, concepts, and techniques presented.

Most Reverend William Francis Murphy
Bishop of Rockville Centre

When it comes to the fundamentals of Church management—especially at the parish level—this book is destined to become an indispensable resource. It is well-written, practical, theologically informed, and divided into easily referenced chapters.

Rev. Edward A. Malloy, C.S.C.
President Emeritus
University of Notre Dame

Quite valuable for both its pastoral perspective and its practical suggestions! A profoundly wise compilation of lived experience useful to both ordained and lay Church administrators, no matter how many years are notched to their credit. Reflection guides make it ideal for both personal and group use. Kudos to St. John's Vincentian Center for Church and Society!

Honora Remes, D.C.
Provincial
Daughters of Charity, East Central Province

D1446619

The authors have skillfully blended real-life ministry experiences with sound ecclesial insight to generate this resource suitable for anyone seeking to learn or improve fundamental Church management techniques.

Rev. William J. Lechnar
Director for Planning
Diocese of Greensburg

The most comprehensive guide available for both experienced and beginning Church leaders. This book is packed with timely and beneficial suggestions to deal with rapidly changing Church structures, personnel, and membership. It provides the equivalent of a full continuing education program for those serving in leadership positions, whether ordained or lay.

Katarina Schuth, O.S.F.
Endowed Chair for the Social Scientific Study of Religion
St. Paul Seminary School of Divinity
University of St. Thomas

This excellent book is a must-read for lay and ordained leaders faced with the challenging task of management in parishes today. From servant leadership to employment law and accounting procedures, it's all here.

Michael Brough
Director of Planning and Programs
National Leadership Roundtable on Church Management

In response to a common concern about the lack of financial and management training among the clergy and other Catholic leaders, the Vincentian Center for Church and Society is providing priests and other administrators with a valuable aid in navigating the management components of parish life. The formational focus of "priests in training" has been the spiritual dimension. The evolution and the complexities of the parish life call for new tools at the disposal of the parish priest. Now—along with the Lectionary, the Roman Missal, and the Code of Canon Law—we have another valuable tool in the pastoral arsenal for responding to the evolving landscape of Catholic ministry.

Rev. Richard Vega
President
National Federation of Priests' Councils

a concise guide to

Catholic Church Management

The Vincentian Center for Church and Society
St. John's University, New York

Larry W. Boone, PhD
Mary Ann Dantuono, JD
Margaret John Kelly, D.C., PhD
Brenda Massetti, PhD
James W. Thompson, EdD, CPA

Kevin E. McKenna, Series Editor

ave maria press AmP notre dame, indiana

◢ THE CONCISE GUIDE SERIES

The Concise Guide series, edited by Kevin E. McKenna, tackles questions of central importance for contemporary Catholicism. Each book in the series carefully outlines the issues, references the necessary documents, and sketches answers to pressing pastoral questions.

© 2010 by Ave Maria Press, Inc.

All rights reserved. No part of this book may be used or reproduced in any manner whatsoever, except in the case of reprints in the context of reviews, without written permission from Ave Maria Press®, Inc., P.O. Box 428, Notre Dame, IN 46556.

Founded in 1865, Ave Maria Press is a ministry of the Indiana Province of Holy Cross.

www.avemariapress.com

ISBN-10 1-59471-227-1   ISBN-13 978-1-59471-227-2

Cover and text design by John R. Carson.

Printed and bound in the United States of America.

Library of Congress Cataloging-in-Publication Data

A concise guide to Catholic Church management / the Vincentian Center for Church and Society; contributing authors, Larry W. Boone . . . [et al.].

    p. cm.

Includes bibliographical references and index.

ISBN-13: 978-1-59471-227-2 (pbk. : alk. paper)

ISBN-10: 1-59471-227-1 (pbk. : alk. paper)

1. Church management. 2. Catholic Church--Government. I. Boone, Larry W.

BX1803.C66 2010

254'.02--dc22

2010015461

In this year marking the three-hundred-fiftieth anniversary of the deaths of St. Vincent de Paul and St. Louise de Marillac, this book is dedicated to these two courageous innovators, organizational geniuses, and servant-leaders who continue to inspire individuals and influence institutions around the world.

CONTENTS

Preface

While management as a science is less than a century old, the pages of the New Testament are replete with examples of management expertise enhancing ministerial competence. To announce his ministry, Jesus opened the scriptures and quoted the prophet Isaiah:

> The Spirit of the Lord is upon me, because he has anointed me to bring glad tidings to the poor. He has sent me to proclaim liberty to captives and recovery of sight to the blind, to let the oppressed go free, and to proclaim a year acceptable to the Lord.
> —Luke 4:18–20

In this single act he established the model for mission-focused management and a "coming not to be served but to serve" leadership style. From that day until the gathering of his ministry team on Holy Thursday evening, Christ focused on the mission, inspired the vision, recruited key personnel, implemented a succession plan, and modeled the corporate culture that he desired. In that final staff meeting, he delegated responsibility to those whom he had recruited, motivated, served, and "formed" in love. He offered an organizational blueprint for all ages (see John 13–17).

The mission and servant leadership of Jesus remain relevant today, but demands on contemporary Church leaders have greatly expanded over the two millennia since he lived on this earth. Legislation, regulation, and even litigation are growing at an accelerating rate. These demands threaten all faith-based organizations, which are generally limited in resources and can't always afford additional personnel to meet expanding expectations, external requirements, and unfunded mandates. The demand for organizational transparency and accountability has also increased geometrically. Thus, greater knowledge and more efficient oversight are being demanded of Church leaders and managers even when resources are contracting.

Furthermore, in this new millennium, there is an increasing expectation that leaders in Church institutions and organizations will have the same level of expertise and will employ managerial skills comparable to commercial enterprises. The high performance standard that Jesus consistently set forth as the goal for the stewards of Gospel values has remained the same. However, calls for meeting that standard have become increasingly more public, complicated, insistent, and universal. Lapses in good management (disappearance of funds, the hiring of persons without appropriate scrutiny, or the deterioration of a faith community into interest groups) can cause not only embarrassment but deeply damaging scandal to the Church. Reputational risk must be avoided just as carefully as financial risk and quality shortfalls.

Today then, bishops, pastors, and other administrators in Church organizations must be both inspiring leaders and successful managers. They must balance budgets larger than many small businesses; inspire generous monetary support; maintain buildings and campuses; monitor investments; develop realistic planning documents; make good hiring decisions; implement just salary and benefits programs; monitor compliance at multiple levels; assure effective communication systems; motivate the sympathetic, apathetic, and cynical within the organization; avoid litigation; meet the service expectations of very diverse publics; preserve the nonprofit tax status; and perform a host of other tasks. Large or small, each parish, diocese, and Church agency demands responsible oversight of personnel—the greatest resource—ranging from entry-level workers to licensed professionals, each of whom has individual motivational and developmental needs.

The Contemporary Challenge

The teaching of the Second Vatican Council called for greater participation of the laity in Church leadership and accelerated the need for management training for both clergy and lay staff of all

Church organizations. The priest shortage brings priests to parish leadership with considerably less experience than in the past. Promotion from within also catapults persons from service positions to management roles. Staff workers move to supervision, teachers become principals, social workers become agency administrators, associate pastors become pastors, seminary professors become bishops, all within quite short timeframes. While some seek out formal management training, most adopt a "trial and error" approach, a very inefficient method that saps morale, threatens self-confidence, and drains resources. Sadly, it can also encourage defensive behaviors that block communication and inhibit community-building, which is so essential in Church organizations.

The Purpose of This Concise Guide

Those challenges are the reason for this publication, which has evolved from over ten years of St. John's University faculty offering management education to pastors, seminarians, and other Church managers. This concise guidebook provides an overview of management theory and presents specific management skills to complement already acquired theological knowledge, pastoral abilities, and specialized competencies. It is offered as one means to assist managers within the Church to fulfill their stewardship responsibilities with competence and accountability as well as with satisfaction. While the book grew out of programs in parish management, and much of the focus is on parishes, the material is relevant to all Church organizations and can be accommodated to a variety of Church structures and services.

Structurally, each chapter of the guide begins with a statement of key concepts related to the topic that is then developed both thematically and practically. The activities section at the end of each chapter provides the opportunity to apply the learned materials to real situations. While the various chapters contribute to an integrated whole, each chapter is complete in itself and can be read in any order, thus increasing its value as a tool for the busy manager.

Most of the charts, tables, and sample worksheets are available for free download in 8.5"x11" format. Go to avemariapress.com, search under the book's title, then click "Downloads."

This guide is not designed to make one an accountant, a paralegal, a human resource specialist, a planning expert, or genius communicator. Rather, it is designed to help the reader ask the right questions, understand the basics of specialized vocabularies, and develop proven skills. It also heightens sensitivity to the elements of organizational health and responsible stewardship. This guide is offered in the hope that it will help readers gain deepened confidence, increased productivity, and greater satisfaction in the noble task of ministering *to, within,* and *for* the people of God.

The authors are grateful to the many pastors, beginning with John Cardinal O'Connor, and Church managers who have encouraged the publication of these materials, as well as to the many priests, seminarians, and lay persons who have participated in seminars and shared their experiences. We are grateful to Ave Maria Press and especially to Eileen M. Ponder and Fr. Kevin E. McKenna for their encouragement and direction. Gratitude is expressed to the authors who over the years not only have taught well, but have listened well to their students so that their work meets the dual standard of relevance and practice. Special thanks are offered as well to Rosemarie McTigue, executive secretary, Vincentian Center for Church and Society, who patiently and carefully managed the various iterations of the material; to Kathryn Shaughnessy of Instructional Services, whose technological expertise expedited collaboration; and to Natalie Boone, whose generous help and sense of humor lightened many tasks.

CHAPTER 1

Leadership

Margaret John Kelly, D.C., PhD

> If anyone wishes to be first, he shall be the last of all
> and the servant of all.
>
> —Mark 9:35
>
> Just so, the Son of Man did not come to be served
> but to serve.
>
> —Matthew 20:28

Key Concepts

1. Scripture offers many types of leadership and reveals Jesus as the servant-leader par excellence.

2. Servant leadership is the Christian approach to organizational tasks, interpersonal relationships, formation, and community-building.

3. Robert Greenleaf popularized the scriptural concept of servant leadership and has influenced both religious and secular organizations as well as the academic management community for several decades.

4. Leadership and management functions are distinct but related and exert mutual influence.

5. Theorists and practitioners provide varying profiles of the successful leader in both the religious and business sectors, but they generally cite vision, self-awareness, empathy, passion, integrity, and credibility as essential qualities for both venues.

6. While certain personal traits prepare and assist one to develop as a leader, much of what is considered effective leadership can be acquired through ongoing study and continuing effort.

Introduction

One of the most persistent questions raised throughout history has been the nature-nurture influence on the development of human persons. Does nature (genetic inheritance) or nurture (environment and opportunity) determine one's abilities and life activities? Historians, biographers, anthropologists, sociologists, and psychologists have raised this question in terms of leadership and have probed the lives and performance of personalities as diverse as Stalin and Mother Teresa. The precise degree of influence each factor exerts on an individual's leadership ability will always remain elusive. However, there is general agreement that while some persons appear to have a natural propensity to be leaders even from early childhood days, there is no one personality type or a typical age when the leader emerges fully prepared for the role. On the contrary, leaders tend to experience a series of rises and falls in their careers, especially those who have risen too quickly or have not "earned" stripes. It is also generally accepted that, given the desire to lead and a willingness to learn how to lead, many have grown into the knowledge, skills, confidence, and wisdom demanded of leaders no matter the field of endeavor or scope of activity.

Others have questioned whether there is or should be a difference in the leadership practiced within secular and religious groups. While overly simplistic, there has been a tendency to identify soft human-relations skills with religious leaders and the harder skills of productivity and profit-making with business leaders. However, in recent decades those perceived differences have diminished greatly as religious leaders put more emphasis on structures and systems and business leaders focus on the human, personal aspects of motivation and satisfaction. Also during that time, the traditional sharp distinction between leadership as "doing the right things" (effectiveness) and management as "doing things right" (operational efficiency) has been challenged because organizational success requires mutuality and integration of both. It is interesting that during that same period, the business world converted its off-site "meetings" to "retreats" and began to write and speak of "workplace spirituality" and "doing good while doing well." At the same time, some religious institutions replaced the Gospel language of "ministry" (administration and administrator) with the corporate vocabulary of "chief executive officer" as they also struggled with "acting business-like" or "becoming a business."

Servant Leadership

Within this shifting context, a small book appeared in 1970 that related leadership to one's character and one's desire to serve. Robert Greenleaf's seminal essay, "The Servant as Leader," offered a unique and holistic approach to the nature of leadership and the behaviors distinguishing good leadership. Religious groups were early adopters of this new quasi-religious approach because of its scriptural value of service, its call to personal transformation, and its emphasis on community. Many in the business world were slower to join the swell because some corporate leaders thought the "servant" approach was "upside down" or "soft," lacking the rigor and control required in the competitive world. However, in time many came to understand that being "a gentle and humble servant" was not the same as being weak. Greenleaf offered a throwback to the wisdom of St. Francis de Sales, who reminded his friends that honey will always draw more bees than vinegar. Greenleaf and Francis de Sales, despite dramatic differences in their historical periods, vocations, and styles, understood that interest in others and affirmation laced with challenge or challenge marked by affirmation will enlist others to advance the vision. Both recognized that the servant-leader frees and engages others while the dominant leader deadens motivation and freezes progress.

Today, there is considerable agreement that Greenleaf's approach of "servant as leader" and "servant leadership" draws on and develops the best within individuals and within organizations, whether they are religious or commercial. In some affluent corporate settings where the trappings of worldly success are very apparent, Greenleaf has become a guru. His people-growing and community-building tenets are admired and imitated. Also, over the years, academics, practitioners, and consultants in both leadership and management have not only expressed respect for Greenleaf's work but have built on his insights. Greenleaf himself developed a whole organization and industry on the concept of servant leadership.

Today, there also is significant agreement across the for–profit and nonprofit, and the religious and secular sectors that an organization's leadership quality and its organizational performance are directly related. Leadership accounts for the difference between success and failure, however defined in financial, quality service, or growth terms. Workers are willing to follow and carry their share of responsibility, but they also expect a clear direction in which all can walk together. Vision is the role of the leader.

Biblical Images of Leadership

In introducing "servant leadership," Greenleaf was not inventing something new but rather applying a scriptural model to the contemporary organization. He was fond of reminding people that "service," "serve," and "servant" appear over thirteen hundred times in the Bible. Indeed, Jesus chose to articulate his own mission as simply service: "Just so, the Son of Man did not come to be served but to serve and to give his life as a ransom for many" (Mt. 20:28). In that brief statement, vision, mission, and method are aligned and accessible. It is helpful to remember in this regard that Jesus' original workforce was probably no more or no less talented than the ones available in the Church today. Because he modeled the behaviors (habits of acting) inherent in service leadership, he facilitated both the education and formation of his staff. It is only when the rhetoric and praxis are congruent and integrated that followers take the leap of trust and join their lot with the leader's.

The Old Testament reads as a textbook of leadership styles as we move through the epic experiences of Moses, David, Solomon, Joshua, Jonah, Esther, and so many others. We meet the reticent and the ambitious, the arrogant and the humble, the negotiating and compliant, the victorious and the vanquished. The New Testament is rich with other archetypes like Herod, Pilate, Nicodemus, Peter, Joseph, Paul, Mary, the Samaritan woman, and Tabitha. Those interested in leadership will find Jesus' individualized responses to human need and his organizational commentaries both compelling and practical.

The gospels show Jesus as the servant-leader par excellence, advocating vision rather than structure, service rather than power, persuasion rather than control, team participation rather than individual performance, and collaboration rather than competition. John the Baptist offers an interesting example as he moves from servant-leader preparing the way of the Lord to servant-follower acknowledging that "he must increase; I must decrease" (Jn 3:30). They also teach us much about the operational aspects of servant leadership. Christ called his disciples to put the good of the other before one's own good. He taught them that a shared vision gives direction and unites disparate people in a common mission. He demonstrated the need for ongoing formation as he utilized direct instruction, encouragement, and guidance as well as an occasional reprimand blending firmness and kindness. He reminded them that motivations wither and die if not occasionally stirred up, so they had to learn to be strong-hearted to strengthen the weak-hearted. He challenged them to be "prudent as serpents" and "simple as doves," a challenge as paradoxical as the concept of servant-leader itself. At the interpersonal level, Jesus mediated disputes among his followers because he knew that competition born of personal ambition is destructive. He taught the necessity and method of drawing out the gifts of others and investing these talents wisely. He recommended responsible planning, telling stories of building one's house on a firm foundation, assuring sufficient storage space for harvests, and securing adequate fuel for the inevitable pre-dawn vigils.

Application of Servant-Leader Theory

Greenleaf's appropriation of the Gospel message of "service" has met with great success and exerted great influence in religious and secular circles. The simplicity of the teachings has resonated in people of various ages and cultures. Basically, Greenleaf presented leadership not as the source of power, authority, control, or dominance but as an attitude and perspective about the self, the other, and the meaning of life. Like Jesus, he defined servant leadership more as a *way of being than a way of doing*. He believed that by first learning to follow well, the servant-leader acquired "habits" (ways of being with and for others), or what ethicists would call "virtues." Emanating from self-awareness and social consciousness, these other-centered personal habits translate into positive organizational behaviors. They coalesce into a distinctive posture that allows one to be both leader-servant and servant-leader at one and the same time. From this dual position, the questions of "For whom do I work?" or "Whom do I serve?" and "Why do I work?" or "For what purpose do I serve?" are always present to keep one on track and focused on the vision.

Greenleaf's relational and communal emphasis is especially appropriate for faith-based organizations that have community as both their means and end. Both Greenleaf and Steven Covey (*Seven Habits of Effective People*) recognized that the goal of servant leadership is to institutionalize servant habits or virtues (behaviors). Both also cautioned that these will only be institutionalized if the leader "leads" with a compelling vision, sets clear behavioral expectations, and serves as an authentic practitioner of the values proclaimed. Greenleaf further claimed that when servanthood becomes the shared goal and experience of all the workers, the institution becomes a servant to itself and to the community. This "servant institution" is really a role and witness definition of the parish, the Catholic hospital, the university, or shelter in any geographic setting. The concept is also at the heart of *Ex Corde Ecclesiae*, in which John Paul II encouraged Catholic universities, with their vast intellectual and material resources, "to be in service" within the greater Church.

The Core Values of the Servant-Leader

What led Greenleaf to develop this concept that has gained such reception and has dominated the organizational landscape for these past decades? In a college course called "Sociology of the Labor Problem" he accepted the challenge of his professor to make the world a better place. This professor, neither dynamic nor charismatic (traits generally but falsely associated with leadership) but a quiet, elderly gentleman, insisted that social change occurs only when persons within institutions, not outside of them, choose to make the institutions forces for the public good. Greenleaf accepted the challenge and became such an internal and external force during his own business career with American Telephone and Telegraph. The professor's advice rings true today. A few theoretical passages from Greenleaf will illustrate his penetrating knowledge of human nature and the wisdom of servant leadership.

> The servant-leader is servant first. It begins with the natural feeling that one wants to serve, to serve *first*. That conscious choice brings one to aspire to lead. In that awareness two things emerge, the desire to serve others and a desire to serve a purpose or goal beyond themselves.
>
> —*Servant Leadership*, p. 7

> That person (one who chooses to serve first) is sharply different from one who is leader *first*, perhaps because of the need to assuage an unusual power drive or to acquire material possessions. For such it will be a later choice to serve—after leadership is established. The *leader-first* and the *servant-first* are two extreme types. . . . The difference manifests itself in the care taken by the servant-first to make sure that other peoples' highest-priority

needs are being served. The best test but difficult to administer is: Do those served grow as persons? Do they, while being served, become healthier, wiser, freer, more autonomous, more likely themselves to become servants? And what is the effect on the less privileged in society; will they benefit, or at least, not be further deprived?

—*Servant Leadership*, pp. 13–14

The leader always knows what the direction is and can articulate it for any who are unsure. By clearly stating and restating the goal, the leader gives certainty and purpose to others who may have difficulty in achieving it for themselves."

—*Servant Leadership*, p. 15

But if one is a servant, either leader or follower, one is always searching, listening, expecting that a better wheel for these times is in the making. It may emerge any day.

—*Servant Leadership*, p. 9

A fresh critical look is being taken at the issues of power and authority, and people are beginning to learn, however haltingly, to relate to one another in less coercive and more creatively supporting ways. A new moral principle is emerging, which holds that the only authority deserving one's allegiance is that which is freely and knowingly granted by the led to the leader in response to, and in proportion to, the clearly evident servant stature of the leader.

—*Servant Leadership*, p. 10

Personal Behaviors of the Servant-Leader

Throughout the 1970s in corporate boardrooms and in church meetings, Greenleaf elaborated on the behaviors practiced by the servant-leader. These grow out of the basic convictions of the dignity of the human person and the respect that is owed to each person because of that dignity and his or her community desires. While the following distillation is an injustice to Greenleaf, it captures the servant-leader.

The servant-leader:
- listens well and seeks to understand the other;
- uses language that encourages the imagination of others;
- accepts the role of "seeker" and searcher for truth;
- withdraws regularly to renew self;
- uses power of persuasion, not coercion;
- tries to create opportunity for others;
- seeks to remediate organizational flaws from the inside;
- adopts attitude of solution-finding rather than assigning blame in difficult situations;
- deals with persons as individuals with unique talents, not as functions;
- accepts others and empathizes with them;
- senses the unknowable and foresees the foreseeable;
- practices foresight and has a good sense of right timing;
- stays aware of the environment both physical and psychological;
- conceptualizes what "can be" and communicates it well;
- keeps the vision at the center of all activity.

Models of the Servant-Leader

Consistent with his behavioral and role-model emphases, Greenleaf uses examples from the ambit of religious conviction and civil society to illustrate these qualities. A few examples of awareness, foresight, timing, and persuasion will show the enfleshed concepts. He used the story of the woman taken in adultery to show Jesus' acceptance of and trust in others as well as his full awareness of the environment. The situation led Jesus to decide to assist the woman but not to engage in any verbal attacks or defensive tactics. He chose, rather, to awaken the individual consciences of the elders and brought them to see themselves alongside the woman in the sinful human community, with no right to accuse.

Greenleaf chose John Woolman to demonstrate the power of vision and "one-at-a-time" leadership. John Woolman, the quiet abolitionist, traveled the East Coast seeking to persuade his Quaker associates of the evil of slavery. His individual converts to racial justice amalgamated and resulted in the Quakers being the first religious group to take up the abolitionist cause. Greenleaf presented Thomas Jefferson as the self-aware and patient servant-leader who has a clear vision of what is needed, knows his own abilities, and prepares well but waits for the appropriate moment for action. When others joined the revolutionary army, Jefferson chose to withdraw to Virginia because he foresaw that if he could draft statutes for the Virginia legislature during the war, these could become the foundation for the much-hoped-for federal constitution. Greenleaf describes N. F. S. Grundtvig, who saw the peasant class in Denmark in need and recognized the opportunity to work for systemic change. Passionate about social and economic progress, he initiated a creative educational system that in just a few generations raised up the peasant class of Denmark. Each of these examples reveal the servant-leader providing individual service but also creating "servant institutions" (Greenleaf, *Servant Leadership*, 28–34).

Characteristics of Servant-Leaders

The early success of his concepts caused Greenleaf to elaborate core beliefs and present servant leadership from both the conceptual and implementation perspectives. The latter stage is more important, even though the first is foundational. These descriptors, indicators, or organizational virtues require of the leader enormous measures of passion, commitment, creativity, self-restraint, wisdom, and courage. Implementation calls servant-leaders to:

- tell the vision constantly and promote it in such a way that others want to play a part in actualizing it;

- regularly assess self-motivation and one's impact on others;

- create organizational climates where respect and trust are palpable and there is consistency between talk about the core values and the lived experience;

- help others to see their work as vocation or call to a higher good and not just employment for survival;

- call forth the gifts of others rather than show their own;

- assist others to find their own future and follow it;

- engage and empower others to pursue personal transformation;

- lead others to extend personal transformation into the social realm;

- remain curious about new ideas and things;

- live with integrity (self-awareness and truth);

- be committed to continuous personal learning and growth;

- master the heart and head elements of following and leading;

- have the courage to pursue the common good in good times and bad.

Leadership Styles

These expectations of the servant-leader elude the categories in the traditional three-fold classification of leadership styles presented by many organizational theorists:

1. Authoritarian (autocratic)

2. Participative (democratic)

3. Laissez-faire (totally delegative)

For special situations it may be appropriate to adopt the authoritarian or laissez-faire style, but the servant-leader would seldom call on these. Rather, conscious of the value of each person, servant-leaders rely on the participative style, which respects the individual, calls out the talents of each, strengthens community, and provides a structure for ongoing assessment and recommitment.

Servant leadership does not abuse power, as is possible with the authoritarian "boss" model; nor does it abdicate authority, as in the laissez-faire model. Rather it respects subsidiarity and encourages corporate responsibility. The aware servant-leader depends on others so that he or she is always assessing situations and personnel potential. This maintains flexibility and makes adaptability possible—what has come to be called "the nimble organization." Camus, a writer of great interest to Greenleaf, understood this when he advised that one should not walk ahead because he might not follow, should not walk behind because he might not lead, but should walk beside him. The servant-leader stands equal to and close to servant-followers in a circular rather than pyramidal relationship.

Commentators on Greenleaf

Forty years after Greenleaf's first work, one still finds the major writers on leadership and management relating their own particular insights to Greenleaf's basic theory. The authors of *Reflections on Leadership: How Robert K. Greenleaf's Theory of Servant Leadership Influenced Today's Top Management Thinkers* (1995) and *Insights on Leadership* (1998) form a veritable Who's Who of twentieth-century management experts. Writers across the business and religious sectors find Greenleaf's work rich in inspiration and eminently applicable to the twenty-first century. Several have commented that servant leadership remains more relevant today than ever before. It offers a holistic approach at this point in history when interest in spiritual subjects is growing, the "bottom line" philosophy has proven destructive to many companies and individuals, many are looking for more humane work environments, technology is gaining ascendancy over the human person, and many seek greater meaning in their work and more integration in their lives. Here are just a few of the tributes or interpretations offered by current experts in the field.

Thomas Bausch, an authority on effective leadership in the Catholic Church, wrote this of Greenleaf:

> Just as the large organization, properly implemented, that Greenleaf loved allowed a specialization that grew people in community, so the technological and organizational development of a new century can do the same—if harnessed by the true servant-leader committed to the growth of all involved with the organization. The spiritualization of work in no way calls for a soft approach to leadership. The servant-leader is in no way relieved of the ever harder options facing those in leadership. The characteristics of foresight and reflection will be demanded.
>
> —*Insights on Leadership*, p. 243

In this regard it is helpful to remember the Native American wisdom that in decision-making one must consider the effect of each choice on the next seven generations.

Ken Blanchard, a professor of management, offers a pragmatic appreciation of Greenleaf:

> My aim in talking about servant leadership has always been to encourage managers to move from the traditional "direct, control, and supervise" approach to the roles of cheerleader, encourager, listener, and facilitator. In the past, managers have emphasized judgment, criticism, and evaluation rather than providing the support and encouragement that people need to be at their best.
>
> —*Insights on Leadership*, p. 21

Stephen Covey writes in "Servant Leadership from the Inside Out":

> I have found Greenleaf's teaching on servant leadership to be so enormously inspiring, so uplifting so ennobling. The idea of servant leadership will continue to dramatically increase in its relevance. There is growing awareness and consciousness about it around the world. The only way you get empowerment is through high-trust culture and through an empowerment philosophy that turns bosses into servants and coaches.
>
> —*Insights on Leadership*, p. xi

Kouzes and Posner cite the reciprocal relationship between those who lead and those who follow and identify credibility as central to the cultivation and maintenance of such relationships. In their acclaimed books *The Leadership Challenge* and *Credibility,* they refer to credibility as the foundation of leadership. "If you don't believe in the messenger, you won't believe the message"(*Credibility* 33). "Credibility is about how leaders earn the trust and confidence of their constituents. It's about what people demand of their leaders as a prerequisite to willingly contribute their hearts, minds, bodies, and souls. It's about the actions leaders must take to intensify constituents' commitment" (*The Leadership Challenge*, xiii).

Kouzes and Posner recommend thinking and speaking of "we," not "I," and claim that "We become more powerful when we give our power away" (*Credibility*, 284). They also claim that leaders must be perceived by followers as honest, forward-looking, competent, and inspiring.

Catholic Social Thought and Servant Leadership

Greenleaf spoke out of his scriptural knowledge and Quaker culture. It is possible to read Greenleaf through the lens of Catholic social teaching as well. There are several parallels between the seven major themes of Catholic social teaching articulated by the United States Conference of Catholic Bishops in their 1998 document, *Sharing Catholic Social Teaching,* and the values expressed in the servant-leadership literature.

Themes of Catholic Social Teaching

- Life and dignity of the human person
- Call to family, community, and participation
- Rights and responsibilities
- Option for the poor and vulnerable
- Dignity of work and the rights of workers
- Solidarity
- Care for God's creation

The dignity of the human person, the call to community and participation, rights and responsibilities, dignity of work and the rights of workers, and solidarity, are intrinsic to servant leadership. The option for the poor and care for God's creation are consequences of active reflection and attention to others, which is fundamental to servant leadership. In addition to the parallels between the bishops' statement and Greenleaf's approach, there is also congruence between Greenleaf and those social justice writers who construct a four-pillared approach to social justice: dignity of the human person, the common good, subsidiarity, and solidarity. The first two are the ends and the second two are the means to being a "servant-institution." They also are the foundation for businesses to live with authenticity, corporate responsibility, and accountability.

Conclusion

Servant leadership offers a model that is accessible to all and able to be implemented in various organizational situations. It is especially appropriate for Catholic institutions and organizations, whose mission is to carry on the work of Jesus. At its core is respect for the human person and the dignity of all work. A good metaphor for leadership within the Church is found at St. Peter's Square at the Vatican. The passionate, dynamic, culturally sophisticated, and self-aware Paul stands next to the impetuous, brash, earthy, penitent Peter. Peter—cowardly at the time of Christ's passion and death—emerges after Pentecost as the stalwart leader of The Way. Paul—on the other hand—committed to righteousness, converted from being a divider and destroyer of people into one who stressed the obligation of "mutual up-building" in the one Body of Christ. In his writings, Paul leaves us a prolific record of his leadership efforts within his diverse communities. Peter left a very small literary record, but the Acts of the Apostles chronicles his courage, conviction, collegiality, and credibility in a very hostile environment. These massive but mute figures standing before the parish church of the world speak loudly of servant leadership, its unity and its universality in Christ, The Way, The Truth, and The Life who came "not to be served, but to serve" even to death.

Exercises

1. Reflect on your past experiences and identify one person with whom you have worked and consider a very effective leader. Cite the qualities that you think made him or her successful. Then choose one pastor or supervisor to whom you have reported whose performance was not so effective, and identify the qualities that you think detracted from his or her success as a servant-leader to you.

2. Select a leader figure from the Bible, such as Moses, Joshua, John the Baptist, Peter, Paul, Esther, Tabitha, the woman at the well, Pilate, or Herod, and submit them to the servant-leader test by reflecting on their credibility and their ability to engage others. If one of them asked you to coach him or her for a while, what would you advise? If you had been alive, would you have been inspired to follow her or him? Why? Share your reflection with a colleague.

3. Make a list of the servant-leadership traits presented in this chapter. Identify the traits to which you can lay claim, and cite a particular event in which you practiced servant leadership. If it is feasible, ask a colleague to cite the three traits where you seem to have servant-leader competence and two where you need to place more effort. Establish a leadership development goal for yourself for the next three months.

BIBLIOGRAPHY

Alford, Helen, O.P., and Michael J. Naughton. *Managing as if Faith Mattered*. Notre Dame: University of Notre Dame Press, 2001.

Bausch, Thomas. "Servant-Leaders Making Human New Models of Work and Organization." In Spears, *Insights on Leadership*, 230–245.

Blanchard, Ken. "Servant-Leadership Revisited." In Spears, *Insights on Leadership*, 21–28.

Collins, Jim. "Level 5 Leadership: The Triumph of Humility and Fierce Resolve." *Harvard Business Review*, January 2001, 19–28.

Covey, Stephen R. "Servant-leadership from the Inside Out." In Spears, *Insights on Leadership*, xi–xviii.

Drucker, Peter F. *The Effective Executive: The Definitive Guide to Getting the Right Things Done.* New York: Harper Collins, 2006.

Greenleaf, Robert K. *The Servant as Leader.* Indianapolis: The Robert K. Greenleaf Center, 1970.

———. *Servant Leadership: A Journey into The Nature of Legitimate Power and Greatness.* New York: Paulist Press, 1977.

Kouzes, James M., and Barry Z. Posner. *Credibility.* San Francisco: Jossey-Bass, 2002.

———. *The Leadership Challenge.* San Francisco: Jossey-Bass, 2003.

Phelps, Owen. *The Catholic Vision of Leading Like Jesus: Introducing S3 Leadership—Servant, Steward, Shepherd.* Huntington, IN: Our Sunday Visitor, 2009.

Senge, Peter M. *The Fifth Discipline: The Art and Practice of the Learning Organization.* New York: Doubleday, 1990.

Sofield, Loughlan, and Donald H. Kuhn. *The Collaborative Leader.* Notre Dame: Ave Maria Press, 1995.

Spears, Larry C., ed. *Reflections on Leadership: How Robert K. Greenleaf's Theory of Servant-Leadership Influenced Today's Top Management Thinkers.* New York: John Wiley and Sons, 1995.

———. *Insights on Leadership: Service, Stewardship, Spirit and Servant-Leadership.* New York: John Wiley and Sons, 1998.

CHAPTER 2

Fundamentals of Management

Brenda Massetti, PhD

Since we have gifts that differ according to the grace given to us, let us exercise them: if prophecy, in proportion to the faith; if ministry, in ministering; if one is a teacher, in teaching; if one exhorts, in exhortation; if one contributes, in generosity; if one is over others, with diligence; if one does acts of mercy, with cheerfulness.

—Romans 12:6–8

Key Concepts

1. Management at its most basic meaning is achieving goals *with* and *through* others.

2. Managers are principally responsible for the success or failure of an organization whether it be a parish, Church agency, or a commercial enterprise.

3. Unless an organization has a vision and clear goals that are SMART, there can be no management.

4. Management encompasses the four basic and interrelated functions of planning, organizing, influencing, and controlling.

5. The skill types for management are technical, human, and conceptual, with the human always being essential and the conceptual growing in importance as one moves up the organizational ladder.

6. Creativity can be developed, and it can enhance managerial effectiveness individually and collectively.

7. Managerial resources are categorized as human, capital, monetary, material, information, and time.

8. Management needs to be measured by both effectiveness and efficiency standards.

Introduction

As Richard Templar so aptly points out in his book *The Rules of Management*, few, if any, of us grow up wishing to become managers. However, we learn quickly as adults the powerful role management actually plays in our lives. Any organization, whether a parish, a Church agency, a doctor's office, or a nation, succeeds or fails based on the actions of management. Just think of a time, for example, when you genuinely enjoyed something as simple as having dinner in a restaurant. Perhaps the hostess was welcoming, the waiter was attentive, the menu choices were interesting, the atmosphere was appealing, the food was spectacular, and the bill was reasonable. *Successful* management was at the core of that experience. Someone worked hard to bring those components together at just the right moments to produce an enjoyable dining experience. And what is even more fascinating about the power of management is the extent to which such experiences impact one's life beyond the event. Not only was something as mundane as your desire to dine out affected by that experience, but your sense of value, your belief in the way things ought to be, and your expectations of how humans should interact were also shaped by the well-placed efforts of that restaurant manager. Moreover, the manager influenced the values, beliefs, and expectations of the employees involved in producing that experience.

So, whether one is born to be a manager, chooses to become one, or simply has the role thrust upon him or her, by becoming a manager one acquires the power to directly and indirectly affect the lives of others. However subtle the impacts of management may seem for a given experience, they create lasting impressions. For example, consider a *bad* dining experience. Perhaps the host seemed rude, the waiter indifferent, the food unattractive, or the atmosphere dreary. Fundamentally, that experience too was the result of management, but this time a management *failure* was at the core. Whether improper training, material use, and/or system support are touted as culprits, managers are always ultimately responsible for any and all failings. Moreover, since negative experiences tend to be more memorable, one bad experience can easily lead to a lasting, unenthusiastic impression of the service provider.

Management ultimately impacts not only how we feel about a given organization but also how well that organization can produce positive outcomes. Defined generally as the process of working with and through people and other organizational resources to achieve goals, management is in some way fundamentally connected to everything an organization accomplishes or fails to accomplish. Whether a restaurant, a hospital, a shelter, a Wall Street investment firm, or a parish, organizations that are well managed thrive while those that are poorly managed falter. Consequently, any organization stands to gain as those within it enhance their abilities to manage—the purpose of this book.

The Practice of Management

Management is an extremely challenging process, requiring patience, financial wisdom, human skills, and well-developed organizational ability (Templar). However, the reward for becoming a better manager more than outweighs the effort required. Good managers are not only respected, admired, and followed by those around them but are also comfortable, confident, and content with their ability to improve their organizations, and thus have high satisfaction levels.

While some people naturally possess the skills required to be a successful manager, most need some degree of training. The following sections present the fundamentals needed to be a successful manager. First, goals and goal setting are discussed. Then the functions of management are defined. Next, the requisite skill sets and resource options are described. Finally, the measures used to assess managerial performance are defined and discussed.

Managerial Goals

By definition, a *goal* is "the state of affairs that a plan is intended to achieve and that (when achieved) terminates the behavior intended to achieve it" (thefreedictionary.com). While somewhat complex in nature, this definition offers valuable insights into the powerful role goals play in the management process. Basically, goals serve as both beginning and ending points for managers. Without a goal to guide action, there is no cause for management. Why deploy the troops and expend all that effort for nothing? Once a goal is set, management can begin. If well-constructed, the goal soon becomes the main cause for management. In general, a well-determined goal is one designed to bring about a positive result for a critical challenge. How many of us continue to strive for goals that seem trivial and uninteresting? Moreover, how many of us continue to strive for any goal without consistent support and guidance? Consequently, without management keeping organizations focused on important goals, it is unlikely that many would be reached.

Interestingly, once a goal has been achieved, the cause for management comes to an end. Why keep climbing the mountain once you have reached the top? Hence, in order to stay useful, management must continually create new goals to replace those that have been achieved. The challenge is to ensure that the new goal is as motivating and important as the one just achieved. In other words, to maintain the momentum of success, the next goal often matters more than the one before it. This is the challenge of management.

Managerial Goals in Practice

Gene Donohue, from Top Achievement, has developed a useful acronym that both conveys the value of goals and offers guidance on how best to make them. He argues that they must be SMART:

> *Specific:* answers the "Six Ws" of who, what, where, when, which, and why
> *Measurable:* must be quantifiable and observable
> *Attainable:* must be important to all involved so that necessary effort is put forth
> *Realistic:* must be something all involved can achieve
> *Timely:* must be time-conditioned for end of achievement

Consider *if* and *how* the following goals illustrate the SMART method:

1. Increase enrollment in the parish school for fall to assure a break-even budget.

2. By September 2012, use the Harrison bequest to replace current ramp access for the handicapped with an elevator on the east side of the church to accommodate both individuals and funeral needs of the parish.

3. By Spring 2011, pastor and pastoral council will present plans (architectural and financial) to diocesan council requesting permission to build a community center on parish property so as to expand space for religious education and social activities, and have the center operative eighteen months after diocesan approval.

The second goal is the most SMART. The first one is not expressly measurable or timely, while the third one is not clearly attainable or realistic because it is actually multiple goals rolled into one. One goal is developing and presenting the architectural and financial plans to the diocesan council, another is gaining the approval of the council, and yet another is actually creating the community center.

Managerial Functions

Whether managing a soup kitchen, a multinational conference on poverty eradication, or simply managing to get out of bed in the morning, the management process encompasses four basic functions: *planning, organizing, influencing,* and *controlling* (Certo and Certo). Each has a critical role to play in managerial success and, because each relies upon the other, all must be done well. The purpose behind the functions is to establish processes and procedures to help the organization reach its goals.

Planning is considered the primary function of management, as it starts the overall process. In its simplest conception, planning is nothing more than picking a future. It is the function where the leader-managers take their visions for organizational success and articulate them clearly enough for everyone to not only see the same future but also to accept the organization's envisioned place in that future. Depending on the organization, the act of planning can be more or less formal, more or less habitual, and more or less participative. Some managers create planning departments or committees, others periodically have planning retreats, and still others keep their visions to themselves. Planning is complete when there is a believable vision for the future and a clear idea of where the organization is to be in that future. This aspect of management is more fully treated in another book in this series, *A Concise Guide to Pastoral Planning* by Dr. William L. Pickett.

Organizing is the managerial function where all of the tasks necessary to realize the organization's envisioned future are identified and prioritized. It is an important function because it must show exactly how much effort will be required to bring about the organization's desired future state. Depending on the resources available, management's experience level, and the technology support available, organizing can be more or less straightforward. In general, it should be a fairly inclusive activity, involving those people with specific knowledge of how the organization *actually* operates and those who may implement the plan. Rather than generate numerous lists of extremely detailed activities, however, the main purpose of organizing is to develop a plausible sense of what needs to be done when. The focus is on outcomes and timelines more than on specific methods and ways. For example, focus on "have a contractor in place by June," rather than the process by which the contractor will be selected.

Influencing is the function most people think of when they hear the term "managing." Basically, it entails doing every ethical thing conceivable to get as many people as possible to both believe in the envisioned future and to change as needed to have that future actually occur. "Influencing activities" include communicating, leading, negotiating, motivating, and training. Depending on the belief structures, personalities, physical and mental capabilities, and basic desires of those involved in the process of creating the organization's future, influencing will be more or less challenging. It is important to get this step right because it is really the only way the future envisioned for the organization can ever be realized.

Controlling is the "reality check" function. Here, managers compare where the organization actually is to where their plans want it to be and then act accordingly. If the organization has achieved its goal, successfully placed in its chosen future, then it is time for management to create a new future for the organization. Organizations do not stand still; if they are not progressing, they are regressing. If the organization has not yet attained its future existence, then management uses the controlling function to take different actions. Depending on the nature of the discrepancies between the plan and reality, management has a number of different options for proper controlling. For example, the problem may lie in the organizing function. Perhaps new tasks need to be identified, or old ones need to be reprioritized. If the problem lies in the influencing function, perhaps new motivational or training efforts are needed. Finally, it may simply be that the plan is no longer viable. Perhaps management needs to take the organization in a different direction because the future they envisioned really should not or cannot be.

While the managerial functions were described above in a serial fashion, rarely, if ever, do they take place so smoothly or separately. In reality, managers may perform them in any order, including simultaneously, to ensure goal attainment.

Managerial Skills

While the specific skills a manager needs for success can vary tremendously depending on the nature and goals of the organization, researchers have categorized the myriad potential skills into three broad types, making more straightforward the identification and consideration of any particular skill a manager might need. The skill types are *technical, human,* and *conceptual.*

Technical skills are all the knowledge requirements and expertise needed for a manager to perform the core tasks within a given organization. For example, individuals wishing to manage in the Church should understand the mission of the Church, its overall structure, and the values animating its work; teachers must have the requisite abilities to motivate learners and share knowledge; bookkeepers must be able to accurately maintain accounts and report on them in an accepted system.

Human skills are all of the talents one has for getting along well with others, such as communication, delegation, leadership, and negotiation.

Conceptual skills involve those capacities that allow a person to think deeply and abstractly about complex ideas and issues. Creativity, analysis, synthesis, and logical reasoning would fall into this category.

Depending on one's managerial role within an organization, the relative importance of the skill set varies. Technical skills are more important at the beginning of one's career, as it is necessary to really understand the nature of the work one has chosen in order to be good at managing that work. Moreover, in order to move up the organizational hierarchy, one must clearly demonstrate that he can perform most of the fundamental organization-specific tasks. Human skills are important at any and every phase of one's managerial career, as they determine who becomes, sustains, and improves management. Finally, conceptual skills are most important for those in strategic planning positions because these are the skills needed for ensuring the long-term health and survival of the organization.

Creativity as a Managerial Skill

Successful management requires a broad variety of skills. Fortunately, every skill is learnable and can be improved significantly with proper training and practice. Even the conceptual skill of *creativity*, one of those skills many people think is innate and rare, can be developed. It is not true that one is either creative or not creative and there is little to be done about it. Years of research suggest that there is much one can do to grow in this skill. Creativity—the act of producing something novel and useful—has four learnable components: *fluency, flexibility, originality,* and *elaboration.*

Fluency is the ability to generate large numbers of ideas. Statistically speaking, the more ideas are generated, the more likely one will be creative. Brainstorming is a great way to increase fluency.

Flexibility is the ability to change one's thinking. The more one changes perspective, the more likely one is to think of something novel and useful. Humor is great way to develop flexibility. Making and/or laughing at jokes basically require one to shift perspective (deBono).

Originality is the ability to produce something unique. It is what most people consider to be the fundamental skill of creativity. However, originality can be determined only relative to the ideas already generated. How original an idea is deemed to be depends directly on how many ideas one already has. The more concepts one is familiar with, the *less* likely a given idea will be considered truly unique and vice versa. So, originality, rather than being innate, is easy to accomplish when ideas are few, and difficult to achieve when ideas are plentiful.

Elaboration is the ability to take a creative idea and turn it into something everyone can accept. Regardless of how useful a new idea may be, few of us are willing to accept it without a clear and meaningful explanation of its value (Amabile). By openly demonstrating the connections between the old and new way, it becomes more possible for people to adapt. Resistance to change is almost universal, but the more openness is sought, the more creativity grows.

Managerial Resources

In addition to working toward goals through and with others, managers must also use resources in service to the goals of the organization. They have the following resources available to use for goal accomplishment: *human, capital, monetary, material, information,* and *time.* Managerial success depends on the effective use of these resources as separate entities but also in relationship.

- *Human resources.* All the people directly involved in the day-to-day functioning of the organization, such as employees and boards, as well as those indirectly involved, such as parishioners, clients, and community members.

- *Capital resources.* All physical assets owned or at the manager's disposal, such as buildings, land, and equipment.

- *Monetary resources.* The funds available for use, such as donations, loans, savings, investments, and income from sales.

- *Material resources.* All the material things an organization uses to achieve goals, such as inventory, and basic support, such as electricity.

- *Information.* All the meaningful data and publications that advance the goals of the organization, such as lists of services, budgets, financial reports, list of donations or contributions, and publicity materials.

- *Time.* Starting points, ending points, and length of time absorbed (used, delayed, or saved) by activities like decision-making, dealing with employees, meetings, etc.

One of the interesting things about managerial resources is that they are interrelated and can often substitute for one another. Selecting and deploying resources carefully is the hallmark of successful management. In general, the most frequent consideration for choosing between and among them is cost. Not only can managers mix and match resources in myriad ways to accomplish organizational goals, but how they use the resources they choose also impacts future goals and resource availability. For example, technology offers many opportunities in terms of using resources in such a way that both the long- and short-term views are well served. In the same way, the choice of construction, purchase, or lease of facilities requires great discernment of immediate and future benefits.

Management Measures: Effectiveness and Efficiency

While countless books, newscasts, editorial pages, and other documented reports discuss the success or failure of manager after manager, there are really only two ways to judge managers: *effectiveness* and *efficiency*. *Effectiveness* is the extent to which goals are achieved. *Efficiency* is the number and amount of resources used in achieving those goals (Certo and Certo). For example, if the parish goal were to increase Mass attendance by 10 percent over the course of a year, and Mass attendance did increase by 10 percent over that time span, then you have been effective. Moreover, if you did not have to expend any significant resources, other than to remind people to attend Mass regularly when you happened to run into them, then you were also efficient.

While clearly the two are related, excelling in one does not necessarily mean excellence in the other. It is possible to achieve goals (effective) but waste resources (inefficient). For example, if you spend hundreds of dollars sending weekly formal invitations to Mass attendance, have taxis carry otherwise healthy parishioners to and from Mass, and throw festive "after parties" to get that 10 percent increase in Mass attendance, then you have been effective while being extremely inefficient. It is also possible to be extremely frugal (efficient) but miss goals (ineffective). Refusing to take any action other than occasionally requesting a better attendance record from your parishioners minimizes resource use, but makes the likelihood of reaching the 10 percent increase in Mass attendance less likely as well. It is also possible to fail at both.

For example, focusing your efforts only on those parishioners who already attend Mass regularly ("preaching to the choir") is likely to be both ineffective and inefficient.

Multiple standards can help to measure effectiveness and efficiency. For example, a parish will be interested in Mass attendance, collections, parish committee membership, participation in parish activities, number of "new" and "lost" parishioners, satisfaction surveys of various age cohorts, budgeting allocations, etc. Schools will have indicators like enrollment, achievement, family involvement, public recognition, recruitment, applications, and retention. This topic is addressed more fully in chapter 9, Evaluating Parish Performance. The measures one uses to assess effectiveness and efficiency make all the difference in determining success, so it is important to pay attention to what is actually being measured to assure validity and reliability.

Conclusion

As good management practices have the power to transform any organization for the better, all managers need to improve their managerial abilities. Because the Church is a value-oriented organization committed to community-building and quality performance, Church administrators have a particular call to manage with foresight, wisdom, and prudence, as well as with charity and justice. Fortunately, the skills needed to be a successful manager are learnable. Successful managers are those who are both effective and efficient in their relationships and use of resources. Fundamentally, successful management begins with setting meaningful goals and continues successfully as long as those goals are achieved with efficient and effective use of resources.

Exercises

These exercises can be conducted by individuals or by groups composed of organizational leaders. They are available for free reproducible download, in worksheet format, at www.avemariapress.com.

Exercise 1:
Setting Goals: Identify a few key things that matter.

List the three biggest challenges facing your parish or organization today.

1. _____
2. _____
3. _____

Create one SMART (*specific, measurable, attainable, realistic,* and *timely* [see page 27]) goal for each of the challenges you listed above.

1. _____
2. _____
3. _____

Exercise 2: The Managerial Functions

Refer to pages 28–29 to answer the following questions.

Practice with Planning

1. Based on the challenges you described in *Exercise 1*, describe what you envision for the future of your parish or organization.

2. What place would you like your parish or organization to have in the Church of the future?

Practice with Organizing

3. How much effort do you believe will be required to realize the future you described above?

4. What are some specific milestones that must be reached in order for your vision to be realized?

Practice with Influencing

5. What are three ways you might communicate, motivate, and train those around you to get them to help bring the future you described in #1 into reality?

Practice with Controlling

6. Describe two ways to compare your plan to reality.

7. What are three mechanisms you can use to determine whether any discrepancies noted are the fault of the plan itself, the organizing effort, or influencing tactics used?

Exercise 3: Identifying Relevant Managerial Skills.

1. What do you see as three specific skills in each of the following categories that are most relevant for anyone trying to successfully manage your parish or organization? Write them in the first column.

Rating Managerial Skills

Skill	Personal Rating
Technical:	
Technical Total:	
Human:	
Human Total:	
Conceptual:	
Conceptual Total:	

2. In the second column, rate yourself on each of the skills you listed using a scale of 1 to 10, with 1 being very weak and 10 very strong. Sum the totals for each category.

    Which skill category is your strongest? _____
    Which skill category is your weakest? _____

3. Describe two ways you can develop the skills listed in your weakest category.

4. What is one way that you might share your strongest skill?

Exercise 4: Consider Your Resources

Refer to pages 32–33 to complete this exercise.

Select the goal defined in *Exercise 1* that you believe should be accomplished first, and then describe the resources you think are needed to reach that goal.

Goal: _____

Resource Requirements

Human:	
Capital:	
Monetary:	
Material:	
Information:	
Time:	

Exercise 5: Defining Effectiveness and Efficiency

Refer to pages 33–34 to complete this exercise.

Describe two measures of effectiveness and two measures of efficiency for each of the goals you listed in *Exercise 1*.

Effectiveness _____

_____

Efficiency _____

_____

Exercise 6: Conceptualizing Management

Read the following quotations and describe the concept of management each presents.

"If a man knows not what harbor he seeks, any wind is the right wind." (Seneca)

"Do not turn back when you are just at the goal." (Publilius Syrus)

"Those who know how to win are much more numerous than those who know how to make proper use of their victories."(Polybius)

"A goal without a plan is just a wish." (Antoine de Saint-Exupéry)

"A vision without resources is an hallucination." (Friedman 2008)

BIBLIOGRAPHY

Amabile, Teresa M. *Creativity in Context: Update to the Social Psychology of Creativity*. Boulder, Colorado: Westview Press, 1996.

Certo, Samuel C., and Trevis Certo. *Modern Management: Concepts and Skills*. 11th ed. Upper Saddle River, New Jersey: Prentice Hall, 2008.

Dayton, S. "Entrepreneur of the Year Acceptance Speech." USC Marshall School's Lloyd Greif Center for Entrepreneurial Studies, University of Southern California, February 1999.

DeBono, Edward. *DeBono's Thinking Course*. New York: Facts on File, 1985.

Donohue, Gene. Creating SMART Goals. Top Achievement, 1993–2007. www .topachievement.com / smart.html.

Friedman, Thomas L. *Hot, Flat and Crowded: Why We Need a Green Revolution and How It Can Renew America*. New York: Farrar, Straus, and Giroux, 2008.

Pickett, William L. *A Concise Guide to Pastoral Planning*. Notre Dame: Ave Maria Press, 2007.

The Quotations Page and Michael Moncur. "The Quotations Page." 1994–2007. www .QuotationsPage.com.

Templar, Richard. *The Rules of Work: The Unspoken Truth About Getting Ahead in Business*. Upper Saddle River, New Jersey: Pearson Education, FT Press, 2005.

Zimbardo, Philip, and John Boyd. *The Time Paradox: The New Psychology of Time That Will Change Your Life*. New York: Free Press, 2008.

CHAPTER 3

Time Management

Larry W. Boone, PhD

But wisdom is vindicated by her works.
—Matthew 11:19

Key Concepts

1. Attitudes toward time, its value, and its use are culturally conditioned.

2. Management experts indicate that one can save 10 percent of a typical workweek by either doing less or working faster, and they suggest ways to do both.

3. The art of delegation demands effective communication skills and is an essential tool of the secure administrator who manages time well.

4. Saying "no" at the appropriate times and knowing the best people from whom to seek help allows a manager to spend time on activities where he or she is the best resource, doing what no one else can or should do.

5. Some very simple ground rules on interruptions, materials-flow, priority setting, calendaring, "to do" lists, and technology can add greatly to one's productivity.

6. "Doing nothing" occasionally can be a very productive exercise.

Introduction

Citizens of the United States often appear to persons from other nations to be extremely time-conscious and "in a great hurry." One often hears that "time is money" and "you can't make up for lost time." This emphasis on "keeping busy" derives from the high importance U.S. culture places on productivity and recognition. The "consumer character and time imperative" of this culture causes many parishioners to expect efficiency and effectiveness from their parishes and faith-based organizations as well as from businesses. It is helpful to remember that parishes and Church institutions are indeed communities and faith-based, but they are also "business" operations. Staff form both a community and a work force; and the pastor or administrator serves as pastoral leader and organizational manager. This chapter offers some insights into the theory and practice of "time management" from both the personal and organizational perspectives. The pastor or administrator is ultimately responsible for stewardship of all assets and talents; all on staff assume the responsibility to assure that time is spent productively.

In our society time takes on a variety of meanings. One can *keep time, do time, spend time, save time, invest time,* or *waste time.* It is important to get in touch with one's own definition of time so that one can align attitudes and feelings toward it. Everyone's relationship with time can be different; therefore, effective strategies for managing time will vary (Bolton).

A person afraid of losing time will have different strategies from the one who challenges time by trying to make the most of it. The time-management system of an individual who has a spouse and several children will differ from a person who lives alone. The number of organizations with which you have contact, their importance in your life scheme, and the work organization's own systems, goals, and priorities will impact your approach to the management of your time.

Author Lesley Bolton suggests that before you try to hone your time-management skills, you engage in a little self-reflection by asking yourself the following questions:

- What time constraints did I experience growing up?
- How do I handle situations when I'm running late?
- Does it seem as though time is always working against me?
- Do I feel lost without my watch?
- Do I have leisure time?
- How well do I handle leisure time?
- Does time control me?
- How do I define "on time"? Early? To the second? Is half an hour late close enough?
- Is managing time a desperate act for me?

—Bolton, p. 5

Honest answers to these queries will help uncover some underlying influences that have shaped your awareness of time. For example, if you were raised in a very organized and time-efficient atmosphere, your attitude will be quite different from that of an individual who grew up in a less organized and random environment. It is very likely that your early notions of time have influenced your current attitudes.

Attitudes Toward Time

What are some common attitudes toward time? Bolton suggests the following five categories: the enemy, at your leisure, fear of work time, perpetually late, and disregard for time.

The Enemy. People may see time working against them. No matter how hard they try to exercise control, time seems to get the best of them. Obviously, that's a self-defeating attitude. Time can be neither an enemy nor an ally. Time is just there; it's a constant. Because time won't bend to your will, you may believe you are powerless within its unyielding grasp. However, you can learn to improve your management of time, as will be demonstrated later.

At Your Leisure. Some people feel comfortable controlling their time at work, but they abuse their leisure time because they just aren't sure what to do with themselves. Leisure time can lead an otherwise well-organized worker to panic. Time does not create this tension. The problem is caused by lack of value recognition. Many people who fear leisure are just afraid of wasting it. Typically, these people will take one of two paths. They will either fill their days and nights with work to eliminate the leisure issue altogether, or they will preserve their leisure time but fritter it away by doing absolutely nothing with it. A *New Yorker* cartoon humorously captures the first type as it shows an executive at the beach who built an office desk with sand and sat at it using a seashell for a telephone.

Fear of Work Time. Some take the opposite approach. They value their leisure time but fear work. Often, they aren't satisfied with their jobs, or they feel like work is forced upon them. They create resistance, either subconsciously—or sometimes quite overtly. Leisure time is spent in a very fulfilling manner, but work time is spent in chaos. Little is accomplished. These people may well consider time spent working to be time taken away from their "real" lives, the pursuit of happiness through leisure. With this approach, leisure time passes very quickly but, when at work, time stands still. Again, attitude is the key. People may still find leisure preferable to work, but if a more positive attitude toward work is developed, work time won't seem to take on such grand proportions within one's life.

Perpetually Late. Some people make a habit of being late to everything—work, social functions, appointments, etc. Being late becomes part of their personality. Friends and coworkers recognize it as a defining characteristic: "Oh, yes, Marie is always late. That's just Marie." But it can backfire. Chronically late individuals may find themselves stuck in a rut of constant tardiness because it is expected of them. Some may always be on time for work but late for social and family functions, or vice versa. One's sense of responsibility or fear can often influence arrival time. A person may feel a strong responsibility toward his employer, so he shows up on time. If he is afraid of being reprimanded, he gets into the office before starting time. However, such responsibility or fear of negative repercussions may not exist with family or friend relationships. No matter the reason for tardiness, one thing is certain: many people perceive late-arriving behavior as disrespectful. Others may decide not to rely on "the tardy" and exclude them from future activities or even dismiss them from their employment relationships.

Disregarding Time. Lastly, some people seem to simply have no regard for time. They like to interpret this attitude as adopting a carefree, "free spirit" way of life. Some in this category may proudly present themselves as fully liberated. Unfortunately, having no sense of time may mean that they have no guidelines for accomplishing things. With them, *"goal"* may be a foreign word and deadlines may not exist. It's good not to obsess about time, but ignoring it completely can disassociate one from the people and organizations in one's life. Better to recognize time's effects and seek to establish reasonable control over time and self.

Time Management Techniques

Dennis P. Slevin, a professor, consultant, and practicing manager, has written extensively on the concept of time management. He suggests that busy administrators can easily save four hours per week (10 percent of a typical forty-hour schedule) if they adopt one or two of the following time management techniques. As you read through the following approaches, keep an open mind and select a few "favorites" to try out. The four hours saved per week could represent

- one week of vacation every ten weeks;
- five extra weeks of productivity each year;

- seventeen more hours per month to spend with your family and friends.

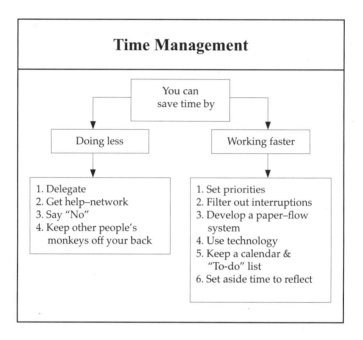

Doing Less

There are several approaches one can adopt to save time by doing less: *delegating tasks to qualified others, getting expert help through one's own personal network, saying "No" when appropriate,* and *keeping other people's monkeys off your back.*

Delegating

The most effective way to do less in your job is to delegate. The only reason administrators have other individuals in their organizations is that they cannot do all of the work themselves. If the pastor were Superman and could run the pastoral office, preside at worship, lead meetings, maintain the facilities, do the accounting, and handle all necessary interpersonal interactions with all parishioners, there would be no need for an organization.

But there are no Supermen. Therefore, the better one delegates, the more effective all are going to be. It is important to remember, however, that one cannot delegate one's responsibility. Delegation implies ongoing interest and oversight.

Virtually every manager fails to delegate as effectively as possible. Consider this typical example. An office manager realized that she spent about one day each month compiling the "Monthly Operations Report" demanded by her superior. Yet, when challenged to examine the last six months' reports, it was evident that each report was pretty much the same. The only differences involved a few specific performance statistics relevant to that month (which were available from anyone in the department who possessed basic math skills) and a couple of "special issues" that required communicating her opinions on a few matters of immediate importance each month. She realized that all the "routine" elements of the report could be compiled by her assistant for her review and approval. She retained the task of writing the "special issues." The result: half a day's time saved each month.

The use of delegation is probably the single most effective step toward improved time management. There are added benefits:

- Subordinates are more motivated, and their job satisfaction is higher · because their jobs have been enriched.

- You are doing a better job of planning and organizing because delegation forces you to pay more attention to planning and organizing.

```
┌─────────────────────────────────────────────────────┐
│                    Delegate                          │
├─────────────────────────────────────────────────────┤
│  "Push down" decision making; empower others; let    │
│  them be comfortable doing things in "your place."   │
│                                                      │
│  Delegation involves:        Why delegate?           │
│  Allocation of duties        Frees up a manager's    │
│    tasks a manager desires     time                  │
│    someone else to do        Improves decision       │
│  Delegation of authority       making                │
│    empowering someone else     decision maker is     │
│    to act for you              "closer" to the       │
│  Assignment of responsibility  problem               │
│    assigning the equivalent  Helps develop others    │
│    "obligation" to perform     stimulates personal   │
│  Creation of accountability    growth and            │
│    making the person answer-   development           │
│    able for carrying out the Enhances commitment     │
│    tasks                       "buy in" enhances     │
│                                implementation        │
│                              Improves relationships  │
│                                exhibits trust and    │
│                                confidence            │
└─────────────────────────────────────────────────────┘
```

Effective delegation requires communication skill. To be a good delegator, you must communicate two messages:

1. What you expect the subordinate to accomplish.

2. How much authority the subordinate has to carry out the assignment.

By delegating, the administrator tells the subordinate what task he is to carry out, how long he has to accomplish it, when he or she will be checking back with him, and how much freedom he has to get the task done.

Most administrators do an adequate job of explaining objectives to subordinates. However, many fail to provide an explicit directive clarifying the level of decision-making authority the subordinate has. This can inhibit an employee from taking initiative because he or she fears overstepping his or her bounds. When you assign tasks to subordinates, also assign one of these three authority levels:

Type of Decision-making Authority	Subordinate's Authority Level
1. Take action on your own, but notify me routinely (daily, weekly, monthly)	Most authority
2. Take action on your own, but notify me immediately	↕
3. Recommend potential actions only, take no action without approval	Least authority

Building a Network

Research conducted by management expert John Kotter and others has led to a clear recognition that effective administrators use a widespread network to accomplish their work. This network may consist of hundreds, even thousands, of members. If you look at a busy manager's Rolodex or electronic file, you will see the names, contact information, and areas of expertise of many people who can be called upon for support. And, importantly, the manager's name will be included as a support person on the files of those individuals. A typical Help and Communication Network for a pastor or parish administrator follows.

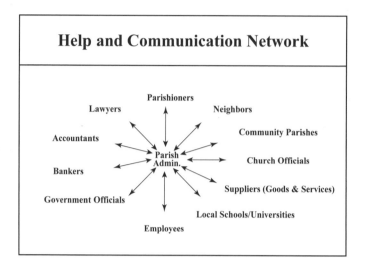

Help and Communication Network

Parishioners

Lawyers   Neighbors

Accountants   Community Parishes

Parish Admin.   Church Officials

Bankers

Suppliers (Goods & Services)

Government Officials

Local Schools/Universities

Employees

The administrator's job is not as simple as arriving at the office each day and dealing directly with each office-related task and parishioner request. If an administrator attempted to behave in this manner, his or her time would not be well spent toward achieving the parish's goals and objectives. Let's look at a very obvious example. Imagine that a parish member slipped on the sidewalk in front of the church and broke his leg. What would an effective administrator do? It's quite clear: call an ambulance and obtain the expert assistance of people trained to provide the kind of help required to best support the parishioner in need. Good administrators would not use their time to learn as quickly as possible how to mend a broken leg so that they could perform the task themselves. The injured party's interests would not be served by such an approach, and neither would the interests of the parish or the administrator.

The lesson, then, is obvious. Know a lot of experts. Contact them and solicit their assistance when they can perform a task better than you can. This is not "shirking" your duty—it is your duty.

A Concise Guide to Catholic Church Management

Get the job done as well as possible and as quickly as possible. Then move on to the next task.

Persons who care about getting the organization's work accomplished and managing their own time effectively invest some of their time each week cultivating a network. They meet new people at every opportunity, exchange contact information, and note each new acquaintance's area(s) of expertise. They know that at some future point, this person may well be the best individual to handle or advise on a problem or issue that crosses the administrator's desk. It is the quality of work that matters, not the idea that you perform the work yourself.

Saying "No"

Another way to manage your time by doing less is to learn to say "no." This is an important communication skill. It requires personal discipline and a strong sense of priority. Learn to say "no" cleanly and quickly. Responses such as "I'll think about it" or "I'll get back to you" simply raise hopes, draw out the decision, and waste time. Many people find it hard to say "no" to others and to opportunities, especially interesting ones, they have the chance to accept. Refusal goes against the grain of a generous person who believes it is right to support others in need.

Learn to Say "No"

- **Know your priorities.**

  Decide what tasks are most important to meet your objectives. Say "no" to other requests.

- **Don't say, "I'll think about it" or "I'll get back to you."**

  They are time wasters.

- **Connect those in need to others in your network who can provide the best support possible.**

  You are not always the best person to help others in need.

"No" is an appropriate response for low-priority tasks for which you don't have time or for tasks that *others can do better and faster than you* (see the previous section on network-building). The habit of saying "No" to low-priority tasks or to tasks for which others are better suited will allow you the free time to say "yes" to tasks that will be more important to the organization, more helpful to others in need, emerge unexpectedly, or are more personally exciting or satisfying to you.

Keeping Other People's Monkeys Off Your Back

An interesting aspect of this "saying no" approach is the concept of "monkeys" introduced in the mid-1970s by Oncken and Wass. A monkey is a task to be accomplished. Once a task has been assigned, picture it as a monkey sitting on the back of the employee responsible for its care and feeding until the task is done. Consider the following situation:

A secretary enters the pastor's office and says, "Monsignor, we've got a problem. You assigned me the task of setting up a meeting next Friday with the Finance Committee. I have been able to contact only four of the six members. I cannot seem to reach the others no matter what I try, and I've been working at it for hours." A short pause ensues. "OK," the pastor says, "just leave the names and numbers of the other members on my desk. I'll try to get through to them."

Before the secretary entered the office, she carried the monkey. Who has the monkey now? Intentionally or unintentionally, it was delegated up to the pastor. Further, if you have five employees, and each one executes a monkey leap each day, you will have five new screaming monkeys on your back howling to be fed.

Keep Other People's Monkeys Off Your Back

- Do not let employees "delegate up" to you.

- Don't agree to proofread or fact-check employees' work.

- Don't accept tasks from your employees.

- Let subordinates know it's their responsibility to do the work assigned to them—and to do it well.

The moral of this story is straightforward: keep subordinates' monkeys on subordinates' backs. Any tasks delegated to workers should continue to be their responsibilities until completion. The monkey concept is a handy visualization trick. When subordinates approach to discuss problems related to their tasks, picture the monkeys on their backs. When they turn to leave, make sure every monkey is still on their shoulders.

Working Faster

Another approach to time management is *working faster*. By "working faster" Slevin does not imply that you should take vitamins, drink lots of coffee, and in general speed up the frantic pace at which you may already be living. Rather, he offers some techniques to help you get more mileage from your existing time by using it wisely. They are: *setting priorities, filtering out interruptions, developing a paper-flow system, using technology, keeping a calendar and a "to-do" list,* and *setting aside time to reflect.*

Setting Priorities

Management is a job of setting priorities. No successful person needs to be convinced of the necessity for setting priorities and using them as guidelines for how to spend one's time. Many unsuccessful managers are hard-working and enthusiastic, but somehow they can't seem to get the right things done because their priorities are not clear and consistent. Examine the *Priority Planning* chart below for a useful overview of the priority-setting task.

Priority Planning	
Annually	Set global objectives for the year, dividing them into: a) routine things that must be accomplished, b) problem-solving tasks to improve performance, c) innovations that would make a difference, and d) personal development and life goals.
Monthly	Evaluate progress toward your global objectives, revising them as necessary.
Weekly	Have a specific idea of what you want to accomplish this week.
Daily	Create a "to-do" list.

Every action that you take as a manager concerning the allocation of your time is at least implicitly evaluated against the following priorities:

- Controlling your time
- Controlling your job
- Putting a high priority on managing the stress you are under

- Managing smarter and more effectively
- Giving your personal life the value it deserves

If you evaluate and, potentially, change your priorities, you may find yourself to be not only happier, but also more effective as a manager.

Filtering Out Interruptions

One of the most significant problems facing every administrator involves interruptions. Every time you start a project, are interrupted, and return to the project, you lose valuable set-up time. The telephone is the worst interrupter. When the phone rings, it might be someone calling to congratulate you on a job well done or news about a family member's illness or an unhappy parishioner with a complaint. Because of the unknown and random nature of telephone calls, the telephone is extremely powerful; it can throw your management life into confusion. Thus you should establish a filter system. Establish guidelines to protect yourself as much as possible from unwanted interruptions while leaving yourself accessible to people who need to get in touch with you. Of course, you don't want to be like the executive who will simply not talk on the telephone before noon to save the morning for staff meetings, planning functions, and so on. Calls are returned only after lunch. This technique works fine until one wants to talk to a person who will not accept telephone calls in the afternoon. The point is, make sure that you control the telephone and not vice versa.

Filter Out Interruptions

Most common interruptions are:

- Telephone calls

- People dropping by

Establish guidelines for when, for whom, and for what you will accept interruptions.

A second major source of interruptions is people. Subordinates, peers, superiors and others may wander by and engage in discussions on both work and nonwork matters. One administrator turned his desk away from the door and toward the wall. He discovered that a number of interruptions were caused by his subordinates who, walking past and making eye contact, felt compelled to acknowledge his presence and exchange a few words. By facing the wall, he saved a few hours every week. Although he still maintained his open door policy, he managed to reduce his number of unnecessary informal conversations.

Developing a Paper-Flow System

If anything has had more adverse effect on management time than the telephone, it is probably e-mail and the copier. You can now get copies of everything—and probably do. The average manager is confronted by an ever-increasing digital file and paper flow. When one executive was asked to identify his biggest "management" problem, his answer was surprising. He had guided his organization through a major crisis and was enjoying due regard. Yet he responded, "Dealing with the paper flow across my desk." If a high-level executive who is supposed to be buffered from day-to-day details finds problems with paper flow, imagine the dilemma of the average parish administrator with a very small staff. Still, you *can* develop an efficient and straightforward system for handling paper flow.

First convince yourself that there are only three kinds of paper: (A) important; (B) worthwhile; and (C) junk. Important paper should be acted upon. Worthwhile paper should be read. Junk paper should be tossed.

Paper-Flow System Goal: Handle each piece of paper <u>only once.</u>	
A. IMPORTANT	Take action
• Immediately:	Take appropriate and complete action, and dispense with the paper.
• Pending:	Initiate some action – only then put the paper in a pending file.
B. WORTHWHILE	Read
• Distribute:	Only if it is significant to others; be considerate – they get enough junk.
• File:	Only if you'll need to see it again.
• Toss:	When you have gained all its information.
C. JUNK	Toss

Remember, the ultimate aim is to handle each piece of paper only once. You are going to have to spend the same amount of time dealing with the paper whether you've looked at it five times previously or not, so you might as well deal with it the first time you see it.

If you have access to a secretary or assistant, have him or her sort your incoming e-mail or mail into the category A, B, or C. Also, have the assistant act directly on as much mail as possible.

Using Technology

Most people can achieve much faster work rates by employing some or all of the variety of technological tools available today, such as beepers, cell phones, e-mail, fax machines, pagers, text-messaging devices, videoconferencing setups, voice mail, and voice-recognition software—to name just a few. Application of all these tools is far beyond the scope of this material, but investing one's time in a few classes to learn how to use these technological time-savers is well worth the cost.

As an example, let's look at the use of dictation equipment and/or voice-recognition software. You may dictate to tape or to an audio file for later transcription, or you may dictate through voice-recognition software to create an electronic file directly. People write at the speed of about twenty-five words-per-minute, but they can speak quite easily at two hundred words-per-minute. For the bulk of your correspondence, it's faster and more efficient to use dictating resources.

Keeping a Calendar and "To-do" List

On a daily, weekly, and monthly basis, know what is important and what you will be doing. Do you know what your schedule is for the rest of the week? Are you hitting the important tasks? Effective administrators have a mental image (or an electronic image on an e-calendar) of the total picture of their time and expectations, as well as a moment-by-moment awareness of what they should be doing.

A daily "to-do" list helps a busy administrator manage both time and stress. At the end of each workday, consider all the things that must be accomplished tomorrow. Don't make it a long "laundry" list. Include only five to ten truly "must" tasks. Referring to your personal and organizational priorities helps with this identification. Write down the things that must be done tomorrow, and leave the list on your desk or anywhere it can be accessed easily first thing in the morning. Then, forget the list. Forget work. Get on with the other (nonwork) parts of your life that help you maintain a healthy balance of mind, body, and soul. The list will wait for you, and you can pick up right where you need to.

When work resumes the next day, focus on the list. Accomplish every one of those tasks—or take them as far as you can before you "hit a wall." Say "no" to people who try to knock you off track. You can always go back and say "yes" to their requests after your list is finished. Do the math here. If you accomplish (I mean truly "accomplish") five to ten tasks each day, how many is that per week, per month, per year? It's enough accomplishments to convince everyone, including yourself, that you are a highly productive person.

Setting Aside Time to Reflect

Schedule a little time every day or a couple of times a week to sit down and reflect. Ask yourself frequently, "Am I getting the important things done?" Determine whether or not you should refocus your priorities and tasks. There is constant pressure to spend time on lower-priority issues. Resist it. Your job is to think as well as act.

Conclusion

While attitudes toward time are strongly influenced by culture, and the supply of time never seems quite adequate to the demand, it is possible to "make the most of every minute" and actually save 10 percent of the typical work week. This can be achieved by doing less or working faster, or better still—doing both. One can set ground rules and develop very specific skills that will achieve both of these goals and still allow time for that highly productive activity of "doing nothing." Developing such rules and skills is a valuable investment of time that can yield dividends in productivity and satisfaction.

Exercises

1. Reflect on your own attitude toward time—the situations in which you feel most harried or pressured by the clock, as well as your attitude toward "doing nothing." Share those reflections with another person who has read this chapter, and consider if there are areas where you would profit from modifying your attitude or behavior.

2. For two workdays keep a log of all your activities, and review it to see where you have spent your time. Identify the activities as "something I must do myself," "something I can delegate to another," "someone else's monkey."

3. Consider "the working faster" techniques presented in this chapter on pages 53–59. Evaluate how many you use and how well you use them. Begin immediately to adopt one technique you are not currently using.

4. Review your current schedule and communication systems. Are they efficient as well as respectful of staff and visitors? Is there clear separation of business and personal time for those who live and work in the same place?

5. Decide on your best (most personally productive) time of the day (early morning, late morning, early afternoon, etc). Plan a schedule that protects that time from all interruptions and distractions. Try it for a week, and see how much more productive you are.

6. Develop a calendar for once-a-year events and for regular parish activities that require your final approval. Identify all activities, specific dates, and accountabilities for review and sign-off by all parish staff involved.

BIBLIOGRAPHY

Bolton, Leslie. *Fastread Time Management: Get Organized and Accomplish More in Less Time.* Cincinnati: Adams Media Corporation, 2002.

Oncken, Jr., William, Donald L. Wass, and Stephen R. Covey. "Management Time: Who's Got the Monkey?" *Harvard Business Review* 52, November 1999/1974, 76–78.

Slevin, Dennis P. *The Whole Manager: How to Increase Your Professional and Personal Effectiveness.* New York: American Management Association, AMACOM, 1989.

CHAPTER 4

Communication:
The Oxygen of an Organization

Margaret John Kelly, D.C., PhD

Go and tell John what you hear and see.
—Matthew 11:4

Key Concepts

1. Communication is a very complicated human activity and is strongly conditioned by one's culture, maturity level, and personality type, as well as by one's knowledge and skill.

2. Nonverbal communication outweighs verbal communication by a ratio of four to one.

3. The effective manager will vary his or her communication style according to the content of the message, the environment, and the receiver.

4. Emotional static can be destructive of communication in the same way that static distorts sound on the airwaves.

5. The medium (e-mail, personalized letter, memo, phone call, personal visit, group session, large assembly, etc.) can be as important as content in communication.

6. A wise manager pays attention to the unofficial communication structures (grapevines) in the organization and uses official structures (spoken and written) to prevent "information hunger" and "gossip."

7. Intercultural communication requires an awareness of how the two cultures are alike and where they are different, as well as respect for the differences.

8. The litigious and pluralistic nature of our contemporary society dictates that careful attention be paid to communication within an organization.

9. Communication is facilitated by active listening, paraphrasing, and openness to sharing information and feelings.

Introduction

The pages of scripture are a veritable treasure trove of samples of both effective and ineffective communication, but it is Jesus' encounter with the Samaritan woman at Jacob's well that is particularly instructive (Jn 4:5–30). It serves to demonstrate the theory of communication and to model effective communication in its many aspects. First, because the Samaritans were disdained by the Jews, this encounter between the woman and Jesus starts out with an intercultural challenge that has to be overcome. In addition, this woman must have carried much resentment because she had to come alone to this central meeting place for women at high noon. This would be a daily reminder that her less-than-exemplary life caused her to be scorned by the other women who could draw water at other times and so avoid the oppressive midday heat.

This woman probably was not very receptive to the dialogue that this Jewish man, Jesus, was initiating. It is probable that both were uncomfortable because the cultural mores of their day would expose both Jesus and the woman to criticism. Yet with all those impediments to communication, the two engage in an open, sincere, respectful dialogue that concludes with the woman recognizing Jesus as the Messiah and announcing this to others. Here we have a perfect model of good communication: message given; message received; message acted on.

A closer look at this exchange offers additional insight into the principles of communication. First, a familiar setting around the common well put both participants on equal footing despite their divergent and conflicting backgrounds. To establish rapport, Jesus simply asks a favor, a cup of water. This draws attention to their shared need for water and also serves as a symbol for the message that he progressively unfolds. The woman's initial hesitancy flows into an openness that slowly yields to trust as Jesus directly, but kindly, confronts both her social and moral predicament. In his communication style, Jesus is simple, focused, and directive, which facilitates the engagement of the Samaritan woman. Overcoming her initial defensiveness, she follows point for point Jesus' line of logic. Jesus leads her to look beyond the well and water, reflect on her irregular life, admit to her past with candor, and in the end also express hope in the Messiah. At this point of readiness, Jesus declares himself to her. The message is received according to the intention of the sender and is then translated into an active response. The Samaritan woman leaves her water jar and runs to communicate the message to others in much the way Mary runs from the tomb of Jesus to announce that it was empty. Both women complete the circle, showing that the truth not only sets us free, but that in sharing truth an ever-expanding circle of meaning opens up. A great deal of communication is directed to that end: searching for truth and the true. It is the heart of evangelization.

It is interesting to note that throughout his ministry, Jesus often relies on a simple question to engage another in dialogue, just as he did in this encounter with the Samaritan woman. To draw attention to mission, Jesus asked the disciples that very simple question, "Who do people say that I am?" In conferring leadership on Peter, Jesus challenged him with threefold intensity, "Do you love me?" With great poignancy, he lamented the weakness of his disciples with "Could you not watch one hour with me?" These brief but well-formed questions engage the others by focusing on a precise and personal experience.

Through the careful formulation of these questions and so many others, Jesus opened reflection and dialogue in such a way that the individual questioned came to a deeper understanding of his or her own world for having been invited into Jesus' world.

This merging, this "coming together as one" is the essence of communication and remains a pillar of ministry, the structural support for effective ministry today.

Communication and Organizational Vitality

Communication is universally considered one of the most complex actions humans perform. Some would opine that it is *the most* complex activity. Its complexity is matched by its centrality to both interpersonal relationships and organizational vitality. While communication skills have generally been a predictor of managerial success even of despots, they are even more critical in a "community" or "team" environment such as that which the Church seeks to create in its organizations. Many images are used to capture the critical role of communication in an organization. Some liken communication to glue because it holds together units as small as the family and as large as corporations, universities, and parishes. Others prefer the image of oxygen because they consider communication essential for organizational survival. Weakened commitment and dysfunctional behaviors within organizations can often be traced to "poor communication" or to "information hunger," which causes persons to feed on conjecture. These two conditions invite suspicion, speculation, alienation, gossip, and mistrust within any organization, secular or ecclesial.

It should not be surprising then that a whole consulting and publishing industry has grown up around organizational communications. Communication is the number one cause of both success and happiness as well as failure and unhappiness, on the job and in the family. There is a full continuum of communications sin—of both commission and omission—that can affect organizational morale and productivity. The mere recognition and greeting of a subordinate on a Monday morning could cause that individual to engage in healthy and productive behaviors for the remainder of the week. A perceived slight, such as a perfunctory greeting or indifferent look, could have the opposite effect. Failure to ask for and listen to feedback could result in projects continuing far beyond their natural lives and absorbing energies that should more appropriately be dedicated to other activities. Failing to respond to the uniqueness of the person during an evaluation conference can make the encounter not only meaningless in terms of improvement but counterproductive for the ongoing relationship as well. Positive communication, such as a grateful e-mail or note from a supervisor, can generate new enthusiasm and dedication. Such rapport saves valuable time, builds confidence, raises morale, and contributes to quality performance.

The Communication Process

The following diagram illustrates the complexity of communication and the difficulty of offering a simple definition of the process. The following commonly used definitions hint at this difficulty and point up the three interactive elements of Sender, Receiver, Message:

- The act by which one enters the mind and heart of another to experience the world as the other sees, hears, and responds to it.

- The process of stimulating meaning in the mind of another through verbal or nonverbal images.

Both of these definitions assume reciprocity and the shared grasp of one meaning. The definitions, however, fail to include the added influences of image of the other and environment. These ancillary factors can alter or offset greatly "the message," which is meant to bring the communicator and interpreter together in a shared understanding, shared meaning. It is safe to say that seldom are words the only component of communication, and seldom is there a one-to-one correlation between message sent and message received. Past interpersonal relationships, current concerns about the topic, or environmental issues can be equivalent to or more influential than the actual word message.

In effective communication two beings come into relationship either directly (through face-to-face or electronic dialogue) or indirectly (packaged messages, such as reports, letters, symbols, advertising, news, mass e-mails). Each of those individuals brings his or her history as well as his or her image of the other to the encounter. In addition, the environment in which each operates impacts the degree to which the sent message corresponds to the received message. Much human static and environmental distortion can occur as messages are sent from one individual to another.

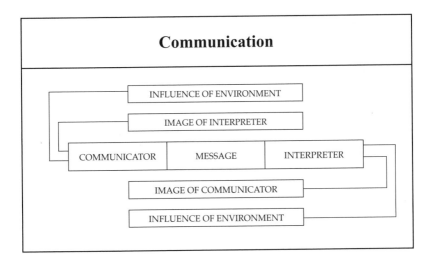

Multi-level Messages

Consider the following groupings, each of which has similar content but also a distinctive tone caused by the pronoun usage:

a. I agree with you.
   You're right.

b. I don't think you are listening.
   Perhaps I need to go over this again.
   Will you summarize my point to get us on the same page?

c. Just forget about it.
   There is no point in discussing it.

    d. We've been through this before.
       I don't think you are able to handle this now.

An actual story captures the levels of relationship and meaning contained in a single encounter and demonstrates that communication is not just about words. In a philosophy class at a Catholic university, a revered priest-professor decided to challenge a sister who apparently had difficulty getting to a morning class on time. One day when she entered late, Father turned to her and said, "How will you have your tea, Sister?" Without a moment's hesitation the sister replied, "With a little less lemon please, Father." Effective communication even though expressed in code! From below the polite words, the annoyed professor and the affronted student surface. One wonders how the encounter affected future relations within the class and communication between the professor and other students. In addition to the words that are expressed, interpersonal communication includes a nonverbal component, and one can only speculate on the posture and facial expressions of the two in their mutual sarcasm.

Another story suggests the power of nonverbal communication, which will be discussed later. During a marriage counseling session, a priest sought to make the couple more self-aware of how each communicated his or her feelings, especially after some tension had been experienced. After some probing, the wife revealed that she used the closing of doors to signal her mood. A slam meant "I'm still angry." A moderate push meant "I'm unhappy." A soft, gentle closing meant "Things are okay now." The husband admitted: "I go silent and don't talk until she asks me for something." Neither invoked the spoken word, but the message was clear.

The nonverbals of posture, dress, gesture, facial expressions, etc. send messages that may or may not be consistent with the verbal message that is being transmitted, as in the classroom scenario, or in place of words, as in the counseling scenario above. Nonverbals can send out sub-messages that distort or override the intended spoken message.

When we look at communication in the context of the parish or any Church organization, it is hard to ignore its centrality.

The full range of management and ministerial activities depends upon effective communication: counseling, planning, supervising, interviewing, visioning, teaching, advising, evaluating, preaching, and facilitating groups and meetings, etc. All demand conscious attention to the *what, how, who, when,* and *why* of messages sent and received. It is essential then that pastors and administrators be aware of both the complexity and centrality of communication to their ministry as well as of their personal communication strengths and weaknesses.

Communication Style

People differ greatly both in their preferences for initiating communication with others and in receiving input from others. Over the past twenty years a great deal of attention has been given to styles of learning and communicating. Research findings confirm that there is a wide range of individual differences in the learning process, which frequently extend to sending and receiving information as well. Some persons learn best aurally, others visually, others kinesthetically, still others through context or gestalt. Some persons need to read information to retain it; others have only to listen to grasp concepts. Some persons need some physical involvement to internalize meaning. Some administrators find the telephone or e-mail a buffering influence, while others reject these "cold" modes and prefer face-to-face conversation. Some function well in teleconferencing, while others are frustrated by the absence of nonverbals beyond voice tone and speed. One simple way to evaluate one's own style of receiving or sharing information is to consider what type of directions we like to receive and the kind we give. Although today the options of route numbers, landmarks, mileage, street names, or a carefully drawn map are becoming irrelevant thanks to global positioning systems (GPS), personal insight can still be gained by reflecting on one's preferred method. Even with GPS, research on "recorded voices" has found that gendered voices affect the reception of messages, either positively or negatively, as do "digitized personalities."

Interpersonal Communication

At the interpersonal level, communication brings together two different persons with different experiences and views of the other into one message or meaning, as shown in the previous diagram. A communicator sends a message that he or she expects will be received by the interpreter in the same way that it was intended to be received, with point-to-point correlation of intention and reception. As noted earlier, this is difficult if not impossible to achieve except with very simple messages like "stand" or "place it there," but even with these simple commands, tone of voice can affect the receiver. The sender comes out of a specific experiential background, which may be different from the receiver's, and has an image, correct or incorrect, partial or complete, of the receiver. The environment—formal or casual, supportive or hostile—in which the communicator sends the message can affirm, distort, or negate the message, as shown in the class vignette of the priest-professor and sister-student.

At the receiver level, we have the same three factors (experiential background, image of the other, and influence of the environment) affecting the meaning or message that has been transmitted. In groups where the members know each other well, the receiver may anticipate what the message will be and not hear what is actually communicated. Even the posture of standing or sitting when sending a verbal message can influence strongly how a message is received. To be at eye level with another enhances mutual openness and facilitates communication, while looking down at another signals superiority and evokes caution. The amount of physical space between the two involved in the communication process can assist or hinder, as does a physical barrier such as a desk or table.

Every communication has a history. There are no blank pages. Emotional residue from past encounters (or even from pressures unrelated to the present encounter) can create static. Just as with radio static, emotions have the potential to distort the message. Furthermore, some words carry heavy emotional baggage that can add positive or negative ballast to the message. No wonder misunderstandings often occur! One theorist has facetiously observed that because it is harder to receive a message and get it right than to give one, God designed the human body with one mouth and two ears. Is this an anatomical reminder that our listening and attentiveness should outweigh our speaking?

Verbal and Nonverbal Communication

Communication is classified as verbal and nonverbal. Verbal communication uses words to transmit a message, while nonverbal communication refers to everything except the words used to transmit a message. As noted earlier, nonverbal messages (75 to 90 percent of daily communication) can enhance or disturb interpersonal relationships and effective communication, although they frequently are overlooked. These include posture, dress, gesture, facial expressions, touch, punctuality, space, etc. Some specialized areas of nonverbal communication, such as touch and eye contact, which are strongly conditioned by culture, need to be studied carefully when one functions in a multicultural setting. There are special classifications of nonverbals: *haptics, proxemics,* and *chronemics*.

Haptics

Haptics relates touch to communication. A touch can send a message of sympathy, affection, aggression, punishment, camaraderie, etc. Culture dictates the use of touch in communication. A slap on the back as a sign of friendship may be well received in the Bronx but rejected in Bangkok. A bow is the more appropriate greeting in some areas of the world rather than a handshake. In some cultures, women do not extend their hands in greeting. Rubbing a child's head in play or opening a gift in the presence of others can be a social transgression in some cultures in Asia and Africa. A failure to respect these differences can erect communication barriers for one encounter, but the effect lasts much, much longer.

Proxemics

Proxemics relates space to communication. Being close to another implies familiarity, while distance can signal respect, fear, or indifference. Private and public zones are determined by cultures, settings, and relationships. Generally, within eighteen inches is private space, and twelve feet and beyond is public space, with intermediate areas of social propriety depending upon the relationship of those communicating. Even the amount of table space one takes with materials during a meeting may send a message about the individual's desire for control and power. The general custom of a subordinate going to the office of a superior rather than the reverse is a statement of status in the same way a corner office communicates power.

Chronemics

Chronemics relates time to communication. As in our vignette of the philosophy class, punctuality sends a message not only about the self but also how one regards others. It is said that anxious people arrive early; compulsive people come on time; hostile people arrive late. In the United States arriving late for a meeting is generally interpreted as a lack of respect or commitment. Many Americans are obsessed by time because for us, "time is money." But some cultures, in the southern hemisphere especially, attach lesser importance to being "on time." An individual's practice of punctuality communicates different messages within different cultures and settings. (See chapter 3 on time management.)

It is the power of these various nonverbals that justifies observations such as the following:

> "What you *are* is speaking so loudly that I cannot
> hear what you are *saying*."
> "If looks could kill, you would be a murderer."
> "When he keeps standing when he enters my office,
> I know there is big trouble."
> "I can tell what kind of a day it will be from the way
> he opens the door."
> "You seem different on dress-down days."

It is good to remember that even when our voices are silent, we are still sending many messages.

Intercultural Communication

Intercultural communication, whether verbal or nonverbal, holds many challenges because all communication is shaped by culture and embedded in culture. Language reveals the values and beliefs under-girding culture. Intercultural communication offers an excellent opportunity to broaden knowledge and understanding of others. It is mutually beneficial and growth-producing as it moves us toward that goal of human solidarity so frequently presented by Pope John Paul II. However, in a pluralistic setting, the potential for misunderstanding increases with the addition of each new culture, so there is a responsibility to seek to understand one's own culture in relation to other cultures. There is wisdom in the claim that one only understands his/her own culture by living in another culture for at least six months. Often, a lack of experience with other cultures makes us yield to the temptation to think our experience is normative. In this mindset, we perceive a difference as a point of inferiority rather than simply a cultural distinction. A lack of awareness of differences can create grave misunderstandings and can also offend others to the point where communication becomes ineffective or problematic in an ongoing way. This danger exists at the interpersonal level but also at the international level, where poor choice of vocabulary as well as the shape of a conference table can ignite wars and cancel trade agreements as well as simply inhibit communication.

Culture not only determines the appropriateness of subject matter, but also offers standards for the nonverbals of posture, tone, touch, proximity, gesture, and even vocabulary. As already noted, certain behaviors and references acceptable in one culture are offensive in another. For example, as noted in the chapter on time management, people in the United States value efficient and economic use of time. When Americans meet others, they may minimize socializing and get right down to business, while other cultures will emphasize relationship-building. Where viewpoints can be very different, such as with interreligious dialogue and even parish councils, a social event or dinner before the work session enhances communication and minimizes cultural differences.

In the United States, attention to a sermon or homily may well deteriorate after just five to eight minutes, while in other cultures a congregation will sustain attention for an extended time period. In western cultures in general, to look someone in the eye is to exude honesty and simplicity, while not looking directly at another is considered suspicious or a sign of guilt. On the other hand, in some eastern cultures to lower one's eyes is a mark of respect to the other. To question or challenge an authority figure, such as a parent, professor, or priest, is considered disrespectful in eastern cultures and is avoided, while in the West it generally indicates interest and openness and is encouraged.

An example here will help illustrate a specific difference and the effect of nonverbals. An African student attending a U.S. university entered a classroom where two students were already in their seats. As he took a place next to one of them, customary in his country, he sensed discomfort and was uncomfortable himself. Then he was amazed to see how as other students entered, they chose places scattered throughout the room. Americans like space and their own turf. They don't like to be fenced in and often choose seats on the margins rather than in the center.

From the management perspective, the desire for public praise is culturally influenced as well. Some cultures work to be lauded openly, while others prefer quiet commendations, such as a letter in the personnel file, because they have been taught not to stand out. Acceptance of these as "differences" can build respect and understanding of others and facilitate communication.

Rules for Good Communication

From the massive amount of literature available on communication, a few plain rules that apply to all human interaction have emerged and are stated very simply here as the foundation stones for good communication:

1. Treat others with respect.

2. Be willing to listen well, and be interested in others.

3. Listen to the complete message; separate what you want or expect to hear from what is actually communicated.

4. Be honest but not brutal in expressing views, especially about and to others.

5. Trust that others are serious and sincere in their views and have come to their position by study and reflection. Do not dismiss or trivialize their views.

6. Take the time to communicate; don't be in a hurry to "get things done."

7. Track emotional interference to avoid filtering or distorting the message.

8. Ask facilitative questions by using "how," "what," and "when" rather than "why," which can be threatening.

9. Realize cultural differences are just different; one is not necessarily superior or inferior to the other.

10. Speak simply and clearly without exaggeration or under-statement.

Modes of Communication in the Organization

At the beginning of massive technological change in the United States in the late 1960s, communications authority Marshall McLuhan made famous the expression, "The medium is the message." He pointed out that how we say something or what medium we use may have more impact than the words selected for the message. Varying messages call for varying media. McLuhan also noted that our contemporary society, particularly our younger generation, responds better to the visual image and sound than to the printed word. Since the sixties, major attention has also been given to the social influence of the sound bite and the headline. News stations now differentiate themselves on the depth of information disseminated (*PBS Newshour*) or the speed and efficiency with which it is communicated (*CNN Headline News*). The Web has quickly become a major resource for Church personnel not only for materials on theology and spirituality but also for internal and external communication. Communication changes have rapidly penetrated all of society, including the Church, and must be factored into organizational planning. The scope and speed of the Web heighten the urge for more information and a desire for speed as well as control over all forms of communication.

Purpose influences—and in many cases dictates—the choice of medium. The medium will differ if the goal is pure information sharing, motivating, brainstorming, or decision-making. When we apply the effectiveness standard (do the sender and receiver meet in the message?), we find the following ascending hierarchy: nonpersonalized memo; e-mail; personalized letter; telephone call; face-to-face interaction. Obviously, time availability helps determine the format as well. For example, if it is necessary to get one message out to many people within a short period of time, a memo or e-mail is efficient and economical, although it suffers by its impersonal nature and the inability for discussion or feedback. When we need to observe the way the message is being received, the telephone or face-to-face meeting is more time consuming but also more respectful of the individual and also allows for feedback. A termination interview is preferred to a pink slip in an envelope. In face-to-face encounters, communication is enhanced dramatically when questions are raised or the addressee repeats what he or she has heard. This practice is especially helpful in the United States when dealing with persons who are not fluent in English. For certain legal or supervisory purposes, it may be necessary to follow up face-to-face communications with written documentation. In a litigious society such as ours, written documentation, while considered by many as too formal, is necessary for evaluation sessions and reports of policy deviations. A written follow-up to an employee conference or supervisor-subordinate meeting can help to assure common understanding of the interview because emotional pressures often dominate these encounters even when there are no points of conflict.

Dialogue or Debate

The dawning of both moral pluralism and ecumenism in the 1960s heightened the need for dialogue rather than debate within Church organizations and with other publics. Organizational success as well as multicultural harmony depend upon the ability to address issues openly, objectively, and nondogmatically so that hearts and minds are united in the search for truth or the best-practice solution to a problem. Many of our television and radio shows adopt a crossfire and over-talking style, which impedes communication and unfortunately is very easily imitated. As secularity increases it is especially important that Catholic institutions clearly, respectfully communicate the convictions foundational to our beliefs and listen attentively as others share their convictions.

Jesus offers a model. On various issues with his disciples, and prototypically with the Samaritan woman at the well, Jesus shows how empathy and trust can lead to good dialogue and good pastoral results. His parables employed the method of introducing basic experiences before venturing into the unknown of his message. He also avoided confusing justice and love when presenting the generous employer who treated all day-workers the same no matter the hours worked and in the father who welcomed back his errant son. Jesus used questions to stimulate thinking and to reduce threat, and he preferred dialogue to debate except when necessary. He understood that at the human level debate polarizes and freezes views, while dialogue encourages openness.

It is helpful then to consider how dialogue and debate differ. We can summarize the distinctions as follows:

Debate	Dialogue
Assumes I have the right answer.	Many people have contributions to make.
I need to prove the other wrong.	Effort to find mutual understanding.
Winning is all.	Search for common ground.
Listen for counter-arguments.	Listen to understand the other.
Defensive attitude.	Separate persons from ideas.
Desirous of closure.	Willingness to continue, not close.

Organizations profit from open dialogue sessions that bring forth a range of views and develop informed readiness for decision-making. Leaders who are sincerely interested in engaging in dialogue and profiting from others' perspectives need to focus on the shared interests of the group while acknowledging the divisive ones. All must assume that all are motivated by good purposes and that ideas must be separated from personalities. It is also helpful to honestly face and identify emotional pressures, related or unrelated to the issue, that affect one's responses and relationships. Dialogue on any issue should always be separated from the decision-making on that issue, preferably by at least a week for serious questions. This allows for both the extraverts and the introverts to process the issue before taking a stand and also offers opportunity for integrating the dialogue experience and, if necessary, re-ordering one's values or changing one's judgments.

Conclusion

To be effective, Church managers must understand that communication serves as the oxygen of the organization and is a very complex process. They must also be conscious of their own communication style and recognize that different situations require different approaches and different media. This demands that managers spend time getting to know how associates communicate and how they wish to be communicated with. The administrator must also realize that the medium selected must be assessed and guided by the situation and the person.

Exercises

1. Reflect on a recent total-parish or organizational communication experience that went extremely well. Using the diagram of communication on page 67, consider the elements that made the effort successful (sender, message, receiver, image, environment).

2. Reflect on a recent encounter with a co-worker or subordinate that did not go well. Using the Rules for Good Communication presented on pages 74–75, consider how you will change your approach if a similar situation comes up again with that employee.

3. Perform a communications audit for your parish, using the Communication Needs Assessment (see page 81) and Parish Communications Audit forms. These are available in worksheet format at avemariapress.com. They can help you identify all the types, frequency, distribution, cost, etc. the parish currently uses to communicate various types of information with personnel, committees, parishioners, and the public.

   After completing the needs assessment and audit either alone or within a parish staff meeting, decide how to evaluate the effectiveness of each means of communication and whether or not changes should be made. After gathering and evaluating this information, you can be confident in creating an effective communications plan.

4. Study the following two mini-cases that have actually occurred, and identify the communication issues that are being revealed. Indicate what you would do if you were the associate pastor in Case A. In Case B, point out the advantages and disadvantages of the three suggestions, and then develop your own proposal.

A. Neighborly Competition

In St. Zachary parish there are four priests; two work in the parish, one is diocesan administrator, and one is a professor at a nearby university. Over the past few weeks, the associate pastor has been visiting homes and has heard comments like the following about the professor: "Some mornings I leave before communion at the early Mass because Father H. gives a three-credit homily every day." "Does Father realize that many of us at the early Mass have to work?" "I have been going to St. Tobias because they have a fast early Mass." "I wish the bulletin would list who has each Mass so you could choose your priest."

At dinner one evening the pastor noted that the pastor of St. Tobias had thanked him for sending his parishioners over for the early Mass. The associate remained silent. The pastor said, "We should find out if they go over on Sundays, too." The competition ended.

B. Consolidation of Mass Schedule

The pastors of three parishes in a heavily populated area with a decreasing Catholic population have decided to decrease the number of Masses offered each Sunday. They develop a schedule that assures the usual times for Masses will be maintained, but the Masses will be scheduled for the three parishes as a region or unit. For example, not every parish will have a 4:00 or 6:30 Mass on Saturday evenings. A generous schedule of area Masses will be retained, but not at each site. In effect, there will be a reduction of six Masses in total, but the time availabilities will be maintained. After lengthy discussion, one pastor recommended that they send out one joint announcement and promise to publish the three schedules in all three parish bulletins in the future. Another thinks a meeting in each parish would be better. Another suggests getting the parish councils on board first.

Sample Communication Needs Assessment

1. On the **left** of the Audit list below, what you believe are information sources that need to be generally available within the parish.

2. On the **right** check what is currently available in your parish.

Need		Current Status
_____	Weekly Bulletin	_____
_____	E-mail Directory	_____
_____	Web site	_____
_____	Telephone Relay – "Phone Chain"	_____
_____	Scheduled Mailings	_____
_____	Parish Information Sheet	_____
_____	Parish Newsletter	_____
_____	Adequate and Effective External Signage	_____
_____	School Calendar	_____
_____	Home Visits – General Schedule	_____
_____	Monthly or Quarterly Publications	_____
_____	Display of Press Releases	_____
_____	Parish Calendar	_____
_____	Diocesan Paper	_____
_____	Religious Publications	_____
_____	Annual Report	_____
_____	Parish Organization / Personnel / Authority Matrix	_____
_____	Budget	_____
_____	Financial Statements	_____
_____	Parish Planning Process and Plan	_____
_____	Parish Services	_____
_____	Service Programs	_____
_____	Parish Organizations	_____
_____	Ministry Opportunities in Parish	_____
_____	Parish Profile / Demographics	_____
_____	Parish Calendar	_____
_____	Mass Intentions by Week / Month	_____
_____	Liturgical Readings for Week / Month	_____
_____	Pastor's Letters or Messages	_____
_____	Spiritual Reflections	_____
_____	News of Parishioners	_____
_____	Issues / Events of Diocese	_____
_____	Other	_____

On the "Parish Communication Audit" (available online at avemariapress.com), list your current communications and complete the audit.

After review of your list with the audit, develop a communication plan.

BIBLIOGRAPHY

Buber, Martin. *I and Thou*. Translated by Walter Kaufman. New York: Scribners, 1970.

Jandt, Fred E., ed. *Intercultural Communication: A Global Reader*. Thousand Oaks, CA: Sage Publications, 2004.

Levine, Deena R., and Mara B. Adelman. *Beyond Language: Cross-Cultural Communication*. Upper Saddle River: Prentice-Hall, 1993.

Martin, Judith N., and Thomas K. Nakayama. *Intercultural Communication in Contexts*. New York: McGraw-Hill, 2007.

Pickett, William L. *A Concise Guide to Pastoral Planning*. Notre Dame: Ave Maria Press, 2007.

Wood, Julia T. *Interpersonal Communication: Everyday Encounters*. Belmont, CA: Thomson/Wadsworth, 2007.

CHAPTER 5

Meetings

Margaret John Kelly, D.C., PhD

The apostles and the presbyters met together to see
about this matter.
—Acts 15:6

It is the decision of the holy Spirit and of us not to
place on you any burden beyond these necessities.
—Acts 15:28

Key Concepts

1. Both post–Vatican II ecclesiology and contemporary management theory recognize the importance of broad participation to
   assure organizational vitality and personal commitment to the
   mission.

2. Meetings are a direct way of gaining participation and support within an organization, but they are time-consuming and
   must, therefore, contribute proportionately to the organizational mission.

3. A meeting's effectiveness is affected by preparation, participation, and meaningful follow-up.

4. The environment (physical and psychological) created for a
   meeting is a critical success factor.

5. The purpose of each meeting (idea-generating, decision-making,
   morale-building, brainstorming, information-sharing, supervision, conflict management, etc.) and the scope of authority

(advisory or decisive) should be made clear in the announcement of the meeting and again as the meeting begins so that all participants have the same understanding of their roles. The demands of confidentiality should also be explained.

6. An agenda must be prepared and distributed well in advance of the meeting.

7. The skills required of both the meeting leader and the meeting participants can be acquired and measured.

8. The learning, personality, and communication styles of the participants need to be considered when planning meeting activities.

9. Minutes provide a record of deliberations and decisions as well as attendance, and should be carefully recorded and documented. A written summary should be developed after each supervisory encounter even when formal minutes are not required.

10. Well-planned opening prayers or reflections set the tone of a meeting and sensitize participants to their shared responsibilities for mission.

11. Group meetings should not be used as a way to avoid one-on-one confrontations with employees.

Introduction

The quotations from the Acts of the Apostles that open this chapter remind us that meetings held a place of honor in the early Church. They were used not only to achieve sound decision-making but also to maintain unity within the community. The Second Vatican Council (Vatican II) affirmed that emphasis with its stress on active participation and responsibility at all levels of the Church, especially among the laity. The Vatican II council called clerical leaders to share their leadership with a significantly broader group and to serve as motivators and conveners who identify, encourage, and mobilize all the gifts within the community. The 1983 Code of

Canon Law also stressed the contribution each member of a parish must make to the life of the faith community. It mandated financial advisory committees to the pastor and bishop and advocated pastoral councils for the parish and the diocese. The United States Conference of Catholic Bishops expressed this in their 1980 pastoral *Called and Gifted*, which was updated in 1995 as *Called and Gifted for the Third Millennium*, highlighting again the role of the laity within the Church. The need to develop a participative leadership style and to discover ways to engage all within the parish and other Church organizations took on new importance. Meetings became a major means of achieving this goal of participation and shared responsibility.

Concurrent with this post–Vatican II call for greater involvement and responsibility on the part of all in the Church, management practitioners and researchers demonstrated that organizational ventures are more successful when members are kept well informed and personally involved in the corporate mission and overall goals. They also found that vertical and horizontal communication, referred to in this book as the oxygen of a parish, greatly enhances ministry and organizational vitality. Meetings, whether *in vivo* or virtual, remain a central means to dispense and gather information, to educate and animate communities, and to make good decisions. Meetings also exert a positive force on morale and productivity and are a key means of expanding the knowledge and commitment of the participants. Generally speaking, people prefer circles to pyramids and democratic structures to layered or hierarchical ones. Meetings can create such circular structures as they bring together some or all levels of the organization as well as peer groups within the organization. This chapter presents an overview of the importance of meetings and some practical means to make them instruments of community-building and organizational strength.

The Value of Meetings

While there is consensus that effective meetings yield great organizational benefits, this does not suggest that productive meetings are easy to plan, conduct, or follow up. In fact, noted moral theologian Bernard Haring, in the early post–Vatican II era, noted that Church meetings, principally because of their frequency, length, and poor leadership, had become the modern replacement for hair shirts. Others lament the divisiveness that meetings can bring to the surface as well as the challenge created by the wide range of interests and backgrounds existing in most parishes and other Church organizations. One pastor gave meetings the proverbial left-handed compliment while also capturing their value: "I hate to spend good time sitting around listening to them, but the parishioners really seem to enjoy coming together at meetings, and they seem more cooperative now in volunteering in the parish." Another Church administrator missing the point lamented, "At the end of the meeting we took the path I suggested at the beginning, so we could have saved time by accepting my proposal immediately."

Meetings are necessary. It is that coming together and being heard, as well as speaking with and listening to others, that promotes loyalty and engagement and contributes to a Christian community. Meetings demonstrate well the wisdom that process often is more important and contributes more to organizational health than the final product. They are central to achieving the mission and advancing the vision, but they must be both constructive and productive, effective and efficient.

As specialization grows in information technologies, it becomes more and more apparent that no one person can be expected to have all the information needed to make the best decisions. It is also apparent that having a group of people meeting in one place (or electronically present to each other) is superior to a series of one-on-one consultations. Ideas build on other ideas. It is counterproductive at several levels for a pastor or administrator to be satisfied with asking a few "friendly souls" their views on an issue. "Ad hoc social dialogues" cannot substitute for focused meetings where persons come together for the good of the whole. Broad participation almost always enhances buy-in and acceptance even by those who were not directly part of the process. It is helpful to remember that the best decision in the world may be compromised, or even sabotaged, unless those who are affected by it or must implement it are involved at some level and are committed to its purpose. Finally, meetings, along with regular reporting of the business covered, contribute to a culture of transparency and accountability so necessary in today's Church.

Listening

There is great wisdom in the observation that "God created us with two ears but only one tongue, a gentle hint that we should listen more than we speak." The skill of listening is essential to all communication but is of particular importance if meetings are to be goal-oriented and process-driven. Listening in a group setting is a difficult skill to master because the setting makes it so easy to drift, isolate oneself, or, worst of all, prepare what one wants to say as soon as the opportunity arises. In every group there will be one or two individuals who are more concerned about gaining converts to their way of thinking than seeking to appreciate the genius of others. The following points help to cultivate listening competence and listening readiness.

1. *Open Environment.* Remove distractions in the meeting area and arrange furnishings in a practical manner for conversation or interaction. A round or U-shaped table formation encourages attention to other group members, not just to one speaker. When groups are large and opportunity for input is requested, persons need to offer comments from a central place so that all may hear, or the chair should repeat the observations to sustain attention.

2. *Presence/Attitude.* Show through attention, eye contact, and other nonverbals that you respect the other person and want to hear his or her thoughts.

3. *Empathy.* Try to put yourself in the other person's place and experience so that you can appreciate his or her opinions.

4. *Issue Orientation.* Don't judge people on their emotional expressions or presentation styles, but rather on their observations on the issue.

5. *Openness.* Don't assume you know what another will say because of past experience with the individual. Avoid thinking things like "Here he goes again!"

6. *Nonjudgmental Orientation.* Ask questions for clarification, but don't argue on the legitimacy of an opinion held by another.

Pre-meeting Considerations

Before a meeting is called, the convener must determine that bringing people together is the best method for the task at hand and how a group session will be helpful. The chart below distills some of the elements identified by Dennis Sleven in his monumental text, *The Whole Manager.*

Should I Use a Group?		
Factors	**No**	**Yes**
TIME	Little time	No time deadline
RESOURCES	Individual knowledge skill, ability, etc. is sufficient	Greater resources will lead to higher quality decisions
CONFLICT	Will / may be an obstacle	Desirable among members to stimulate problem-solving
IMPLEMENTATION	Group cooperation is not essential	Group cooperation is essential
TYPE OF TASK	Poorly-structured (specific problem unknown)	Well-structured (problem well-defined)

Those who call meetings need to consider the cost of bringing people together (hourly wages, lost opportunities, slowdowns, distractions, and disruptions) against the benefits and anticipated outcomes—both tangible and intangible. Sometimes leaders hesitate to bring issues to meetings because they feel they may be surrendering their authority to the group or that discussions of difficult topics could increase polarization within the organization. Meetings are "low-risk" for polarization and for infringing on authority if the purpose of the meeting is clearly presented and participants know whether they will be involved in brainstorming, gathering information, analyzing proposals, or decision-making. When there is suspicion, or even assurance, that polarization exists on an agenda topic, it is helpful to have a brief social session before the business is taken up. This helps to set the stage because friendly pre-meeting sessions help participants to see others as real persons whose identity is not equivalent to the ideas they express. The pursuit of a common goal, as well as this separating of persons from their ideas, facilitates objectivity. Unfortunately, however, some dialogues and meetings fail because participants view each other as the ideological enemy rather than another human being with some differing viewpoints. It is healthy to get points of division out into the open so that the values and advantages of specific perspectives can be explored and scrutinized. If the pastor or organizational leader wishes to encourage the expression of diverse views, he or she can reinforce this intent to listen to all by not attending the session or by assigning someone else to chair the meeting and refraining from offering any opinions or judgments. At the parish level, when the pastor allows others to take such leadership, the members are less likely to hold back or defer to the cleric—a practice still common in some parish communities and Church organizations.

Meeting Planning

It is not an exaggeration to claim that the most important part of a meeting takes place before the meeting, especially in the development of the agenda and the selection of participants. In work settings, the supervisor of a department may develop the agenda alone, but in parishes and Church organizations that strive for community, it is helpful if a few persons assist in formulating it. The following steps can expedite the planning process and facilitate the meeting itself. They also help to guard against the all-too-common evaluation: "We killed two hours and didn't get anything done," or "It's all talk, a waste of time." After the need for a meeting is affirmed, the following steps can facilitate the planning process.

1. *Purpose:* In just a few words, articulate the reason for the meeting and what "work-product" is desired as a result of the convening. This will identify the topics to be included and suggest the best process and approach.

2. *Previous Minutes:* If the meeting is of an ongoing committee, task force, or work group, review the minutes of the last meeting to assure continuity and follow-up with previous meetings.

3. *Agenda:* Develop the agenda, assuring that the schedule is appropriate for the business issues identified.

4. *Participation:* Identify the people who need to be present because of their office or their expertise. For most organizational administration issues a group of five to eleven is effective. An uneven number is helpful to avoid ties in voting.

5. *Logistics:* Determine location, time frame, and environment (access to meeting area, security, arrangement for chairs, refreshments, etc.).

6. *Materials:* Identify materials needed for the meeting (pre-meeting readings, displays, pens, newsprint, computer, projector, dry-erase board or chalkboard, etc.). Progressive visual recording of ideas facilitates progress and avoids needless repetition.

7. *Communication:* Determine the manner in which the announcement of your meeting will be made (print letter, posters, web site, e-mail, phone) and the timetable needed to do so. Be sure that the announcement includes purpose, beginning and

ending times, location, preparatory materials or advance work needed, and a deadline for confirming attendance. Agenda should be forwarded one week in advance.

8. *Immediate Preparation:* Two people should arrive early to ensure that the facility arrangements are satisfactory and no adjustments need to be made. This uses time well and witnesses to the importance of the meeting and respect for the time and comfort of others.

9. *Recording:* Assign a reporter to take notes or tape the meeting so that minutes can later be developed.

10. *Start and End Time:* Start on time with a prayer (preferably one chosen to support the purpose of the meeting). Meetings generally should not extend beyond ninety minutes. Before closing, provide a brief summation so that all have a common understanding of what the group has done during the meeting and what the next steps should be.

Format for Agenda

The agenda format below is standard and can serve as a model for most meetings. In some cases where several items are to be discussed, time allocations should be cited.

1. Opening prayer
2. Roll call (if appropriate or necessary) or introductions
3. Review of meeting purpose by chair and approval of the agenda
4. Approval of minutes (if relevant to group)
5. Communications (if correspondence for the group has been received)
6. Old business (follow-up from previous meeting)
7. New business (first-time considerations)
8. Summation (review of business covered and assignment of follow-up tasks)

9. Other (while this is not an invitation to add issues for discussion and does not permit the introduction of new matter for immediate discussion, it provides opportunity to raise issues for future consideration and for announcements of interest to the group)

10. Announcement of time, place, and purpose of next meeting

11. Adjournment

Minutes

Minutes direct the follow-up activities much like the agenda directs the actual meeting. Minutes of meetings and other convenings serve as an immediate record for guidance as well as for historical documentation. Honesty in reporting and prudence must guide the development of minutes. While some dioceses and organizations have standardized a format for minutes, the following example can be used as a general model.

General Information. A meeting of the planning committee of St. Mary's Parish was held at Emmitstown, Maryland, on January 1, 2010, from 7:00 to 8:30 p.m. The opening prayer was offered by Msgr. James Flannigan.

Participants. Minutes of boards and committees should identify present, absent, and excused members so that all are accounted for. Guests should also be listed, and the parts of the meeting they attended should be cited. If persons engage by electronic means, this also should be noted.

Approval of Minutes of Previous Meeting. (Standing and ongoing committee meetings)

Summation of Old and New Business. Provide a short, *crisp* summary of issues discussed, each with a topic. All new recommendations for further consideration or for action should provide the vote on the issue if one was taken or the general consensus of the group. For historical purposes, it is helpful to include the rationale for any recommendation or proposed action of the committee.

Follow-up. Describe the actions and responsibilities to be undertaken.

Next Meeting. The next meeting will be held on February 11, 2010, at 7:00 p.m.

Adjournment. The meeting adjourned at 8:35 p.m.

Note: To allow for full freedom of expression during a meeting, attribution of ideas to specific persons should be avoided in the writing of minutes.

Participation

If broad participation is a goal of the post–Vatican II Church, and research has demonstrated that group thinking has many individual and organizational benefits, it is helpful to identify the qualities desired in both the effective meeting leader and the effective meeting member. If a group will remain stable for some time or even if some difficulty or conflict is anticipated for a single meeting, it is helpful to present these criteria as the desired profile of the members. Generally, as people review these descriptors, they engage in a self-evaluation and thus become much more aware of their own styles. While these descriptors are expressed positively, they not only engender reflections on meeting virtues but also elicit reflections on their opposite weaknesses. This dual awareness can encourage imitation of the positive behaviors as well as a desire to avoid their opposites.

Traits of the Effective Meeting Leader
(Planner, Conductor, Facilitator, Integrator, and Evaluator)

- Tactful, calm, respectful, comfortable
- Knowledgeable about purpose and expectations of the meeting
- Authoritative but not authoritarian
- Capable of eliciting participation, relating ideas, tracking common threads, pointing out areas of agreement and disagreement
- Objective and evenhanded in treating people, ideas, and proposals

- Proficient in phrasing questions and issues so that discussion is generated and simple "yes" and "no" responses are avoided
- Capable of summarizing meeting progress and suggesting future activity of the group
- Flexible in responding to a range of personality types and various group sizes

Traits of the Effective Meeting Member
(Contributor, Collaborator, Synthesizer, and Reactor)

- Involved in the meeting either as an active contributor or by visible interest
- Generous in spending time in preparation for the meeting
- Respectful toward others, neither patronizing nor dismissive
- Willing to negotiate
- Disciplined to stay on subject
- Trained in listening to and not prejudging speakers.
- Collaborative, not competitive
- Adaptable to various situations and accepting of various personality types

Aids to Participation

On complex issues it is helpful to get as many ideas on the table as possible without anyone declaring ownership of or commitment to any. Creativity can abound when participants understand that the goal is to explore all possibilities without championing or rejecting any particular one. The more loquacious in the group need restraint, while the timid need encouragement; the extroverts need discipline, while the introverts need time. Consensus (one sense; one understanding) is the goal of most meetings. It also is helpful to have some win-win agreement when there is not consensus. Groups can become unbalanced when one member's role is inflated by "winning" too often. If conducted well, meetings should not result in winners and losers. When a lack of consensus is apparent, a vote could be premature. Therefore, when buy-in is essential, it may be advisable to delay a decision until the next meeting.

In seeking consensus on preferences or in actual group decision-making, it is necessary to assure that every person has an opportunity to express him- or herself to the group. When everyone is given the opportunity to give an opinion, each surrenders the franchise to gripe or to engage in "post-meeting meetings." These post-mortems by a few can be destructive of overall morale and trust in the organization and can sidetrack progress at subsequent meetings.

The following three methods can promote broad participation and creativity in generating ideas and in expressing judgments on specific issues at the appropriate time:

1. *Brainstorming.* In this technique, ideas are called out and listed in view of all on a board, newsprint, or computer, without any judgment of their value being permitted. The process is continued until all ideas are exhausted and all are recorded visually. Persons are encouraged to be creative and not limit themselves to ideas they themselves support. This listing of ideas, issues, solutions, etc., then provides a visual record for discussion and evaluation.

2. *Round Robin.* This provides a more disciplined brainstorming technique. In succession, each member of the group lists a view, idea, or approach that has not already been mentioned. All are recorded without evaluation and the round-robin continues until all reach the "pass" stage when their turn occurs. In this method, as well, the ideas must be recorded visually so that all can view them. This round-robin technique (with or without the physical recording) can also be used effectively to poll individuals on a particular issue so that all will have to express an opinion in a circle of equality. This provides the opportunity to

assess the group. If there is great division, it may be advisable to delay.

3. *Scenario Building.* After time for reflection, each person offers a possible scenario (i.e., the way things could work out in a given situation) for the issue or topic being considered. For example, each person might offer one possible schedule for parish visitation of newcomers or a plan for starting a "welcome home" outreach to inactive Catholics. Each individual can answer questions from the group after presenting the scenario, but no evaluation can be made. All scenarios are recorded in broad strokes. Then in discussion the implications of each are drawn out.

After these steps, the group can identify the strengths and weaknesses of each scenario and select the most and least desirable according to the apparent implications of each scenario. Evaluation may not occur until all scenarios have been discussed so that complete freedom is maintained and no scenario is identified with just one person because all have had the opportunity for input. With serious issues, it is wise to allow a lapse of time between the proposals and decision-making stages because some group members will need more time for reflection.

Again, in these processes visual recording is essential to track the conversation, preclude unnecessary repetition, and retain focus.

Everyone has probably experienced the two extremes of participation in meetings. One extreme is the group where some remain strong and silent, not revealing themselves or their opinions and thus not making a contribution to the discussion. The other extreme occurs where one or two loquacious participants dominate or seek to take the discussion off course. The following leader responses to specific personality types pass the discipline and respect test. They are gently corrective of the individual and offer advice to the group as well. In addition to these specific responses, many consultants now advise groups to establish a "parking lot" somewhere in the room, away from the main discussion area, but visible to all. When any issue is raised that is not relevant to the discussion, the leader asks the speaker to write up the suggestion and put it in the parking lot so the issue will not be lost but the group can move forward on task.

The following techniques can be used to both encourage and to moderate group members:

A. Discouraging the loquacious:

    1. "We will limit each one to a brief comment and allow each person to speak before anyone speaks a second time."

    2. "Once an idea has been presented, it should not be repeated again or expanded on until we have all of our ideas on the table."

B. Encouraging the quiet and/or hesitant:

    1. "Jim, we haven't heard your opinion yet."

    2. "We'd like to hear from those who haven't had a chance to speak yet."

    3. "Has everyone had a chance to give his or her thoughts?

C. Discouraging sidetrackers:

    1. "Let's hold that for later in our discussion."

    2. "Let's reconsider our purpose and limit our discussion to that."

    3. "Could we return to our meeting goals and see if this line of thought will help us achieve the goals?"

    4. "Let's back up and redefine our goal for this meeting."

General Guidelines for Meetings

The following guidelines provide direction on the theory and practice of effective meetings and are also very useful in guiding participants through a post-meeting self-evaluation.

1. *Purpose.* Meeting purpose is focused, expressed in clear language, and reasonable for the timeframe allotted.

2. *Timeframe.* Time parameters and task parameters are announced prior to the meeting. Start on time and end on time. Relevant materials, as well as minutes and agenda, are distributed one week in advance of the meeting. Generally avoid Monday and Friday meetings. Meetings generally should not exceed ninety minutes, with sixty to seventy-five minutes being optimal for most. With large groups the sessions should not exceed eighty minutes.

3. *Clear Expectations.* Clarify expectations so that each participant knows if the task is brainstorming, information-sharing, advisory, or decision-making.

4. *Agenda.* Develop an agenda that relates past work with future goals as well as guides the proceedings. It should be distributed well in advance of the meeting along with any other necessary materials. New material of more than one page should not be presented during a meeting.

5. *Competence/Representation.* Select persons who have an experience and knowledge base to deal with the given subject. If a project is to affect a diverse group, a representative group needs to be involved from the beginning of the discussion.

6. *Implementation.* When the meeting purpose includes decision-making, include at least one person who will be involved with implementation of the decision to assure understanding of the thinking *and* feeling behind the project or issue.

7. *Summations.* At the conclusion of meeting, the chair or designated reporter provides an oral summation to the group. A written report or minutes, including follow-up tasks and responsibilities, is prepared immediately after the meeting and shared with participants and others who need to be kept informed.

8. *Leadership.* The leader or facilitator assumes responsibility for moving the group toward full participation and achieving its

purpose, but does not dominate or control. This person maximizes talents, minimizes eccentricities, encourages consensus, and manages conflict.

9. *Confidentiality.* Clarify the importance of confidentiality and identify an authorized spokesperson—the person who will communicate in the name of the group to other stakeholders in the group's work.

10. *Commitment.* Seek to make good decisions, but remember that the best decisions are empty and futile unless support is generated for their implementation.

11. *Process.* Use visual aids and ongoing written reporting on newsprint, board, etc., to keep the group focused.

12. *Value.* Ensure that meetings are not just an expense of people's time and energy but also a good investment for the individuals and in the organization.

Post-meeting Evaluation
(Available for free download at avemariapress.com)

These questions can be raised and responded to by all participants at the close of a meeting or after a meeting by the leaders. Areas of remediation can be identified for follow-up.

1. Did all members participate?

2. Did participants come prepared for the meeting?

3. Did anyone exert undue influence or pressure so that the atmosphere of openness was affected?

4. Were the agenda and other materials received in time for preparation?

5. Was everyone aware of the purpose and kept focused on the defined tasks?

6. Were the appropriate people at the table?

7. Was time used economically?

8. Were "irrelevancies" noted respectfully without unduly sidetracking the group?

9. Were opinions expressed clearly and received with respect?

10. Was a summary of the meeting presented to assure agreement about conclusions and follow-up?

11. Was the group meeting necessary, and did it achieve its purpose? (Was it necessary for the information shared to be given at one time to all? Did the setting enhance the quality of response? Did the group endorse the project presented or was enthusiasm generated to move projects forward?)

12. Did the setting and seating arrangement facilitate the progress of the meeting?

Conclusion

In the twenty-first-century, post–Vatican II Church, meetings are indispensable aids to Church managers and essential to sustaining organizations, advancing the mission, maintaining solidarity, and actualizing the vision. They can serve as a major medium and meeting ground for planning, sharing, and motivating within the organization. It is important, therefore, to make use of the skills and techniques that can transform meetings into productive, energizing, and positive experiences for all. Meetings are, after all, the place where a group of individuals united in mission become more fully a community.

Some of these observations may appear self-evident to some, but experience has shown that often the most basic and the most obvious are overlooked, ignored, or avoided. Whether a meeting is to plan a parish picnic, develop a long-range plan for an institution or diocese, close parish schools, redecorate the church, or add a wing to the hospital, the outcome will be enhanced by convening those who have the requisite knowledge and commitment to process individually and corporately the goals of the group and thus to advance the vision.

Exercises

1. Using the traits of an effective meeting member or leader, review a recent meeting that you conducted or attended. Identify where you performed well.

2. After the next meeting where you serve as leader, ask the participants to help you evaluate the session using the Post-Meeting Evaluation questionnaire provided in this chapter and available for free download at www.avemariapress.com. From the evaluation process, identify one thing you as leader will do to improve and one that would improve the participation of the group.

3. As pastor, you have identified the need to make your parish more accessible to both the elderly and persons with mobility concerns. Currently they must remain apart from the congregation in a side chapel. You are considering two options: (a) ramping to the current entrance; and (b) installing an external elevator on the side of the church. Both ways have financial and aesthetic implications. You have decided to raise this at the next parish pastoral council for study. What idea-generating techniques will you use? What materials will you assemble to assist the members of the council?

4. Read the following case study, "Convent Share," and critique it from the perspective of good communication and effective meetings. Create a scenario of what happened in the convent as a result of the tour. Suggest how that meeting could have been improved and what follow-up advice you would give to the pastor to improve parish relations and parish meetings.

Mini Case: Convent Share

A convent located in a changing neighborhood was built for eighteen sisters and now houses just six. While the sisters all work outside the parish, they are very active within the parish in liturgical ministries and outreach service areas.

At a recent parish pastoral council meeting, one of the officers recommended to the pastor that parish services be placed in the "excess space" in the convent. It was then recommended by the religious education coordinator that the sisters move to the top floor, as in many other convents, and the parish use the first two floors. The pastor said he would look into it.

The next week, the school principal, who had been present at the council, asked the maintenance man to take her through the convent during the day when the sisters would be at work so as not to disturb them. While they were touring, one of the sisters returned to the convent. The principal told her it had been recommended at the pastoral council meeting that some of the convent space be used for the parish because only six sisters lived there, and that the pastor agreed to look into it. The principal explained that she already had some specific plans and could easily see how the community room and the dining room would make good preschool areas. She asked the sister if she had seen how this has been done in other parishes. She also acknowledged that this change might be hard for the sisters to accept. The sister answered politely but with obvious displeasure.

When the other sisters in the house heard about "the takeover tour," they were all very disturbed at the invasion of privacy and the lack of communication. They asked the sister-coordinator of the house to call the pastor, express their concern, and ask for clarification. They also, among themselves, asked if there could be a rapid eviction.

5. Read the following case study, "Seventy-Fifth Anniversary Planning," and respond to the questions at the end of it.

Mini Case: Seventy-Fifth Anniversary Planning

Father T., the parochial vicar, opens the meeting by asking the group to work on the seventy-fifth anniversary celebration for the parish, which could be a fundraiser. One person asks how this group was selected because it seems to have just the senior members of the parish, who are mostly Irish. Tom McKenna immediately says that if they're going back to celebrate the founding, they should have those who put up the money to build the parish. Mary Pacifica immediately says that they should be equally concerned with the people of other nationalities who currently support the parish. Father answers that he will invite others later. Mary suggests that Mrs. Balboni be included because her family has been in the parish for three generations and she has children in the school. Mrs. Gross says she thinks that before they start naming names, they ought to think about what expertise they want on the committee. Arthur Shed asks Father if this event will be paid for by the parish or if people will have to pay for it because no one should be excluded because of money. Mary Caesari notes that with a Mass they only need coffee afterward, and all can participate.

At that point, Fr. T. says there is a liturgical committee under Fr. Allen who will plan the liturgy. Arthur returns to his point that they can't plan without knowing about finances. Father repeats his point that they must know what they want to do first. Mary suggests that a theme and calendar be developed. Orchid goes to the board and says she will develop a chart so that they can decide how they want to celebrate: as an entire parish or with mini-celebrations for the seniors, the school children, for families, etc. Tom says that people celebrate in different ways, and with a cultural fair the old parishioners can get to know all the newcomers. Arthur remarks that if people bring the food, everyone could buy a meal and the parish wouldn't have to pay for refreshments. Mary observes that they haven't yet decided on a cultural fair, and she thinks Orchid's suggestion was a good start for the discussion. Bill asks Orchid to repeat her suggestion. Mrs. Gross wonders if a committee is looking at doing a history of the parish and if this will be published because she has an attic full of pictures that she could contribute.

Father thanks everyone for participating (even though six did not speak) and says he will think about the suggestions. Arthur offers to give Father the notes he has taken.

1. If Father T. asked you to critique the meeting, what would you say to him?

2. How would you handle at least three of the participants' contributions so that the discussion could continue productively?

3. How would you plan a follow-up meeting?

BIBLIOGRAPHY

Asmub, Birte. "Meeting Talk." *Journal of Business Communication*. January 2009. Vol. 46, Issue 1, p. 3-22.

Brickerhoff, Peter. *Faith-Based Management*. New York: John Wiley, 1999.

Guttman, Howard. "Leading Meetings 101." *Leadership Excellence*. July 2009, Vol. 26, Issue 7, p. 18.

Hiesberger, Jean Maria. *Fostering Leadership Skills in Ministry*. Missouri: Ligouri Press, 2003.

Jan, Antony. "The Good Meeting." *Harvard Business Review*. April 2003, Vol. 81, Issue 4, p. 126 (reprint).

Lauer, Larry. "A New Way to Look at Meetings." *The Nonprofit World*. March-April 1995, Volume 13, p. 55-58.

Lee, Shirley Fine. "How Should Team Meetings Flow?" *Journal for Quality and Participation*. Spring 2008, Vol. 31, Issue 1, p. 25-28.

Pickett, William. *A Concise Guide to Pastoral Planning*. Notre Dame: Ave Maria Press, 2007.

Scanlon, Jessie. "How to Make Meetings Matter." *Business Week Online*. April 29, 2008, p. 9.

Slevin, Dennis. *The Whole Manager: How to Increase Your Personal and Professional Effectiveness*. New York: American Management Association, 1989.

CHAPTER 6

The Parish and Service Quality

Larry W. Boone, PhD

If the work stands that someone built upon the
foundation, that person will receive a wage.
—1 Corinthians 3:14

Key Concepts

1. As service quality becomes a major issue in secular society, it is a growing concern for the Church as it seeks to build and maintain strong communities for worship and service.

2. While parishioners are not really "customers," they do expect an attitude of caring and interest from their Church as well as a response to their needs.

3. The five constituent elements of customer service are empathy, assurance, responsiveness, reliability, and tangibles such as physical environment.

4. Flexible and parishioner-friendly standards are expected because the Church stresses the dignity of each person and the respect due to each one.

5. The hiring and training of personnel are keys to high-quality service.

6. Physical and psychological "comfort" contribute to an environment of respect and caring.

7. Individual involvement and participation in the Church, especially among youth, increases the perception of quality and enhances commitment.

Introduction

For many years the field of service-quality management has received significant attention from both for-profit and nonprofit organizations. From this field of study many well-developed theories of consumer behavior have been applied to improve customer service. Successful organizations have built competitive advantages by providing better customer service than other organizations providing similar products and services. These organizations include not only restaurants, theaters, auto companies, and retail department stores but also hospitals, universities, charitable institutions, and government agencies. Indeed, many state departments of motor vehicles and even the Internal Revenue Service, traditionally the poster children for customer abuse, have made significant strides toward improving their relationships with taxpayers by focusing on customer service.

What is the result of a few decades of spoiling American consumers with improved service? Certainly the tide of consumer expectation has risen. The American public expects organizations with whom they have contact to care—care about their individual wants and desires, care about their comfort, care about their convenience, their time, their need for information . . . in other words, care about *everything*.

Since so many for-profits and nonprofits have improved their levels of service, organizations that have not worked hard to improve their customer service have fallen behind. They stand out. Consciously or subconsciously, customers feel they are not treated well. The perception that they are not treated well leads consumers to develop an uncaring attitude, and this attitude leads to avoidance. "If they don't go out of their way to serve me well, I simply won't go back" is a fundamental consumer stance toward the acquisition of goods and the utilization of services.

Because of this service-quality culture and the importance of mission, Church leaders can and should apply the concept of service quality to their operations. They can do so by putting themselves in the "customer's shoes." That is, they need to adopt the consumer/parishioner perspective and answer the questions: "How am I being treated?" "Are parish service providers glad I'm here?" "Is my comfort and convenience important to them?" "Do they want me to come back?" Certainly, there are many opportunities for parishes and other Church organizations to improve service quality and the extent to which Christian hospitality (welcoming Christ present in each person) is visibly extended. The purpose of this chapter, then, is to highlight some of the methods parishes might implement for improving service to their "customers"—the people who show up (and do not show up) to participate in Mass and programs or to seek support and assistance. While the focus of the discussions is on parishes, the counterpart issues in other Church organizations are easily identified.

A Rationale for Customer Service

Because the parish is in effect a multi-service operation, the issue of quality in a parish has many dimensions. The principles are the same whether we are implementing them in a school, a human-services operation, or a parish. This is *not* to suggest that customer service should be the number one priority of a pastor and his staff. Catholics do not attend Mass to buy a product or to be entertained. Parishioners are not really "customers." But parish leaders certainly recognize that the parish can't serve its members well unless the members choose to show up. Showing up requires proactive behavior on the part of the parishioner and is most often a direct response to feeling welcome, respected, and cared for.

If members begin to believe that their parish doesn't really care about them, they are less likely to put forth the effort to return. In this context, providing excellent customer service is a sign of caring. Over the long run, excellent customer service connects an organization to those it seeks to serve, and it motivates people to come back time after time. Parishes benefit from this type of parishioner behavior. On at least one level, parishioners are indeed "customers," although using that term in a religious context is highly problematic. They consume or utilize services offered by the parish (liturgies, programs, education, events, counseling, and other forms of assistance). If these activities are as user-friendly as possible, parishioners may be more likely to repeat the behaviors of attending and participating.

Do all parishes need to improve parishioner service? No. Many parishes already have strong, positive relationships with their members. Parishioners perceive that the parish cares about them, and they, in turn, care about the parish. This positive attitude results in the behaviors of attending, participating actively, and volunteering. Another result is good citizenship—speaking well of the parish to others both inside and outside the parish.

A fairly low percentage (20 to 30 percent) of Catholics attend Mass and other parish events on a regular basis. This highlights the need for some parishes to think and act differently. Improvement efforts are warranted. Is better customer service the "magic wand" that will solve all parish problems? Certainly not. But a great deal of research on human behavior suggests strongly that it will help. Providing excellent service quality will at least *remove some obstacles* that may be perceived by potential participants.

Customer Service/Customer Satisfaction

Customer satisfaction is achieved by providing customers with quality, convenience, and service *as customers define those terms.* Customer *perception* is key. What the leaders of an organization believe customers *should* desire is inconsequential. General Motors used to believe they knew better than the American automobile consumer. They designed the kinds of cars they wanted to build and assumed customers would buy them. When Japanese manufacturers designed cars that customers really wanted with good gas mileage, quality fit and finish, performance reliability, and long-term warranties (not to mention handy cup holders), many consumers fled from GM into the dealerships of Japanese producers even though they had to pay higher prices and contend with waiting lists. GM got the message and started to collect marketing information to better understand their customers' needs. Since this famous customer-service revolution of the 1970s, many other American organizations have gotten the message: if you want to succeed, put the customer first. There is something scriptural in that theory that resonates with Jesus' style of evangelizing.

The five basic elements of customer service are:

- Empathy: caring, individualized attention; emotional connection

- Assurance: knowledge and courtesy of service providers, ability to convey trust and confidence

- Responsiveness: willingness to help and provide prompt service

- Reliability: ability to perform a promised service dependably and accurately

- Tangibles: appearance, comfort, and convenience of physical facilities, equipment, personnel, and communication materials

As can readily be seen, the first four elements on this list are related to the person-to-person relationship between a customer and a service provider. The most important element of service is the *personal touch*. Calling people by name, making attentive and friendly contact, and demonstrating that the service provider cares about customers' needs and wants are essential to satisfying customers. The *attitude* of the service provider is the essential ingredient here. Service is personal. And the customer's perception of the provider's attitude is key. The fifth element, tangibles, highlights the importance of the physical environment. The comfort and convenience of the physical environment set the stage for customer perceptions. The aesthetics of buildings, organizational artifacts, employee dress/uniforms, printed materials, and the like matter to customers. They project an image of caring and attention, or lack thereof.

Some organizations attempt to achieve more than customer satisfaction. They motivate their employees by striving for a higher goal—sometimes called *customer delight*. No matter what terminology is used, this ultimate level of satisfaction refers to the condition of *exceeding the customer's expectations* regarding services provided. Customer delight is achieved by concentrating on every aspect of the relationship between a customer and organization. This relationship covers the following elements:

- Understanding customer needs: To know what customers desire, an organization must first understand thoroughly who its customers are. This requires market research: knowing how large and diverse an organization's customer base may be. Market segmentation is a key concept here and is dealt with in a subsequent chapter. Frequently, markets are heterogeneous. They consist of many different groups (segments), and each group has its own unique, but predictable, needs. For example, service needs of customers over the age of sixty-five are usually similar, but they differ quite a bit from the needs of customers in the eighteen to thirty-five age group.

- Flexibility in meeting needs: An organization has to realize that "one size doesn't fit all." Customers will be delighted when an organization is willing to adjust its services to meet a special need. Conversely, remember how you felt the last time some disinterested service provider responded to your request by saying, "We can't do that for you. It's against our policy."

- Ease of "doing business": There are two major elements to "doing business" with customers. First, systems and procedures have to be very easy to use—that is, "customer friendly." Methods for placing an order for a product or service, making a contribution, etc., must be transparent, simple, and direct. Second, customers have to be in contact with decision-makers. It is never acceptable to tell a customer that someone else will have to authorize a particular transaction, and he or she will have to wait for "the supervisor (or the pastor)" to be available. A goal for delighting customers is to complete a transaction in just one conversation (or phone call or e-mail) with one person in a very short period of time.

- Providing clear, timely, and relevant information: Information required by customers must be anticipated and prepared in advance. The same, consistent information must be readily available from any representative of the service-provider. And the information must be expressed in terminology customers can understand, with no special jargon. Church people may be especially prone to the use of jargon, assuming that their communication partner is familiar with religious or Biblical terminology.

- Meeting commitments: A promise made is a promise kept. No exceptions to this rule! And when exceptions must be made (and that is inevitable), the organization must be proactive in making up a broken promise to its customers and go out of its way to be accommodating.

In order to focus discussion of parishioner service at liturgies, programs, and other events, this chapter explores three elements of service that seem particularly relevant: *personnel (and their attitude for service), convenience,* and *tangibles and physical layout.*

Personnel and Service Attitude

The key variable in the service equation is people and the attitude of service they bring to their job. There is no substitute for personal friendliness, warmth, and courtesy. Like any organization, a parish expresses its attitude through its personnel—most centrally through the pastor, assistant priests/parochial vicars, deacons, other professional and support staff, lectors, greeters, Eucharistic ministers, ushers, social policy networks, and any other individuals who have contact with parishioners as representatives of the parish. Individuals who project successfully a parish's service attitude are empathetic, flexible, articulate, informed, inventive, and empowered (i.e., capable of meeting parishioners' needs without approval or permission from higher authorities). Three organizational processes contribute critically to the development of service-oriented parish personnel: hiring, training, and listening.

Hiring

When hiring parish staff and recruiting volunteers from among parish members, a pastor or parish administrator needs to pay very careful attention to selecting the personnel who will be in direct contact with parishioners. Some people possess personalities that include the characteristics necessary to provide superior service. Their interactions with others are naturally friendly and welcoming. They are empathetic; they identify intellectually and emotionally with others. These people exude service and, if hired, they will do so in the name of the parish. Assess the service-oriented personalities of candidates in interviews. Look for people who are optimistic and exhibit high levels of self-esteem and positive self-images. Notice whether candidates smile often and sincerely. Judge the evidence of the candidate's success in service positions held in previous employment. Personnel hiring decisions are key events for any organization. Invest time and energy in the recruiting and hiring process. Include service-orientation as a selection criterion along with leadership, planning and decision-making skills, technical ability, and any other attributes a specific position may require. It pays off.

Training

Successful organizations don't leave customer service to chance; they train every employee who comes into contact with customers. Organizations striving for superior service typically devote up to 5 percent of their employees' work hours to training. Training is also important in developing the parishioner-oriented parish. Anyone who deals with parishioners should receive regular training and development focusing on topics such as those shown in the chart below. Training in these general service areas is available at many universities, community colleges, and business education institutions. Group training sessions for all parish personnel held at the parish can be excellent team-building activities for a staff. Alternatively, training sessions at a local university arranged especially for members of several parish staffs can provide staffers with opportunities to exchange ideas with individuals who perform similar staff functions at other local parishes.

Service-Oriented Training and Development

Topics
- Interpersonal Communications
- Meeting and Greeting Parishioners
- Understanding Different Personality Types
- Dealing with Parishioner Dissatisfaction
- Managing and Resolving Conflicts
- Cross-Cultural Relations
- Listening Skills
- Problem-Solving
- Communicating via Telephone and E-mail
- Explaining Parish Policies and Procedures

What's the payoff for hiring and training parish personnel toward the goal of building a strong service attitude? The atmosphere within the parish will engender feelings of belonging, teamwork, and energy among parishioners. Major differences between service and nonservice attitudes in a parish are expressed below. To which type of parish would you prefer to belong?

Service and Non-Service Attitudes in a Parish

Service Attitude
"We are here to serve your needs."
"Welcome! We're glad you're here."
"How can we help you?"

Non-Service Attitude
"You're here to serve us" (the Church, the parish).
"You have to be here. It's required of you."
"This is the way we do things. Don't ask for anything special."

A simple *greetings audit* will test the service attitude in your parish. Watch parishioners arrive at Mass. What happens as they enter the church? Does any representative of the parish greet them? Does anyone say "Welcome, we're glad you're here"? Many for-profit and nonprofit organizations, striving to establish a customer service environment, have made it part of their everyday routine to have greeters stationed at every entrance and exit. They say "Thanks for coming in," and "Glad to see you. Come back soon." Some offer small tokens of appreciation, like a free piece of hard candy as patrons exit a movie theater. In Marketing 101 we learn that customers remember you if you give them something for free, no matter how small. The point here is that the American consumer has grown accustomed to being appreciated. The effort required to organize ushers, parish staff members, religious education teachers, and the like to offer a cheerful greeting to persons arriving at Mass, programs, or events can have a big payoff. Also, parishioners tend to be very appreciative of the opportunity to shake the hand of their priest as they enter or leave the church. A service attitude is reflected in this personal touch. Greetings, like smiles, are the least expensive form of effective public relations.

Listening

Another vital element of a service attitude involves *listening*. The best service organizations constantly listen to those they serve. And most importantly, they respond to what they hear. Listening enables organizations to keep apprised of changing customer needs and expectations. Great organizations know that the only way to discover what customers want and value is to ask them. The service-oriented parish will reflect this same attitude.

Several techniques can be employed to improve listening. Surveys (for example, the Parishioner Satisfaction questionnaire we explore in chapter 8), focus groups, telephone interviews, comment cards, suggestion boxes, chat rooms on websites, and frequent one-on-one conversations are effective tools for tapping into the likes and dislikes of parishioners. Pastors and parish staff or outside consultants can be used to solicit opinions about every aspect of parish operations. Marketing, the science of knowing your customer and what the customer wants, is a very useful tool for organizations of all types. A parish volunteer with expertise in marketing can be a real asset. One warning: once your parish goes to the trouble of listening to what parishioners want, be sure to do something about it. Make *visible* changes, and emphasize that changes are responses to information collected from parishioners. Listening to parishioners without acting on the information you hear may alienate members rather than increase trust and positive perceptions of service. When some desired changes are not possible, the reasons need to be shared, but the issue should not be ignored.

Another reason to implement formal methods for listening is that effective administrators take the pulse of the "silent majority." That is, they avoid making operational changes at the request of the few people who go out of their way to voice their opinions. Often, the most vocal do not represent the feelings of the majority. But, since most parishioners are not involved closely with the parish's operations, they tend to go along with whatever the pastor decides. If they disagree with these decisions, they may keep silent, but they may grow dissatisfied and feel they are badly served.

Being misinformed by the vocal minority is a common occurrence within organizations. The best method for avoiding this is to collect many opinions from all segments of the population through some method of proactive listening. One effective approach is to distribute surveys to a large number of parishioners (perhaps annually). Analyze their responses—their likes and dislikes, what's important to them and what's unimportant. Then hold several focus groups with twenty to thirty individuals in each group. Review survey results, then discuss with the management team and others the ideas for potential changes in operations and/or policies. These focus groups can be organized within a friendly social event such as a Friday evening spaghetti dinner or a pancake breakfast after Sunday Mass. A good consultant (perhaps a parish member who runs focus groups professionally) can elicit many good ideas for improving parish operations at the same time they are building perceptions among parishioners that the parish really does care about them.

Convenience

For many in our contemporary context, caring equals convenience. Understanding parishioners' needs and assigning priority to meeting them when designing parish operations and procedures will result in parishioners perceiving that the parish community cares about them and wants to partner with them in ministry.

Door-to-Door Experience. One key for achieving convenience is to remember that parishioners' experience (attending Mass, for example) begins when they leave their home and ends when they return home—or engage in their next scheduled activity. It includes everything the parishioner has to do to attend. The Mass experience does not begin with the processional hymn; in the mind of the parishioner it is *door-to-door*. To make a positive attendance decision, the churchgoer must say "yes" to every potential obstacle that can just as easily result in a "no" decision. What does this mean?

- *Transportation and parking* matter. Will it be convenient to get to church (and park)?

- *Weather and safety* matter. Is there a chance of getting drenched in the rain between the nearest available parking space and the church door?

- *Safety* matters. Is there a chance of slipping on the church's icy sidewalk? Are the parking lot, church buildings, and grounds well lit and free of unnecessary hazards?

- *Comfort* matters. Will it be too hot or cold or crowded in church?

- *Access* matters. Is it easy to get into and out of church if a parishioner is in a wheelchair or requires other help with mobility? Is it convenient to bring an elderly relative?

- *Time* matters. When does Mass begin? Can a parishioner arrive on time? When will Mass end? Can he or she be on time for the next activity on the daily schedule?

In other words, *everything* the parishioner perceives about attending Mass from door-to-door matters. Some of these can be controlled by parish planners and personnel, others cannot but still must be acknowledged.

Psychological Comfort. Psychological comfort also plays a big role in the overall convenience equation. Will Mass, liturgies, programs, and parish events be *positive experiences* rather than negative ones? Will attending Mass or a program be pleasant? Will parishioners leave feeling better (in one form or another) than when they arrived? Marketing research performed by television networks reveals that many television viewers do not watch the news. It's easy to explain this consumer behavior. Many broadcasts feature news that is perceived by potential viewers as bad or sad. Because viewers feel worse after watching, they don't watch the news. Over time parishioners form clear expectations about the "news" that will be delivered at Mass. They anticipate what the priest and others will say and how they will say it. If they expect positive communication, they will likely be more disposed to attend. If they expect negative messages, their psychological comfort will best be protected by avoiding Mass. Such personal behavior may be interpreted as a reasonable form of self-protection. What can be more inconvenient and uncomfortable than voluntarily attending an event that will make you feel negatively about yourself, your community, or society in general?

Another element of psychological comfort involves parishioners' perception of time and its use. In the 1970s two San Francisco cardiologists, Meyer Friedman and Ray Rosenman, established a relationship among personality type, stress, and health. Their research developed evidence that people with Type A personalities experience much higher levels of stress through exposure to many typical, everyday events. And higher levels of stress lead to negative health effects, such as problems related to the nervous system, high blood pressure, high cholesterol, and increased incidence of heart attack.

Type A people experience a chronic sense of time-urgency, a general impatience with the rate at which most events take place. They tend to move, walk, and eat rapidly. They enjoy engaging in multiple activities at the same time—like watching several TV shows simultaneously with the help of a remote control. Also, Type As feel vaguely guilty when they relax. If you want to make Type As uncomfortable, make them wait in a long line or just take a nap. They perceive the time consumed in such activities could be much better spent in "getting something done." The opposite personality type, termed Type B, does not suffer from a sense of time urgency. Type Bs tend to be patient, undemanding, and easy-going. They can relax without guilt, and they are quite comfortable taking naps or lounging in a chair. Research shows that the American population is split fairly evenly between Type As and Type Bs. The bell-shaped curve applies here. Most people exhibit moderate levels of Type A and B personality traits. But, of course, there are many people who strongly exhibit one set of traits over the other.

Now, how can this knowledge of personality traits be interpreted to enhance personal psychological comfort and convenience at Mass and other parish events? Many parishioners, most likely Type Bs, may be very comfortable with activities that involve waiting—activities such as reflecting in silence upon the completion of a reading or sermon, distributing communion to a large congregation, singing "extra" verses of hymns, or just waiting beyond an event's scheduled start time for the event to begin. In response to the exact same events, other parishioners, most likely Type As, experience stress. Their heart rate increases and their blood pressure rises, their respiration rate increases, their livers produce higher than normal levels of cholesterol. In fact, they are experiencing the fight-or-flight response. Their bodies are preparing to do battle for the purpose of self-preservation because they feel threatened. And they can't simply be told that they shouldn't be stressed. This reaction is part of their personalities.

Organizations that typically require customers to wait in long, time-consuming lines (like the department of motor vehicles or Walt Disney World) have learned through unpleasant experience what it's like to deal with dissatisfied customers. So they try to alleviate customer stress by redesigning their processes and procedures to reduce waiting time. They assign more employees to process customers faster, obtain more efficient equipment, simplify their procedures, establish reservation systems, let customers use websites or 800-numbers to conduct transactions rather than physically traveling to a crowded office, or distract customers by providing free refreshments or entertainment while they wait. Service-oriented organizations do everything they can to eliminate waiting.

Conversely, some parishes choose to build in "waiting times" at Masses and liturgies such as those described above. They do this with the best of intentions; they want to celebrate Mass and liturgies in the most prayerful and meaningful manner they can design.

And, in fact, many parishioners (about half of them who possess Type B tendencies) are quite comfortable with periods of waiting. However, some consideration for the psychological comfort of the Type As in the congregation may lead to incorporating meaningful yet more time-efficient processes. Perhaps more "time-conscious" styles of Masses can be offered at a particular time of the day so that parishioners who are concerned with this element of psychological comfort may choose to attend a liturgy they believe to be more convenient. This is one reason for "church-shopping."

What's the best that can be hoped for in a situation where it's not possible to please everyone? Balance. Consider everyone's needs and try to find a use of time that everyone finds at least minimally convenient.

Effects of Tangibles: Participation and Physical Comfort

Within a parish there are numerous tangible items and materials employed to serve parishioners. There is the appearance of the church building itself—exterior and interior. There are offices; classrooms and conference rooms; crucifixes, statues, and other outward symbols of the faith; weekly bulletins; instructional materials (print and electronic); the parking lot; interior and exterior lighting; vestments; flowers and seasonal decorations; and many other tangible aspects of the parish environment to consider. All of these tangible items affect parishioners' perceptions about the quality of the parish to which they belong.

Here, two specific *effects* of a parish's tangible items and materials will be addressed in regard to the service perceived by parishioners. They are participation and physical comfort.

Participation

It seems safe to say that most parishes assume they operate in a manner that invites all parishioners to participate in liturgies, programs, and events. After all, Catholicism is inclusive. Parishes intend to be inclusive. Yet, the tangibles provided by the parish may not implement this intention—the "rubber may never meet the road"—unless a service orientation is applied consciously to parish facilities and materials.

Some senior members of a parish have specific, predictable needs. Printed materials such as Mass books, hymnals, and weekly bulletins are intended to be useful tools for facilitating participation at liturgy and for communicating with parishioners. However, sometimes the font size used in these printed items is too small for some, mostly older, members of the parish. On a cloudy day, when little natural sunlight penetrates the church windows, interior lighting levels may be too low to permit participants to read comfortably or maneuver safely. Sound systems may be inadequate for carrying the priest's words or the choir leader's voice to parish members with hearing deficiencies. For those who require elevators or ramps, the lack of special access facilities may restrict participation. Facilities and equipment to meet such special needs are readily available. Indeed, there is an expense to remedy these situations, but this expense can provide a recurring dividend.

The financial resources required to remedy these possible deficiencies in parish facilities, equipment, and materials vary. Satisfying some needs can be very expensive and may require consideration within long-term parish planning processes. But some needs can be addressed by parishes in a relatively short time and with few resources. The main point is this: our society has taken great strides in appreciating and attending to *everyone's needs* (note, for example, the numerous improvements spurred by the Americans with Disabilities Act of 1990). When providing facilities for parishioner participation, leaders need to keep the many segments of the parish population in mind and consider everyone's needs.

Younger Catholics will be expected to lead the Church in the future. Young people, as they mature, need to feel well served if they are to continue to experience the desire to participate in Church services and parish activities. Attitudes are formed early in life. Consider for example this reality that makes a lasting impression on many children. In most parish churches, children cannot see over the adults who sit in front of them. Often, the most common sight a young parishioner enjoys while attending a beautiful parish liturgy is the back of the adult positioned in front of him or her. *Vision* is a fundamental service provided to individuals attending an event. A clear view is a consequence of the physical layout of a parish's tangible facilities. For those seeking to build a strong Church for tomorrow, consider how challenging parents may find motivating their children to participate weekly in an event at which the child's basic need to see is poorly served.

All organizations seeking to serve children and their parents have to deal with this same problem. Some provide preferential seating to the young so that they can sit in front of adults in a young person's seating section. Elevated seating aids vision, and an elevated sanctuary supports the centrality of worship. There are many things a parish cannot do about its existing physical facilities, but if creative alternatives are considered, parishes may be surprised at the improvements they can make.

An advanced form of participation involves *independent control*. Adolescent consumers indicate that they feel well served when they can make their own decisions about a product or service. In their years of developing self-image and self-esteem, adolescents are most likely to participate when they can exert some control. For example, research shows that they are most likely to show up at a site (such as a church, parish house, or activities center) when they have their own space—a space they can design, decorate, and use exclusively. Applying this same principle of control to Masses, other liturgies and prayer services, and parish programs, adolescents are most likely to repeat the behavior of participating when they have some control in terms of form or content, or both. Some input into the readings, music, decorations, etc., may improve adolescents' perceptions of service—as well as offer educational value. If we want teenagers to participate, let them interact and have some control. Don't ask them to observe or engage in what others have orchestrated without their input.

Physical Comfort

Many organizations desire to provide their clientele with a comfortable seat—perhaps to eat a meal, enjoy a rest, have a conversation, or just gaze at some pretty scenery. But many of these same organizations desire to turn over their clientele on a frequent basis. That is, customers are welcome to spend ten to twenty minutes in a chair or at a table. Then the organization would prefer that customers vacate the space and allow other customers to use the same resources. There are many examples of this common organizational desire. It's true of fast food restaurants, museums, bus stops, municipal parks, and the like.

These organizations have adopted a very similar and effective strategy to work their will on clientele without alienating patrons by asking them to leave. They motivate clientele to decide on their own to move to another activity by providing comfortably shaped yet hard seating surfaces, such as plastic-molded seats, metal café chairs, or wooden or marble benches. On these seating surfaces, one is comfortable for a short period of time and one feels well served. After a short while, one is happy to vacate the seat.

Aware of this universal seating strategy, how can requiring parishioners to sit on hard wooden pews for a fifty- to sixty-minute Sunday Mass be construed as good service? For many, this is not good service, but is, in fact, the opposite of good service. Parishioners might perceive this, if only on a subconscious level, as lack of comfort and therefore a lack of hospitality. A similar observation can be made about having to sit through Mass or meetings while wearing heavy jackets or coats, as opposed to having easy access to a coat room or coat racks.

Another element of comfort involves the doors one has to use to access a venue. If a client is truly welcome to a service site, easy entry through its doors is assumed. Some houses of worship possess beautifully ornate—and heavy—doors. Their visual impact contributes to the church's sacred environment. Yet parish administrators may not have taken the small amount of trouble necessary to confirm that a properly functioning hydraulic assist would provide the necessary help needed to open the door for a weaker-than-normal worshiper or an elderly or young person. Every obstacle encountered by a parishioner—even one that seems as inconsequential as a door that is challenging to open—delivers a small psychological message. The sum total of these messages can cause a parishioner to conclude, "They really don't welcome me here."

Have you ever observed a worshiper faint during a liturgy? If so, it is quite likely that lack of sufficient oxygen was the cause. And this was likely the result of inadequate ventilation in the church. However, the individual who fainted was simply the weakest person in the congregation at that point in time—perhaps due to age, ill health, or just skipping breakfast that morning. From a general comfort standpoint, consider that everyone in the church was also partially suffering to a lesser degree from a lack of sufficient oxygen. Their symptoms may have included a slight headache, anxiety, and "fidgetyness"—like the child who tugs at her father and asks, "Is it time to go yet?" Children don't know why they may not like to go into a church. They don't realize that they become anxious when they don't receive enough oxygen. After a few Masses they simply realize that they feel better when they are outside. Adequate ventilation assists prayer and worship.

Conclusion

This chapter is intended to encourage parish administrators to *think differently* about how they serve their parishioners: to think in terms of parish service quality and Christian hospitality. If the approaches suggested here are considered and embellished with some creative and compassionate caring from the parishioner's perspective, parish leaders may be surprised at the ideas they will generate to better serve parish members. Think "service," and you will deeply enrich the vibrancy of your parish community.

Exercises

1. Consider your own parish or organizational unit. On a scale of 1 to 10 rate how you believe your parishioners (or others who consume your services) would score your parish on each element of customer service: empathy, assurance, responsiveness,

reliability, and tangibles. Which would be rated highest? Why? Which would be rated lowest? What improvements could you make?

2. Invite a co-worker to join you on a visit to another parish (or any Church organization equivalent to yours). Play the role of "mystery worshipers." Observe their elements of service quality: empathy, assurance, responsiveness, reliability, and tangibles. What do they do better than you? What lessons can you learn for implementation back "home"?

3. Identify one specific service-oriented training and development topic that would be valuable to you and your staff. Invite someone to present a half-day of training at your site for the benefit of all.

4. Stand in the back of church one Sunday and observe all worshipers before, during, and after each Mass. Who appears highly satisfied? Why? Who may appear dissatisfied? Why? Identify a few service-quality improvements that could enhance the experience of the congregation.

BIBLIOGRAPHY

Considine, John J. *Marketing Your Church: Concepts and Strategies.* Lanham, MD: Sheed and Ward, 1995.

DuBrin, Andrew J. *Human Relations: Interpersonal Job-Oriented Skills.* 6th ed. Upper Saddle River, NJ: Prentice Hall, 1997.

Kotler, Philip. *Marketing Management: Millennium Edition.* 10th ed. Upper Saddle River, NJ: Prentice Hall, 2000.

Lussier, Robert N. *Human Relations in Organizations: Applications and Skill Building.* 5th ed. Boston: McGraw-Hill, 2002.

Robbins, Stephen P., and Phillip L. Hunsaker. *Training in Interpersonal Skills: Tips for Managing People at Work.* 2nd ed. Upper Saddle River, NJ: Prentice Hall, 1996.

Robbins, Stephen P., and Timothy A. Judge. *Organizational Behavior.* 9th ed. Upper Saddle River, NJ: Prentice Hall, 2001.

CHAPTER 7

Knowing Whom the Parish Serves: Segmenting the Market

Larry W. Boone, PhD

> He has made everything appropriate to its time, and
> has put the timeless into their hearts, without men's
> ever discovering, from beginning to end, the work
> which God has done.
>
> —Ecclesiastes 3:11

Key Concepts

1. Each parish is composed of different population segments with specific needs, desires, expectations, and distinctive behaviors.

2. The success of a parish depends upon its leaders recognizing these different segments and responding to them.

3. Ministry is enhanced when pastors and parish staff appreciate their "markets" and direct services to specific age, interest, or need cohorts.

4. The parish census and the U.S. Census are valuable tools for parish planning.

Introduction

Effective parish administrators have to make numerous decisions. These decisions must be based in reality and typically involve the following tasks:

- Communicating well and widely with parish members
- Composing committees, task forces, or councils to ensure adequate representation of the parish population
- Planning the parish's future based on current and anticipated parishioner needs
- Determining which programs are most beneficial to parishioners
- Allocating/budgeting the parish's human and financial resources
- Seeking out new members and winning back the inactive

Some basic information about whom the parish serves is needed to guide all of these decisions: knowing the different population segments that make up the parish and the specific needs, desires, expectations, and typical behaviors of each segment.

Consideration of various parish configurations makes this point well. Imagine communicating with a congregation consisting only of women fifty-five years old and older. Choosing specific language and examples that will hit the mark with this population would be a fairly straightforward task since a homogeneous group such as this tends to share many common perspectives and experiences. Now imagine composing a committee to adequately represent the opinions of an entire parish if its membership were mid-career professionals. It would be a rather simple task to gather a small number of people who could represent the concerns of the entire congregation. Imagine constructing a budget to fund programs important to the parish if you knew that all parish members were young, married couples with school-age children. It would be relatively easy to decide to put the lion's share of resources into one or two programs that address the specific needs of this group.

If parishes consisted of homogeneous groups, decision-making would be relatively easy, and managing such a parish would be a highly focused task. However, parishes tend to be geographically based, and consequently, they are composed of *heterogeneous* groups of people who happen to live within their borders. They consist of many population segments, all of whom demonstrate differences: different ways of communicating, different needs, different desires, different behaviors, and different expectations for service. The more diverse the groups comprising the parish, the more challenging the management task. As the cliché goes, "You can't please everyone" with any single decision.

Using simple visual representation, parishes look more like this figure:

PARISH COMPOSITION
(Available for free download at avemariapress.com)

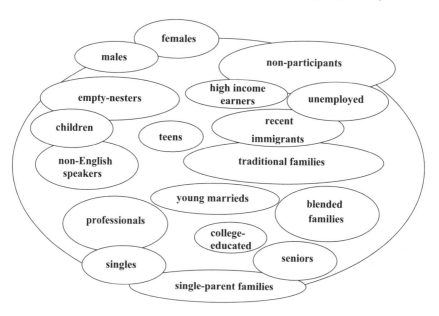

To be effective in making decisions, an administrator has to know whom he or she is serving. *Who makes up the congregation?* An effective parish manager addresses this fundamental question before engaging in other important managerial tasks.

Market Segmentation

Marketing techniques are important to all organizations. The marketing concept of *segmentation* can be applied to address the question of "who makes up my parish?"

Segmenting a market involves dividing a large population of those an organization seeks to serve (whether they are parishioners, customers, clients, patients, students, etc.) into subsets according to their common needs, desires, and habits. The chart below shows common bases for segmenting markets within the parish based on four typical concepts: demographic category, psychographic type, behavioral characteristics, and geographic location. If a parish administrator thinks about decisions in terms of the needs of different parishioner segments, the tasks of communicating, planning, budgeting, etc., become more focused and manageable.

Common Bases for Market Segmentation

Demographic
Age	under 6, 6–11, 12–19, 20–34, 35–49, 50–64, 65+
Gender	male, female
Family Size	1–2, 3–4, 5+
Family Life Cycle	young/older; single/married/divorced/widowed; children (none, young, grown)
Income	$10–19,999; $20–29,999; $30–39,999, $40–49,999, etc.
Occupation	professional, technical, managers, crafts, clerical, sales, farmers, retired, students, housewives, unemployed
Education	grade school, high school, some college, college, advanced
Ethnicity	Asian, Black, Hispanic, White, Middle Eastern

Psychographic
Social Class	lower lowers, upper lowers, lower middles, upper middles, lower uppers, upper uppers
Lifestyle	conservatives, moderates, liberals, change resistors/embracers
Personality	Type A, Type B, compulsive, gregarious, authoritarian, ambitious

Behavioral
Participant	regular, occasional, special event, non-participant
Benefits Sought	spirituality, community, quality-of-life, convenience
Loyalty Status	absolute, strong, medium, low, none
Readiness Status	intending to participate, desirous, interested, informed, aware, unaware
Attitude	enthusiastic, positive, indifferent, negative, hostile

Geographic
Density	urban, suburban, rural
Climate	standard, coastal, resort

Who Is in Your Parish?

The parish census is an invaluable tool for parish managers. An accurate census will provide the information that answers the question, "Whom does the parish serve?" That is, which groups exist today, which groups predominate in terms of numbers or importance of needs, and how have these group sizes changed over the last few years? These questions must be answered to develop a *managerial perspective* so that good *management decision-making* can commence. And, with a little projection, today's census will also help answer the question, "How will parishioners' needs change in the next three, five, or ten years?" This is the stuff good planning is made of! William Pickett's *A Concise Guide to Pastoral Planning* in this series is a very helpful resource for long-range strategic planning at the parish, regional, and diocesan levels.

Establishing and maintaining an accurate census of the members of a specific parish is a big job that requires commitment and resources, but easily attainable and reasonably good substitutes for a parish census do exist. Demographic and sociological data for specific zip codes, towns, and municipal subdivisions are available from the U.S. Census Bureau and from online marketing services. In fact, U.S. Census data can be honed to the specific street address of the parish and its surrounding residential block(s). While these data represent everyone inhabiting a particular area, not exclusively members of a specific parish, parish decision-makers can gain perspective on different categories of people living in their parish area and how many people there are in each category. As the Church ramps up efforts to re-engage the inactive Catholics, these data are becoming more important. Data on historical population trends as well as future projections for population changes are also available.

The U.S. Census Bureau (www.census.gov) offers a wealth of data, which is available online free of charge or can be attained for nominal cost through the Bureau's publications such as *Statistical Abstract* and *Census (year)*. Statistical information can be referenced for the nation, states, counties, cities, towns, and small areas such as census tracts and city blocks. Data on population by age, race and gender is available—as is information on social, economic, and housing characteristics. Social characteristics include information on school enrollment, educational attainment, disability status, language spoken at home, ancestry, and other factors. Economic characteristics include employment status, occupation, income, and poverty status, among others. Housing data covers number and type of units, occupancy, and tenure. Religious affiliation is not included.

Online marketing services can provide very useful data for specific geographic areas for reasonable fees. Among many such services, ESRI Business Information Solutions (www.esribis.com) offers a wealth of information options.

Pickett's *A Concise Guide to Pastoral Planning* recommends Percept's Ministry Area Profile (MAP). Through its website (www .perceptgroup.com) a parish may attain detailed community demographic information specially intended for churches and faith communities. A variety of graphic displays are available for populations in geographic areas specified by the inquirer.

Assessment of Parishioner Needs

Once a clear picture of the parish is developed concerning "who" and "how many," parish leaders can proceed to consider the primary needs of each parishioner category and how the parish can best serve each group now and into the future. With the goal of satisfying the most common needs, as well as needs deemed most important, effective decisions can be made regarding the most appropriate parish policies, programs, events, staffing, facilities, and budget allocations. The Parish Needs Assessment worksheet below helps guide this type of analysis. Typically, a parish planning group can identify major categories of parishioners, the approximate number of members in each category, expected trends in membership (increasing, decreasing, stable) and the current and future needs each group wants to see the parish address. Consideration can then be given to establishing new programs, policies, and/or events (or eliminating/revising current ones), attaining new equipment or facilities, and the like. The objective, of course, is to allocate the parish's scarce resources in the most effective manner to achieve the parish's vision and goals.

Conclusion

Parishes and Church agencies generally have diverse groups in their service populations. To be effective, managers must have a clear idea of whom they wish to serve, which influences how they wish to allocate resources. This clarity of "markets" must precede or be a priority part of any planning process. The segmentation of a market allows providers of services to learn about the needs, desires, and habits of the persons they wish to serve in order to respond effectively. Supplied with this demographic, psychographic, behavioral, and geographic data, providers can then conduct appropriate needs surveys and gain additional information required to respond well in the present and with vision for the future.

Exercises

1. Review the "Parish Composition" graphic on page 128 and determine which representative cohort descriptors are in your parish. Add and delete cohorts as necessary to provide a full scope of your various "markets."

2. Using the chart "Common Bases for Market Segmentation" on page 130, identify the bases that you would like to include in developing a parish profile to assist in parish planning.

3. Assemble the parish staff or a representative group of parishioners and complete the Parish Needs Assessment (available in reproducible format at www.avemariapress.com) for at least four cohorts that you believe need special servicing.

BIBLIOGRAPHY

Percept Group. "Ministry Area Profile." www.perceptgroup.com.

Pickett, William L. *A Concise Guide to Pastoral Planning.* Notre Dame: Ave Maria Press, 2007.

United States Census Bureau. www.census.gov.

CHAPTER 8

Assessing Parishioner Satisfaction

Larry W. Boone, PhD

As best you can, take your neighbors' measure, and
associate with the wise.

—Sirach 9:14

Key Concepts

1. Satisfaction with a product or service affects the willingness of individuals to sustain their relationship with any organization, including their church.

2. The science of measuring satisfaction is a logical response to the "consumer society" that now exists in the developed nations of the world. The need for experienced satisfaction and personal benefit from investing one's time are typical of living in many areas of the world.

3. Satisfaction needs vary across populations and parishes and other organizations.

4. "Customers" respond to the service/product itself, the "price" or cost to self, and the service quality provided.

5. Consumers assess service quality in terms of empathy, assurance, responsiveness, reliability, and tangibles.

6. While some may be uncomfortable with equating parishioners with "consumers" or "customers," the current U.S. culture encourages that identification.

7. Service quality is important in the Church because of the obligation to be instruments of evangelization.

8. Parishioner satisfaction will result in benefit to all and to the Church, particularly in resource-limited situations.

9. The satisfaction of parishioners should be assessed on a regular basis and the findings integrated into parish planning.

Introduction

Satisfaction is a psychological concept representing the fulfillment or gratification of a need, desire, or appetite. Pleasure results from such gratification. People who experience satisfaction with an individual, group, or organization seek to maintain a relationship with that party. The positive feelings of kinship, loyalty, and commitment develop from satisfaction.

Over the last few decades, for-profit and nonprofit organizations of all types have made significant strides in satisfying the people they serve. Whether a particular organization refers to those they serve as applicants, clients, consumers, customers, employees, novices, parishioners, patients, players, recipients, recruits, students, viewers, voters, or what-have-you, organizations want to establish a "satisfaction bond" with them. The science of satisfaction measurement has now been honed to a high degree of reliability. Many organizations have developed valid and reliable survey instruments that facilitate assessing and improving "customer satisfaction." This chapter focusing on the concept of *parishioner satisfaction* offers an assessment instrument. The importance of satisfaction, how it can be measured, and what processes can be adopted to continuously improve the parish-parishioner relationship will be treated here.

Despite trends toward using organizational satisfaction assessments, there is still a degree of discomfort with some who view this practice as a move from a mission-centered approval to a need-centered approval. They raise the possibility of the Church becoming a "mere vendor of religious goods and services" where self-interest can invade the common good (Zech 158). The reader is left to draw his/her own conclusions concerning the usefulness of this approach.

Importance of Parishioner Satisfaction

Needs are deficiencies felt at a point in time, and everyone has needs that present in many forms. Maslow, McClelland, and many other motivation researchers have proposed various types of need such as physiological (hunger, thirst, shelter), psychological (security, self-esteem, growth, self-fulfillment), social (affection, friendship, belongingness), as well as other needs that cut across these categories, such as needs for achievement and power—or spiritual needs.

Needs create internal tension and drive people to act, that is, to seek something that will satisfy their needs (i.e., provide fulfillment). A search will continue until something (food, interpersonal contact, knowledge, etc.) is found to reduce or eliminate the need. Upon fulfillment of a need, the recipient feels satisfaction. As noted earlier, satisfaction produces pleasure. The experience of pleasure leads an individual to repeat the behavior that produced it and sustain the relationships established during the search process.

The Motivation Process

Unsatisfied Need ➡ Tension ➡ Search ➡
Satisfied (fulfilled) Need

Pleasure experienced through need satisfaction can lead to behavior modification; that is, need satisfaction can result in learning and can cause a *relatively permanent* change in behavior. Individuals learn that a particular behavior, such as eating chocolate, meeting with friends, shopping at a particular store, buying a particular brand of cola, attending a liturgy, volunteering at the parish, etc., satisfies a need and results in pleasure. Even after the need is satisfied, people tend to repeat the behavior that led to pleasure. This can be attributed to the learning process: an individual develops patterns of behavior associated with desired outcomes (experiencing pleasure).

However, learning is *not completely* permanent. If the satisfaction is eliminated due to a negative experience or if it extinguishes over time, the behavior will stop. Therefore, continuous reinforcement of the need satisfaction and/or desired outcomes has to be provided to reinforce the behavior. The uneven and diminishing patterns of Mass attendance over age cohorts offer insights here.

Therefore, it is vital that parish administrators and groups understand how their parish satisfies its parishioners. Why do parishioners attend liturgies, participate in events, volunteer for programs, contribute funds, etc.? What satisfactions do they derive from their behaviors? What pleasures? How does the parish reinforce their satisfaction so that their behaviors don't fade over time? Further, effective parish managers consider how parishioners' needs might be changing, so they can plan to meet their changing parishioners' needs.

Many service and product providers fall into a common trap. Over time, providers lose sight of the fact that what they really do for their clients, users, customers, etc., is *satisfy needs*. They become enamored with the particular service or product they provide and assume that their clients are coming to the organization for the specific service or product that the organization has been providing for a long time. They forget that clients are coming to seek the satisfaction of a need; that is, providers associate (or confuse) their standard service/product with their client's needs. When clients stop consuming their service/product, they can't understand why.

Perhaps they don't realize that their "good old" service/product no longer satisfies the changing needs of those they seek to serve. Therefore, effective administrators challenge the assumption that clients are satisfied with current services/products by continuously assessing client satisfaction. Over time, they measure the degree to which clients are satisfied and also determine what new needs or expectations may exist.

Good things happen when people are satisfied. A parish that engenders high satisfaction can expect the following behaviors:

- higher attendance at liturgies and events
- more participation in programs
- higher levels of volunteerism
- higher levels of cooperation with clergy and staff
- better "citizenship behaviors" such as:
    - speaking well of the parish to outsiders
    - providing vocal support for clergy and staff

Satisfaction Factors

We know from years of careful research that three important factors influence customer satisfaction more than anything else:

- the service or product itself
- price
- service quality

Of course, the *service or product itself* relates to need satisfaction. When the customer's needs are not satisfied by the service/product offered, the customer often decides to search for another provider. This may account for the shift from territorial parishes to "intentional" communities. It is important that parish administrators keep in mind that their parish very likely consists of many different sets of parishioners—each with different needs. (See chapter 7, "Knowing Whom the Parish Serves: Segmenting the Market").

Deciding which services, programs, events, etc., a parish will offer determines whether or not most parishioners will favorably rate this component of satisfaction.

Price and *service quality* are other contributors to satisfaction. Price satisfaction is determined by a perception of fairness. Is a fair value being received? (Value = quality and price.) Is the quality received in balance with the price demanded? High price is justified if the service/product quality is high. And low quality is acceptable if a low price is offered. While the price factor is very important in many organizations, it may seem only indirectly related to parish management. However, most parishioners decide for themselves how much parish membership "costs" in a financial sense by setting the level of contribution that is comfortable or "fair" to them. When parishes attempt to implement the practice of tithing, parishioners may have a clear opinion regarding whether or not parish participation is worth 5 or 10 percent of their income. Catholics are generally found in the lowest cohorts of church supporters. Charles Zech's study of the Catholic component of a 1990 study of religious groups in various denominations suggests that the reason for low rates of Catholic giving is a failure of educating parishioners to the meaning of stewardship (Zech 155). However, price may also relate to the value parishioners place on their time. Is the quality of their experience associated with attending a liturgy or parish event worth the cost of personal or family time dedicated to it? In today's society, for example, many families are overscheduled. A variety of events compete for their scarce hours. Parishioners must decide how many hours a particular event may be "worth" by assessing their perceived quality of the experience in relation to time consumed (price).

Service quality is a very important concept to all organizations—including parishes. One of the factors contributing to customer satisfaction is the level of service quality they receive. High service quality leads to high satisfaction and consists of the following five elements:

- *Assurance*: the knowledge and courtesy of personnel and their ability to convey trust and confidence
- *Empathy*: the provision of caring, individualized attention to clients
- *Reliability*: the ability to perform the promised service dependably and accurately
- *Responsiveness*: the willingness to help customers and provide prompt service
- *Tangibles*: the appearance (and performance) of physical facilities, equipment, personnel, and communication materials

For a more complete discussion of this concept, see chapter 6, "The Parish and Service Quality."

The goal of high customer satisfaction will be achieved if customers are satisfied with the service/product itself, the price, and the service quality provided. If any element is missing, the level of client satisfaction will diminish.

At one time or another, we have all been asked to assess a recently purchased service or product. Commonly, organizations seek our input through telephone surveys or questionnaire mailings. The above-mentioned factors of the service or product itself, price, and service quality form the theoretical underpinning of such questionnaires.

For example, use of such a questionnaire by a hotel chain's management should be obvious. When data is provided by hotel guests, a hotel manager can measure each element of customer satisfaction as well as overall satisfaction at a given point in time. Then, the manager can assess trends. If satisfaction with any particular element is trending downward, management identifies this as a specific problem to which staff's attention must be drawn. The problem is investigated, and corrective actions are devised and implemented. This is the process of continuous improvement, and it is good management. Problems can be identified and corrected as they develop, not when major declines in customer satisfaction are experienced. The same method works in Church organizations as well.

Measuring Parishioner Satisfaction

Three researchers at St. John's University, New York—Larry W. Boone, Rev. Patrick D. Primeaux, S.M., and Mary Maury—developed a questionnaire for measuring parishioner satisfaction within Catholic parishes. The parishioner satisfaction questionnaire was developed according to the concepts of customer satisfaction discussed above; that is, the concepts of the *service/product itself* and *service quality* were incorporated into questionnaire statements about various aspects of parish operations. The concept of *price* was not used. Inputs from hundreds of Catholic parish members in several different regions of the United States were used in its development. A copy of the instrument is available in reproducible format at www.avemariapress.com. Interested readers may also refer to Zech's highly useful discussion of "Indicators of Parish Vitality" (Zech 144–151).

The parishioner satisfaction questionnaire was structured to measure satisfaction for eleven different factors:

1. Mass and other liturgies
2. priest(s) of the parish
3. community
4. participation/involvement of parishioners
5. communication
6. homilies
7. service quality and convenience
8. physical facilities
9. Catholic school availability/operation
10. overall impressions of the parish
11. specific programs offered by the parish

Each factor comprises five statements that describe various aspects of parish operations. A satisfaction score for each factor can be produced by summing scores for each set of five statements. Also, a single, total parishioner satisfaction score can be derived by summing scores for the eleven different factors. Additionally, as shown on the last page of the questionnaire, demographic data can be collected, making it possible to assess responses received from different groups separately (e.g., genders, ages, ethnicities, and parishioner activity levels).

For each questionnaire statement, parishioners rate their level of agreement or disagreement that it is indicative of their parish's operations. Parishioners also rate the importance of each item to their overall satisfaction.

Parish administrators can use all or part of this questionnaire to track levels of parishioner satisfaction over time. Low or declining satisfaction scores may be interpreted as problems that should be addressed by the parish staff. Questionnaire statements that receive a high importance score but a low agreement score should be identified as significant problems that, if addressed, can lead to quick improvement in parishioner satisfaction.

The questionnaire can be administered to all parish members or to random samples of parishioners—whichever is desired. After reviewing questionnaire results, parish administrators may wish to hold meetings with groups of twenty to thirty parishioners. At these meetings—commonly called "focus groups"—a discussion leader can present basic results of the questionnaire data collection effort. For example, the top ten items with which there is agreement (or disagreement) or the top ten items in importance can be presented. Then, more specific discussion can be focused on these elements of parish operation. Participants' ideas for potential improvements can be solicited.

Survey-Action Process

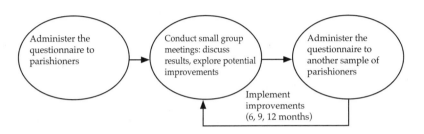

If significant operational changes result from the assessment process, the questionnaire can be administered six, nine, or twelve months later to determine how much parishioner satisfaction has increased. New areas of potential dissatisfaction may be discernible from results, so additional improvements can be considered. This is the process of *continuous improvement*, a management approach that involves iterations of improvements and assessments. With this technique, the parish can engage in a process that stimulates dialogue concerning its operations and stays in touch with changing needs and expectations of its members.

Conclusion

Because the culture of the United States encourages a consumer mentality, the Church must be aware of this and respond with creativity and responsibility. While never compromising the Gospel, the goal is to make the Church a place where Catholics wish to be and a community to which they want to belong. Positive personal experiences are what strengthen bonds with an organization, whether it be a faith community or a any other type of organization. It is important that organizations have valid and reliable survey instruments so that they can capture the opinions of their public and make necessary improvements as they seek to satisfy the needs of those they serve. This willingness to seek feedback on a consistent basis, and to act on it, can strengthen and make firm an individual's or family's bonds with the parish, diocese, and other Church organizations.

Exercise

With your parish management team, pastoral council, or with the leadership of a parish organization, pilot the parishioner satisfaction questionnaire available at www.avemariapress.com. You may want to have the parish team complete it first so that you can check the congruence of your view with the parish sample. Have each person complete it anonymously so that there can be full discussion without concerns about attribution. After tabulating the results, discuss first the "importance" findings and then the "satisfaction" ratings. Begin the discussion with "What are the 'no surprise' statements?" and "What are the surprises?" Are the findings strong enough to suggest any areas for study or for improvement? If so, how will you begin the planning process to make changes?

BIBLIOGRAPHY

Chase, Richard B., and Sriram Dasu. "Want to Perfect Your Company's Service? Use Behavioral Science." *Harvard Business Review* 79, June 2001, 78–84.

Cieslak, Michael. "The Consequences of Pastoral Leadership." In Zech, *The Parish Management Handbook*, 113–153.

Kotler, Philip. *Marketing Management: Millennium Edition.* 10th ed. Upper Saddle River, NJ: Prentice Hall, 2000.

Robbins, Stephen P., and Timothy A. Judge. *Organizational Behavior.* 9th ed. Upper Saddle River, NJ: Prentice Hall, 2000.

Zech, Charles E., ed. *The Parish Management Handbook: A Practical Guide for Pastors, Administrators, and Other Parish Leaders.* Mystic, CT: Twenty-Third Publications, 2003.

CHAPTER 9

Evaluating Parish Performance

Larry W. Boone, PhD

It is the LORD; he created her, has seen her and taken note of her.

—Sirach 7:1

Key Concepts

1. Responsible management demands that all in the parish, but particularly staff and leadership, know the parish performance standards, see their role in achieving them, and are aware of the ongoing progress.

2. While parish outcomes are sometimes difficult to quantify and measure, it is possible to identify key result areas (KRAs) and key performance indicators (KPIs) to assure performance planning, execution, and monitoring.

3. In a results-oriented parish, each member of the organization will be aware of the KRAs of the parish as well as the way he or she assures the achievement of related specific results.

4. KPIs should be measurable, fall within a specific KRA, allow for ongoing tracking, and be cost-effective.

5. A parish performance focus assists in identifying issues and problems in a timely fashion.

6. Problems, part of any living organization, generally come from three sources: change from past performance, change from planned goals, or external criticism.

7. A "walk-through audit," conducted by someone who is friendly toward but not overly familiar with the parish, can offer a new perspective and can bring to light things that have become "invisible" to the onsite managers.

8. In directing and controlling the parish, the pastor will be greatly supported by clear performance standards and a reliable method of keeping score.

Introduction

It's halftime at the Super Bowl. Your team is losing by seventeen points. The head coach enters the locker room and announces, "Men, we're going to change our game plan for the second half." Does that surprise you? Of course not. If your initial plan isn't working, everyone knows you've got to make a change. Why? Because you want to win, and the scoreboard tells you that you're losing. Go to plan B and everyone will follow you. They expect a good leader to know when it's time to do something different. In the other team's locker room, the coach isn't changing the game plan. No surprise here because they're winning.

Now for a hard question for the pastor: "Is your parish team winning?" Perhaps you don't know. Equally as bad, perhaps some of your staff members don't know if the parish is winning or losing because they don't know how to keep score. If the pastor and the staff knew the parish was behind on the scoreboard, all would do something about it. They would try new ideas, different approaches, alternative methods. If the team doesn't know they're losing, there's no stimulus to change.

Good managers never leave their staffs in this quandary because good managers keep score. That is, they evaluate the parish's performance in an ongoing way. When performance isn't good, effective managers and organizations make changes. That much is pretty straightforward, but the bigger challenge is knowing how to keep score. That is the major theme of this chapter—measuring and evaluating performance so that you and your staff know the score.

The focus here is on the parish, but the principles are universal and can be applied to other organizations.

Measuring and Evaluating Performance

Describing exactly what a parish does can be difficult. Therefore, measuring how well the parish is doing can be a very difficult challenge. This is true for every organization that doesn't produce a tangible product or sell a specific service. Hard performance numbers describing sales volume or number of customers served per hour aren't readily available in the parish setting. However, George L. Morrisey offers some very useful ideas for actually measuring organizational results in his book *A Guide to Tactical Planning: Producing Your Short-Term Results*. Morrisey's concepts of key result areas (KRAs) and key performance indicators (KPIs) can be quite helpful. The following discussion is based on his approach.

KRAs are "areas or categories of results that are essential to effective performance in an organization" (Morrisey 27). KRAs cover accomplishments that must be achieved if the parish is to carry out its mission successfully and meet the expectations of its members. KRAs do not specify everything the parish accomplishes. Rather, they are intended to serve as "broad headings" that cover major parish objectives and organize performance assessment.

KPIs are "measurable factors within a given KRA on which it may be worthwhile to set objectives" (Morrisey 49). They serve as tangible indicators that help identify success within each desired category of parish results. *Indicators* is a key word. While indicators are measurable, they suggest only the probability of worthwhile results and are not absolute measures of successful operation. Also, KPIs aren't restricted to quantitative measures; they can be qualitative as well.

> **Key Performance Indicators have at least four uses:**
>
> 1. Identifying a list of potential measurable factors in each KRA.
> 2. Selecting measurable factors on which objectives should be set at the present time.
> 3. Establishing specific action steps for accomplishing those objectives.
> 4. Tracking performance related to objectives and action plans.
>
> Morrisey, 49

Creating KPIs helps parishes focus on the *results* they intend to achieve, not on the *effort* required to produce the results. KPIs help parishes track results over time and help managers and staff to answer the question, "Are we winning?"

Key result areas and key performance indicators help parish administrators and staff stretch their minds in terms of thinking about what the parish does—as well as what the parish could be doing. Thinking is focused on questions such as:

- What is the mission of the parish?

- What purposes does the parish serve?

- How do we know the job is getting done to achieve the purposes?

- What results do we (as administrators and staff) expect on a daily, weekly, quarterly, and annual basis?

- What results are visible to parishioners over the same time frames?

Identifying Key Result Areas

Identifying KRAs is the first step. A planning council or assessment committee usually does this job best. They bring many different perspectives and experiences to the task. This group may find it helpful to concentrate on each major segment of the parish population (see chapter 7, "Knowing Whom the Parish Serves: Segmenting the Market") while deciding which performance areas will cover the broad range of performance expected by parish leaders and members.

The following guidelines for determining key result areas will help with this task:

1. Identify five to eight major areas in which your parish must achieve meaningful results during the coming year.

2. Identify both financial and nonfinancial areas.

3. Choose areas that directly or indirectly support the parish's long-range or strategic plan and other higher-level plans.

4. Don't expect your KRAs to cover your parish's entire operation; instead, identify the *vital few areas* where priority efforts should be directed.

5. Realize that many KRAs will require cross-functional effort.

6. Each KRA should be limited generally to two to three words and should not be measurable as stated but should contain factors that could be made measurable.

—Morrisey

```
┌────────────────────────────────────────────────────────────┐
│                                                              │
│       Examples of Key Result Areas for a Parish              │
│  ──────────────────────────────────────────────────────     │
│                                                              │
│   • Communal life              • Legislative relations       │
│   • Education                  • Liturgical life             │
│   • Efficiency                 • Missionary spirit           │
│   • Employee development       • Moral formation             │
│   • Evangelization             • Parishioner involvement     │
│   • Growth                     • Prayer                      │
│   • Image in the community     • Quality of liturgies        │
│   • Image in the diocese       • Quality of parish relationships │
│   • Innovation/Improvement     • Quality of parishioner services │
│   • Knowledge of the faith     • Revenue                     │
│                                                              │
└────────────────────────────────────────────────────────────┘
```

Identifying Key Performance Indicators

Several KPIs should be identified for each KRA. Since no single measurement will serve as a perfect indicator for success in each KRA, the parish should "triangulate" around the KRA concept by specifying a few ways of assessing performance within each critical performance area.

Key performance indicators should meet the following criteria:

1. They should be measurable factors, falling logically within a given KRA, on which objectives may be set.

2. They may be selected from any or all of the following types:

   a. *Hard numbers*, such as revenue dollars, number of active families, enrollment in parish school, number of civic events attended by staff.

   b. *Percentages*, such as percent of revenue spent on education, percent growth in membership, percent increase in communications with parishioners.

   c. *Significant achievements*, such as major project completions (or milestones), new events sponsored, recognition/awards from the diocese or local community.

A Concise Guide to Catholic Church Management

d. *Service factors,* such as response time to parishioner requests, cooperative projects with other local clergy/parishes, accuracy of parishioner contribution statements.

e. *Problems to be overcome,* such as low attendance at religious education programs, insufficient inventory of religious literature, project schedule slippages, cost overruns for programs, uneven attendance at Sunday liturgies.

f. *Soft or indirect indicators,* which may suggest effectiveness levels in subjective areas such as turnover or absenteeism among staff/volunteers (related to morale) and survey results (related to parishioner satisfaction/service).

3. They should identify *what* will be measured, not how much or in what direction.

4. They should represent factors that can be tracked on an ongoing basis to the extent possible—not only after results have been accomplished. For example, measuring the number of vocations emerging from a parish population may not be an effective assessment. It may be more helpful to assess the number of times clergy address vocations from the pulpit, number of inquiries received, or number of attendees at information sessions.

5. The cost of identifying and monitoring KPIs should not exceed the value of the information. This is a judgment call. For example, measuring improvement in parishioner service resulting from staff use of new software might provide valuable insight in terms of value of the software. However, the cost of obtaining that information may be prohibitive.

Examples of Key Result Areas and Key Performance Indicators

Key Result Areas	Key Performance Indicators
Revenue	Sunday collections Rebates from the diocese Special collections Major gifts / contributions Building fund donations Tuition
Parishioner involvement	Attendance at weekend liturgies Attendance at special liturgies Number of volunteers for programs (education, committees, services) Attendance at education programs Participation at social events
Employee/Volunteer development	Training investment as percentage of revenue Number of training classes attended by staff Development of a cross-training plan Number of backups per position
Quality of parish relationships	Number of contacts with diocese Number of contacts with local clergy Events co-sponsored with neighboring parishes

Quality of parishioner services	Percentage of error-free contribution
	   statements
	Parishioner satisfaction survey results
	Number of complaints received from
	   parishioners
	Response time for special requests (weddings,
	   funerals, visits to homebound, etc.)

Innovation/Improvement	Dollars spent on facility improvement Number of new ideas received from staff Number of new ideas approved by planning committee
Image in the community	Number of civic events attended by staff Favorable mentions in media Public information programs Civic events hosted by the parish Blood drive participation
Legislative relations	Number of contacts with legislators Response time to legislators Special event participation

Identifying Problems

One of the most important skills of a good administrator is to identify exactly what problems the parish must recognize and solve. Unfortunately, parish problems don't come with flashing neon lights. Only after a parish manager has focused attention and resources toward solving a particular problem will improvement take place. Therefore, identifying problems is a primary task of effective administration.

One of the best techniques top-level managers (in any type of organization) have to determine whether or not lower-level workers and managers are performing their job well is very simple: while passing a lower-level manager in the hallway or sharing an elevator ride, the top-level manager will ask, "How are things going?" Then, the top-level manager will listen carefully to the subordinate's answer. If the subordinate can articulate a clear response to this intentionally vague and open-ended question, the superior can be confident the subordinate has a handle on his/her job. If the subordinate cannot provide a well-structured response, the superior will suspect there is something to worry about.

So what is a good response to the seemingly innocuous question, "How are things going?" Off the top of his or her head a good administrator as well as each worker should be able to articulate the few important goals he or she is currently focusing attention on. Then the individual should be able to summarize what progress is being made toward these goals and what significant obstacles still have to be overcome. In other words, effective workers always know and can communicate what they want to achieve, what progress has been made, and what problems still have to be resolved. If top-level managers hear answers structured in this manner, they can be confident their subordinates are getting the job done.

It's important to note that no superior expects that all problems will be eliminated. Everyone has problems. No stigma is attached to having them. Superiors have cause for concern when subordinates don't know what their problems are. That's a big red flag! Therefore, good parish administrators should never be afraid to admit their parish has problems. Identifying your specific problems and focusing the parish's attention and resources on resolutions is what good parish management is all about. Here are some practical suggestions for recognizing problems.

Typically, problems in organizations come from three sources:

- changes from past performance
- changes from planned performance (parish goals)
- outside criticism

Changes from Past Parish Performance

Unless the doors just opened yesterday, parishes have measures of their past performance. This might be the amount of money collected every Sunday for the last year, or it might be the number of people who have volunteered to teach in the religious education program in past semesters. Effective managers identify their KPIs and keep track of performance levels that have been reached in the past. They monitor these indicators to determine whether they are *trending up or down*. If, for example, collections have been trending downward for the last ten Sundays, an aware administrator should recognize a potential problem and should investigate. Effective administrators take note of negative trends in their KPIs and look for specific causes to determine whether or not corrective actions are necessary. If they determine corrective actions are required, they make sure this problem is brought to the attention of the parish staff.

One of the physical manifestations of good management is a highly visible series of graphs somewhere near or within an administrator's desk—posted on the wall, kept in the top drawer, or stored on an easily accessible computer file. These graphs should represent the parish's KPIs and indicate performance over a recent time frame. The graphs serve as continuous, visible reminders to the administrator and staff of how the parish keeps score and whether or not the parish is winning. This can serve as a simple yet effective means of focusing attention on those elements of performance that must be achieved to ensure the parish's success. As can be readily seen, KPIs serve as a foundation for an effective parish management information system whose purpose is to highlight what is going right in the parish—and what requires management's immediate attention. (For examples of performance graphs, see the "Monitoring Performance" section below.)

Changes from Planned Parish Performance (Goals)

Effective administrators plan. That is, they establish future directions and goals for their parish in the short term and long term. Desired future performance levels are set to provide new direction and communicate the need for change in the parish, as opposed to benchmarking against previously attained levels of performance. As described in the section above, graphs of actual performance should be established and monitored constantly to determine whether or not the parish's performance levels are lagging, approaching, meeting, or exceeding planned goals. Actual performance lagging indicates a problem that the parish administrator should recognize and address as quickly as possible.

Outside Criticism

Have you ever had the experience of visiting a relative whom you see only occasionally—let's say annually—and seeing their young, growing daughter? What is the first thing you say? Of course, it is something like, "My, how Mary has changed! She's really growing up." Your relatives may look at you with a slightly puzzled expression because Mary doesn't look that different to them. Mary, and all their other children, look pretty much the same every day. That's because parents are so close to the situation. They see their children continuously, so they don't recognize incremental changes, but over time these small changes add up to big differences. But you see Mary only once a year, so Mary has changed a lot. This is a limitation in human perception that affects all of us. Our five senses don't register small changes very well; big changes do register.

How does this perception phenomenon relate to receiving outside criticism and identifying parish problems? Parish managers deal with the same things every day—the same challenges, same staff, same parishioners (same people who always complain), same facilities, same everything. They are just like parents raising children. Small changes aren't perceived; they don't register. Yet, over time, small changes add up to big differences. Sometimes these differences are significant but unnoticed problems—a lack of personal enthusiasm during liturgies; low morale among staff members; fading paint and fraying carpets throughout the facilities; or more seriously, cracks in the sidewalks. This problem-recognition dilemma strikes managers in *all* organizations.

To counteract this insensitivity phenomenon, it can be very helpful to have a person, such as an acquaintance from another parish, visit your parish every six, nine, or twelve months. Allow your visitor to observe liturgies, interact with staff members, look over your facilities, observe interactions between parish staff and parishioners, etc. At the end of the visit, this "outsider" may well be able to pick up differences that have occurred since the last visit. That is, the visitor can identify problems that may be totally imperceptible to "insiders."

This intermittent "auditing" can be a very effective way to identify problems that are difficult to measure quantitatively. A good "auditor" can provide a significant service by identifying small changes in parish operations that may grow into big problems if they are not addressed. Small, mid-course corrections can be a lot easier to implement than big solutions to significant problems that have been building over long periods. It is much better (i.e., less threatening) to have a friendly, invited visitor identify problems confidentially when the problems are still fairly small than to wait for these problems to become big and to attract attention from parishioners or from the diocesan office.

Monitoring Performance

A few examples will demonstrate the types of performance monitoring of activities identified above. First, a measure of attendance at parish religious education programs can serve as one of several key performance indicators that represent the key result area of

"Parishioner Involvement." Assume that attendance measures are compiled monthly. The chart below provides an easily recognized downward trend that begins in November and continues through January. After a few periods of decline, administrators responsible for the program should recognize that corrective action is required. Of course, identification of the most effective approaches to reverse the trend are left to program administrators. The point here is that a poor manager may not recognize that a problem exists. Effective managers monitor key performance indicators, recognize a problem, and make sure that corrective actions are implemented.

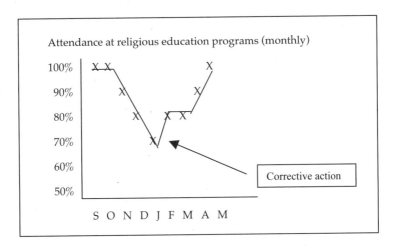

The next example demonstrates use of a planned performance goal that may be established as part of a long-term plan to improve parishioner services. Assume that parishioners complained in the past about inaccuracies in their annual contribution statements, and parish planners established a goal of an error rate of no more than 1 percent. Because improvements have been introduced to the record-keeping system over the last several years, the performance graph below indicates that actions taken to improve accuracy have been effective, but the goal still has not been reached. An effective manager wouldn't dedicate a lot of personal attention to this situation because staff members responsible for this operation seem to now have the situation under control. In other words, there is no problem to be recognized here. Yet monitoring of progress is still required. The goal has not been attained.

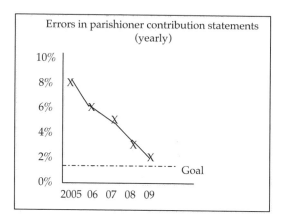

Action Plan Sheets

To keep on top of the numerous improvement projects and corrective actions a parish may be pursuing at any given time, an effective administrator may find it quite helpful to use action plan sheets (adapted from George L. Morrisey, *A Guide to Tactical Planning*). This kind of summary document is a handy tool for tracking progress toward all parish objectives and ensuring that important tasks don't slip through the cracks.

Each objective (for example, improve parish facilities) will have several associated actions (repair the roof, replace conference room furniture, refurbish the boiler, landscape front of church, etc.). All actions related to an objective can be listed on a single sheet along with the person or people who are accountable for carrying out the action plan, the scheduled start and completion dates, budgeted resources, and the success measures to be used for monitoring progress. Through the use of Action Plan Sheets, a parish administrator can organize all the information necessary to monitor major parish activities and keep informed of successful completions as well as developing problems.

Action Plan Sheet
(Available in worksheet format at avemariapress.com)

Objective:							
Action Steps:	**Accountability**	**Schedule**			**Resources**		**Measures of Success**
	Primary and Others	Start	Complete	Staff	Equipment and Facilities	Budget	
Action A							
Action B							
Action C							

Conclusion

Two major functions of all managers involve *directing* and *controlling* their organizations. *Keeping score* and *winning the game* are fundamental to fulfilling these management responsibilities. To direct and control their parishes, effective parish administrators should specify what results are expected and how the parish team will keep score. Staff members and parishioners want their parish to be a winner. Good parish leaders help all to know how the "game is played" and how to maintain a "winning score."

Exercises

1. Identify three key result areas you have emphasized during your tenure and consider how you can measure past progress objectively. If you are satisfied that you have made appropriate progress and can document that progress, determine if new performance indicators need to be set or if other areas should be identified.

2. From the list of key result areas listed on page 152, identify three where you can cite progress, three that are currently not even on the radar, and three that can be considered problematic in your parish or organization. Select one from each category and develop two or three key performance indicators.

3. Within one week, make it a point to find the opportunity to ask persons in your organization, "How are things going?" Reflect on their responses, and determine if the entire organization is working toward the same goals.

4. Select one piece of criticism or complaint (Mass schedule, parking, homilies, high tuition, etc.) that has been raised on a number of occasions over the past year.

   - Has its validity been tested?
   - Has any response been developed as to its validity or its place in parish planning?
   - Does it appear in the current planning process?
   - Have performance indicators for a solution been established?

   If you answered "no" to any of these questions, what actions will you take to address the criticism or complaint?

BIBLIOGRAPHY

Morrisey, George L. *A Guide to Tactical Planning: Producing Your Short-Term Results*. San Francisco: Jossey-Bass, 1996.

Pickett, William L. *A Concise Guide to Pastoral Planning*. Notre Dame: Ave Maria Press, 2007.

Robbins, Stephen P. *Managing Today!* 2nd ed. Upper Saddle River, NJ: Prentice Hall, 2000.

CHAPTER 10:

Human Resources:
The Spine of an Organization

Mary Ann Dantuono, JD

Much will be required of the person entrusted
with much, and still more will be demanded of the
person entrusted with more.

—Luke 12:48

Key Concepts

1. While managers are a key to the effective operation of an
    organization, they depend on others to achieve the mission.

2. Competence in supervision is essential to care for the material
    and spiritual needs of the people in the organization and to be
    effective stewards of the environment of the organization.

3. Employees and "volunteer" workers must meet the same
    standards. Therefore, the employer needs to establish appropri-
    ate screening, training, and supervision of employees and of
    volunteers, who are the hands and heart of many nonprofit
    organizations.

4. Identification and mobilization of the skills and abilities of
    employees and volunteers contributes to their personal and
    professional development as well as to the development of the
    total organization.

5. Affirmation and constructive criticism are important aspects of staff development, but how and when these are offered is critical to achieving the outcomes intended.

6. The roles of ordained, religious, and lay workers need to complement each other and should be clearly articulated.

7. While professional pastoral ministers may use similar skills in their relationships with volunteers and employees as they do with their congregations, the dual role may be confusing to the employee.

8. Personnel records are legal documents and must be carefully constructed and maintained in strict confidence.

Introduction

Within the context of linking effective management to effective ministry, this chapter seeks to recognize the centrality of the human resources function within organizations; identify central principles; and explore processes for hiring, orientation, supervision, development, and evaluation of employees. The human resources function of an organization supports its mission and vision. Understanding some of the basics of hiring and maintaining both paid and volunteer staff can alleviate problems and can build a team of qualified people who serve the organization, its ministries, and services well. This chapter is divided into three sections: Introductory Concepts in Human Resources Principles, Human Resources Functions, and Special Legal Issues.

Work and Ministry

In many ways the Christian perspective on work is expressed in John 3:18: "Let us love not in word or speech but in deed and truth." Kahlil Gibran's simple statement that "work is love made visible" also expresses how faith and work are interconnected. A medical missionary on a poster entitled "Love" offers this quotation about his work: "All you need is a vocation, and all your other skills and qualities will be put to use." He expresses the most important aspect of human resources management. It is about human beings and about being human.

> Work remains a good thing, not only because it is useful and enjoyable, but also because it expresses and increases the worker's dignity. Through work we not only transform the world, we are transformed ourselves, becoming more a human being.
> —Pope John Paul II, *On Human Work*, 9

Basic Principles of Catholic Social Thought

Work is Central to the Social Question
Work is more than a way to make a living; it is an expression of our dignity and a form of continuing participation in God's Creation. "Created in God's image, we were given the mandate to transform the earth. By their work people share in God's creative activity. . . . Awareness that our work is a sharing in God's work ought to permeate even the most ordinary daily activities" (*On Human Work* #25).

Subjective and Objective Dimensions of Labor
Work is for man, not man for work. Everyone should be able to draw from work the means of providing for his life and that of his family and of servicing the human community. (*Catechism of the Catholic Church* #2428)

Priority of Labor Over Capital
Yet the workers' rights cannot be doomed to be the mere result of economic systems aimed at maximum profits. The thing that must shape the whole economy is respect for the workers' rights within each country and all through the world's economy. (*On Human Work* #17).

Just Working Conditions
Catholic social teaching contributes a moral voice to such issues of economic justice as wages, working conditions, relations between employees and employers, the rights of workers to form unions and professional associations, and the duty of workers to develop their skills. (*USCCB Economic Justice for All* #74.)

Participation in Work
It is clear that recognition of the proper position of labor and the worker in the production process demands various adaptations in the sphere of the right to ownership of the means of production. (*On Human Work* #67)

Reflection on a few of the principles of Catholic social thought leads to the conclusion that the human resources function or task is about the development of the human person and the development of community. Church and faith-based organizations are called to build community and shape the world. As the U.S. Catholic Bishops stated in *Co-workers in the Vineyard of the Lord*, the "best organizational practices are consistent with Gospel values. They balance the goals and needs of the organization, its workers, and the community in which it is located" (61). Balancing this call as both a minister and an employer, as in the case of the ordained and religious, is sometimes precarious. The goals may be integrated but the relationships disparate. Managing employees and volunteers is a necessary and also a delicate task for the minister/employer.

Development of a Team

The goal of staffing a parish or other organization is a clear confirmation that a team is necessary to carry out the mission. While leadership is critical, no one person can manage all the various tasks needed for the functioning of a modern parish or organization. The team must understand not only the mission but how their particular skills and talents can be applied in collaboration with others to carry out the mission. There are three major considerations here: mission, competence, and diversity (whether the team reflects the people who are served). There is a delicate balance in the importance of these three considerations, which should be given priority as a starting point. Discussions about "hiring for mission" examine whether the hiring decision should be based on professional skills or formation for mission and which can be "added" if the ideal candidate is not available. In "We Want the Best: Hiring and Keeping an Excellent Church Workforce," J. Patrick Murphy, C.M., argues forcefully that mission is what matters. "Too often we believe our job is to hire the best qualified candidate available, avoiding the burden of hiring for mission. In my experience, the best hires we make are ordinary people, well qualified in all crucial dimensions, who personally connect their own values to ours" (Murphy 1–2). The pros and cons and stories of hiring for mission could fill this chapter. However, the correct answer may be somewhat situational—found in the nature of the position and particularly in the leadership responsibilities it entails. A general rule is that the more influential the position, the more important is mission formation (see Exercise 5.1 at the end of this chapter).

Motivation

Motivation is the starting point for seeking an employment or volunteer position. It is important to explore this dimension and to determine if the motivation of a candidate or volunteer is a fit for the needs of the organization. The starting point is to look inward: "What motivates you?" Why did you direct your career into the job you presently hold? As you examine your motives, you can begin to glimpse the motives of others. Think also about the organization. What is good about the organization—mission, leaders, activities, hours, and location? These factors are all part of the motivation to work in a particular place. Peter Drucker would argue that a clear sense of mission and the existing leadership are critical factors in motivation. Good leaders and staff are the catalysts to motivate others to serve and will invite others into the ministry and empower them to serve. Good leaders with clear mission and purpose attract other good leaders who wish to contribute to the mission and carry out the purposes of the organization.

In drawing a parallel between the "integration of lay ecclesial ministers" and the concept of "employee engagement," Michael Brough of the National Leadership Roundtable of Church Management argues that there are seven key factors that will foster the growth of integration and engagement of Church employees:

1. The purposeful selection of talent
2. Meaningful work
3. Clear work impact
4. Inspired leadership
5. Continuous learning and development
6. A sense of community

7. Results-based recognition and rewards

—Brough, pp. 204–205

The Relationship of Employer and Employee

A correct balance in the mutuality of the relationship between the employee or volunteer and the employer will create a healthy and productive workplace. Additionally, this balance will achieve the mission, respecting the dignity of both the employer and employee. Contemporary management literature and the law outline basic expectations within this relationship of mutuality on the part of employers and employees that can also be modified appropriately and applied to volunteers.

> *Employees may expect:* accurate and current job descriptions that clearly identify reporting responsibility and accountability; a space to work with proper equipment in safe and healthy working conditions; respect for one's dignity; a sense of personal worth gained from using talent, skills and creativity; participation in decisions affecting the work and in developing performance expectations for one's position; fairly applied workplace policies; timely and honest feedback, including periodic performance evaluation; a workplace free from all forms of discrimination and harassment and proactive about addressing and resolving such allegations.
>
> *Employers may expect:* a full day's work and employee contributions to the mission of the organization with commitment, initiative and responsibility; the right to modify assigned duties consistent with the employee's position and/or pay category and the needs of the organization; employees who witness to the values, underlying the mission, treat coworkers and consumers with behavior reflecting those values and observe the

code of conduct of the profession and rules of the employer; honesty, confidentiality; good judgment in the use of the organization's materials and resources; and cooperation when the need arises to perform unusual duties that cannot be foreseen, acceptance of the employers ability to change assigned duties, consistent with job and/or pay category, and acceptance of the organization's need to consider adjustments in its staffing in light of the mission, fiscal resources, and employee performance.

—National Association of
Church Personnel Administrators,
Church Human Resources Administration, pp. 70–71

Organization

A new administrator or supervisor should meet with each person on the staff individually and become familiar with what each employee is doing. If the staff is large, meeting with all who directly report to you is adequate. Determine what each person's responsibilities are, what he or she expects from the supervisor, and what he or she likes about the duties of the position. Ask for job descriptions, if they exist. If they do not, begin a process to create job descriptions in collaboration with the individuals involved in order to clarify respective responsibilities and tasks. Each person should use the same outline so that duplications and contradictions can be discovered and negotiated.

Essential Elements of a Job Description

1. Title/Nature of the position
   How does this person serve the mission of the organization?
2. Role description
3. Reporting/Accountability
4. Responsibilities and tasks
   The Americans with Disabilities Act requires clarification of the essential duties of the position.
5. Qualifications
   Degrees, experience, and continuing education
   Interests
   Skills and competencies
   Decision-making
   Relationships with others
   Administrative supervision, i.e., number and nature of staff
6. Contract/Framework for the position
   Salary
   Benefits
   Hours
   Sick/vacation time

If starting an organization, take time to envision the organizational structure, accountabilities, tasks, and talents needed to serve the mission of the organization before building a team. Using the "Job Description" as a disciplined way to begin to build the organizational structure will avoid competing and conflicting responsibilities among team members.

Human resources management involves practices and skills that can be learned and will ultimately assist you to manage efficiently. Novice administrators may approach the human resources tasks with trepidation and fear of litigation. A step-by-step approach and some foresight and common sense will be good companions for supervising paid or volunteer personnel.

The Four Basic Human Resources Functions

An organization's human resources policies should address both paid employees and volunteers. The policies should be fair, establish clear expectations, and provide for meaningful and effective performance evaluation. There are four basic functions:

- hiring
- orientation and training
- supervision
- assessment

Hiring

> Do not hire a man who does your work for money, but him who does it for love of it.
>
> —Henry David Thoreau

Hiring is probably the most important human resources function. If the person chosen is the "right fit" for the position and the organization, the subsequent functions of orientation and training, supervision, and assessment will be accomplished with ease. In order to begin finding an individual to fill a perceived need within the organization or to fill a vacancy, it is important to think about the pre-hiring tasks of developing a good job description, updating the application form, and determining the process you will use for recruitment.

Pre-hiring Tasks

1. The job description is an important document that will enable the applicant and the employer to determine if the person is right for the job. Review the position, existing needs of the organization, and the present job description. Make changes in the description before you begin recruitment. Be prepared to

answer questions about salary, benefits, and work schedule as well as particular responsibilities of the position.

2. The second pre-hiring task is to design a recruitment process and determine who will be involved in the development of the job description, recruitment, and the interview process.

3. The third task is to review the application for the position. Potential candidates will need to provide their information, including employment history, educational background, and special training or skills that meet the qualifications for the position. This can be done on an application, by providing a resume, or both. Make sure the application is current with employment law. The application may ask the candidate about his or her wage or salary expectations.

The Application
(Sample available at avemariapress.com)

The application becomes part of the employee's or volunteer's personnel file if the applicant is accepted for a position. It is a legal document and is subject to discovery in litigation. The application should not contain any questions prohibited in interviews, such as questions concerning race, ethnicity, citizenship, color, nationality, sex, sexual orientation, marital status, disability, genetic predisposition or carrier status, or any other characteristics prohibited by state or local law in any employment program, policy, or practice. It should contain information about special skills or training, including VIRTUS® Training, languages spoken, and accurate information about education and job history. Additional information may be necessary so the employer can conduct necessary background checks. The application should state that any offer of employment is conditioned on all background checks being completed satisfactorily, as well as having appropriate immigration status documents reviewed and a medical examination, if needed.

If the position requires that the employee be bonded, the applicant must answer questions regarding insurability appropriately. As part of the application or on a separate document, the applicant must provide permission to release information to the prospective employer. This can be "to whom it may concern" but should show the potential employer as the recipient of the information released. The application should require the applicant to acknowledge with his or her signature that the information included is complete and accurate and that the applicant knows that the employer will rely on same. Any inaccuracies or false information will disqualify the applicant or, if hired, may require the employer to take adverse action, including firing the employee for cause.

Recruitment

What kind of person are you looking for? In addition to the qualifications or skills listed on the job description, think about the kind of person who will be a good collaborator with existing staff—a good fit. The Greenleaf Center for Servant Leadership studies nonprofit management and looks to certain character-istics and applies the "outcome test." Researchers ask, "Do those served become healthier, wiser, freer, more autonomous, more likely themselves to become servant-leaders?" This part of the process requires that you exam-ine your own leadership style and communication skills.

How will you find the candi-dates? The most effective recruit-

> **Characteristics of Servant-Leaders**
>
> - Listening to and acceptance of others
> - Foresight and intuition
> - Awareness and perception
> - Powers of persuasion
> - Ability to conceptualize and communicate concepts
> - Healing influence on individuals and institutions
> - Builders of community through teamwork and collaboration
> - Practices the "Art of Contemplation" (prayer)
>   —Greenleaf Center for Servant Leadership

ment technique is networking—asking other staff, leaders of simi-lar organizations, and volunteers. Some professional organizations offer to list opportunities on websites or in professional newsletters. If you choose to advertise, think about where you will advertise. Local or professional newspapers or newsletters may be an option, as are parish bulletins. Web-based recruiting is least expensive and is accessible to most workers. Most nonprofit organizations have an "employment opportunities" link on their websites. Consider the listing opportunities in new professional networking sites, such as LinkedIn, Facebook, and Twitter, among others. However, even in our technological age, 95 percent of people get jobs through word of mouth. Talk to others and network through other parishes and similar organizations. Networking among parishioners is a good strategy, as long as they know they will not be considered for the position.

Special Issue: Employment of Parishioners

Many Church professionals find that the hiring of members of the parish or congregation is not a good practice, particularly in leadership positions. There are many reasons for this policy. One reason is that it often produces difficult conflicts of interest. Another reason is the perception of a lack of confidentiality. A third reason is the difficulty of separating the roles, responsibilities, and relationships of pastor/ employer and the employee/parishioner's relationship to the parish. In the event that a parishioner is hired, the National Association of Church Personnel Administrators recommends that parishes anticipate the confusing, challenging work dynamic.

During the interview process and once employed, regular efforts should be made to assure boundaries are clear, appropriate, and professional. Parishioners who work for the parish should consider themselves employees first and parishioners second.

—*Parish Personnel Administration*, p. 55

Interviewing
(Sample interview questions are available at avemariapress.com)

After a predetermined amount of time or a sufficient number of applicants, the next task is to determine which candidates to interview. Select the most appealing and qualified candidates, set aside time, and prepare for the interview. Prepare by reviewing the application and/or resume and thinking about questions to ask the applicant. The style of interview can be informal or formal. If more than one person conducts the interview, determine areas for questioning prior to the interview. The goal is to get the applicants talking about themselves, their professional qualifications, and personal work styles. Open-ended questions are best. A candidate's responses to questions like "What are you most proud of from your last position?" and "What was the greatest employment challenge you experienced, and how did you handle it?" can reveal much about an individual and supplement the information that appears on the resume and application.

Be prepared for questions the applicant may wish to ask. The applicant should be encouraged to ask questions. Obviously, no matter how mission-driven the individual is, salary, benefits, hours, and location of work are important. If the person will be supervising others, he or she may wish to be introduced to them, or will ask about the people, the duration of their employment, and expectations. Make sure the job application is completed and that all authorizations needed, such as for employment and personal references, criminal background checks, motor vehicle license search, and Child Abuse State Registry Database have been properly completed and are ready for processing.

The Job Offer

After interviewing selected candidates, determine the top three choices. Reference and background checks may help decide between candidates. After these have been received, a formal offer of employment can be made orally and confirmed in writing. If the position does not require a contract of employment, the relationship is an "at will employment," meaning that the employee is hired at the will of the employer. The employee can also be fired at the will of the employer at any time (with a few limited exceptions). No reason is necessary. A contract will outline the terms of the employment relationship and grounds for dismissal.

Orientation and Training

Welcoming the New Employee
(An Orientation Checklist is available at avemariapress.com.)

The first day on any job is stressful. It is important to make the employee or volunteer feel welcome and needed. Preparing a space to work, providing a desk, chair, and necessary equipment in advance of the staff arriving communicates to the person that he or she is a necessary part of the team. Additionally, introducing this person to others and explaining his or her roles in the organization is also very helpful. Basic logistics of parking, lunch or dinner break, and the general order of things indicate a well-structured workplace. The welcome can be delegated to an appropriate person, but it is an appropriate initiation.

Policies and Procedures

As soon as possible, or at least within the first month, all organizational policies and procedures should be reviewed with a new staff person. In a small organization, there may be few written policies, but in general all workplaces have "rules and regulations." Expressing these clearly and reviewing them with the new employee will avoid problems in the future. It also gives the new employee an opportunity to ask questions to better understand the application of the policies. Many employers have a "code of conduct" covering workplace ethics, conflicts of interest, confidentiality, dress codes, inappropriate sexual behavior, etc. The prerequisite for signing such a code is an employee training. One commonly used training to promote appropriate conduct regarding sexual abuse is VIRTUS®. Other programs are available to help employees understand the requirements of the additional ethics of the code of conduct. By completing this preliminary training and orientation in the first weeks, the employee or volunteer recognizes the importance that the employer places on these policies.

The Importance of Training

The failure to provide training can make the learning curve unnecessarily long. Relying on individuals who are self-taught can be disappointing. In many cases, a small employer is not able to have the predecessor available to train a new employee or volunteer. This can be overcome by having the person leaving the position show another employee or volunteer the systems, processes, etc., used and creating a chronological list of tasks. You might also assign someone who has similar hours and responsibilities to mentor the new employee or volunteer for the first few weeks. Knowing the supervisor's needs and priorities can help a new staff member get off to a good start and will enable him or her to be successful. As new ideas and programs develop, encourage employees and volunteers to attend training sessions. It will help them and the entire organization. Many training programs are available on the Internet. Web-based training enables skills to be acquired or enhanced online within the context of a workday in a cost-effective manner.

Supervision

It is important for a supervisor to understand and know employees and volunteers in the organization. Ongoing communication throughout a project can avoid problems and misunderstandings. When assigning tasks, be clear as to the objective, the level of authority delegated, and the reporting responsibilities—what does the supervisor want to know and when? One tool for communication is a meeting. In order for a meeting to be productive, it needs to be scheduled within a specific timeframe, have an agenda distributed ahead of time, and be summarized in writing afterward. A staff person who is expected to report on projects should be well prepared. Written reports can save valuable time and can be distributed to others who are absent. In the chapters on meetings and communications, there are many suggestions that can be used to make staff meetings a valuable tool for all.

An open-door policy of supervisor and staff is a common practice in nonprofits. This practice enables employees and volunteers to feel comfortable asking questions and providing informal reports on various projects. However, if several people report to one supervisor, this can consume valuable time that might be needed to accomplish the priorities of the supervisor. Setting a period of time during the day for informal supervision can be a way to avoid spending the entire day in supervisory tasks.

It is also important to address problems with staff behavior as soon as they appear. Seeing if it "works itself out" or "goes away" is usually an inadequate strategy. As we will see in the next section, this strategy can create legal problems. It is better to attend to simple behavior problems, such as lateness or inappropriate language in the workplace, as soon as they become evident, rather than waiting to see if they self-correct. Establishing a mode of communication as well as times for communication will enable consistency, promote fairness, and avoid constant interruptions. It will also produce better outcomes.

Performance Assessment

(A sample employee performance assessment is available at www.avemariapress.com.)

The purpose of a performance assessment process is to recognize and value what the staff member has accomplished and his/her impact on the organization. It is important to do this in a structured environment in order to communicate openly about job performance, present job description, expectations, and compensation issues. It is a time to look at ways the staff member can improve performance, identify training and educational needs, and plan objectives and goals for the future. It is wise to schedule assessments at designated intervals, such as annually or biannually. An appointment should be set at least a week in advance at a mutually agreeable time and for a predetermined duration of between thirty and sixty minutes. It is good idea for the staff member to complete an assessment form along with the supervisor. This is a good way to determine where there is agreement and any areas that may need clarification. Open, honest discussion is the goal. After the interview a formal summary of it and a plan for growth and improvement is submitted to the employee for signature. The staff member keeps a copy, and one is kept in a *confidential* personnel file within the organization. The process requires confidentiality of both the conversations and the written employee file. It is common practice to separate the performance assessment from any salary review or changes. Most nonprofits have a cost-of-living salary increase that is not reflective of performance. However, performance-based increases are becoming more common in nonprofits, as are bonuses. Either way, it is a good practice to separate the conversations.

Ongoing Employee Development

Employees who are valuable members of the team not only need the reassurance provided by an assessment review but also should be challenged by new and progressively more complex assignments and projects. They should be encouraged to engage in ongoing development. A small budget for staff education and development can bring many rewards, especially where a small staff is responsible for a large and multifaceted organization such as a parish. Creativity and competence in an employee or volunteer is a very valuable asset.

Special Human Resources Issues

The topics discussed in this section are sources of potential litigation, which can be avoided with some foresight:

- legal responsibilities and liabilities of employers
- confidentiality and privacy in the workplace
- diversity and anti-discrimination laws
- persons with disabilities
- sexual harassment in the workplace
- wage and hour laws (Fair Labor Standard Act)
- right to employment
- conflict resolution

Legal Responsibilities and Liabilities of Employers

The employer is legally strictly liable to his employee. This rises from a legal duty to provide a safe place to work, safe equipment for the work, competent coworkers, and sufficient rules for all workers to maintain a safe workplace.

This liability is covered by state labor laws, worker's compensation statutes, and insurance. Volunteers are not covered by this insurance, but most nonprofit organizations have insurance to cover volunteers injured in the course of their service.

The employer is also responsible to third parties for the acts of the employee or volunteer committed in the course of employment. This legal doctrine, known as *respondeat superior,* or "let the master answer," is a key doctrine in the law of agency. The doctrine requires that the principal answer for the acts of the subordinate, such as in the employer-employee, employer-volunteer relationship. As such, churches, schools, and institutions are required to provide adequate supervision of employees and volunteers. This requires proper screening, orientation, instruction in their tasks, and evaluation of the performance in their position. A volunteer's application is as important a record of a volunteer's work history and educational background, as known to the employer, as the employment application is for employees. An agent, either volunteer or paid staff, who signs an agreement to purchase goods for his employer in the name of the employer can create a binding contract between the seller and the employer. If harm comes to a person because of negligence of an employee or volunteer, the employer will be held liable. This doctrine is also extended to independent contractors hired by the church or organization. Contracts with such independent contractors can negotiate this liability. These liabilities are generally insurable risks.

However, if an employee or volunteer commits a crime in the course of the employment, the employer is not liable in a civil suit based on such a crime unless the employer authorized, condoned, or ratified the employee's conduct or knew or had reason to know that the employee had criminal propensities (e.g., history of sexual abuse or a violent criminal background) and retained the employee or volunteer despite knowledge of the unfitness or incompetence. This distinction can be seen in the case of a waiter who got annoyed with a customer and stabbed the customer in the face with a fork, damaging his eye. The employer would not be liable for this assault if there was no history of temper tantrums or violent actions. However, if the waiter expressed his anger by banging a glass on a table and a piece of glass lodged in the customer's eye and caused injury, the court could see the latter action within the context of negligent service, and the employer would be liable (see Exercise 5.2).

Confidentiality and Privacy in the Workplace

An employee has a limited expectation of confidentiality and privacy in the workplace. The one protection that remains strong is privacy of the employment records. An employee's record of employment is confidential. Employers must take precautions to limit access to such records. Health insurance claims must be kept confidential and separate from the personnel records. Additionally, information revealed on health insurance claims cannot be used by an employer against an employee.

Since the personnel records are confidential, the information contained cannot be revealed to third parties. This presents a dilemma in responding to requests for employment references. Employers do well to respond to such requests by confirming only the dates of employment. If the employer undertakes to provide any additional information, the employer may not misrepresent (see Exercise 5.3). The danger in providing information beyond dates of employment is the possibility of a suit being filed by the employee for defamation or negligent misrepresentation.

If the allegation in the above problem involved sexual misconduct, would the answer be different? The standard imposed by the courts is that an employer has a duty not to misrepresent the facts in describing the qualification and character of a former employee if making these misrepresentations presents a substantial foreseeable risk of injury to third parties (see Exercise 5.4).

Employers have an important and legitimate interest in maintaining an efficient and productive work force, and they consequently have substantial latitude in regulating employee on-the-job conduct and working relations. The result is a reduced privacy interest for employees. Private-sector employers are monitoring their employees more than ever before with new surveillance technologies that are available and inexpensive. Activities include recording and review of telephone conversations, storage and review of voice mail messages, storage and review of computer files, storage and review of e-mail messages, monitoring of telephone and computer usage. Other tools that are used are workplace testing of job skills and use of psychological measurement tools to evaluate employees, as well as drug testing.

There are some protections to employees' privacy. While allowing employers to monitor employees, third parties and law enforcement must comply with constitutional safeguards of unreasonable search and seizure. If the employer creates a reasonable basis for the employee to believe he or she has privacy, then the employer may be creating such a right. An example is where the employer allows an employee to purchase a lock for a locker, and does not require the employee to give the employer the combination. The employee may reasonably assume that that area is private, whereas the employer can search desks, even if locked.

Diversity among Employees and Applicable Anti-discrimination Laws

As geographic areas become more diverse, it is generally a desirable goal to have the organization's team reflect the stakeholders or consumers of your parish, diocese, or other organization. Federal and state governments prohibit discrimination of "protected classes." The protected classes are race, color, sex, national origin, and religion. Under federal law there are two additional protected classes: age and disability. These seven are also found in most state civil rights statutes. Some state laws and city ordinances have extended the anti-discrimination protections to sexual preference, marital status, and citizenship status. Disability will be treated in the next section because it has different responsibilities and considerations under the Americans with Disabilities Act of

1990 and state laws. Care must be taken in recruiting, interviewing, and promoting employees to avoid discriminatory language, attitudes, and behavior. Title VII of the Civil Rights Act of 1964 and the Civil Rights Act of 1991 prohibit *discrimination* and also *harassment*, which encompasses but is not limited to sexual harassment. This topic is covered in a subsequent section of this chapter. Anti-discrimination is important to keep in mind in "providing and applying" workplace rules and regulations.

As a job position is created and recruitment commences, where and how one seeks employees will often determine if minorities apply. If speaking a second language is necessary for a position, e.g., a receptionist, that is an acceptable qualification of a job. In an interview, a person may not be asked what country he or she is from but can be asked about language fluency.

Because of First Amendment protections, a church is allowed to "prefer" to hire members of its own religion. Federal civil rights laws contain an exemption for churches concerning discrimination on the basis of religion, as do many states. In addition, courts have held it permissible for a church to refuse to hire a person or to dismiss an employee because he or she is living outside the tenets of the faith. For example, a Catholic parish may not want to hire someone who is in a marriage that the Church does not consider valid or is openly engaged in a homosexual lifestyle. Cases such as these are presently being litigated, and this is a legal area that will need to be watched carefully (see Exercises 5.5 and 5.6).

Employees with Disabilities

The American with Disabilities Act of 1990 (ADA) and related state statutes prohibit discrimination against qualified individuals with disabilities. Under federal law, employers who have more than twenty-five employees must make reasonable accommodation to known physical and mental limitations of an *otherwise qualified applicant* or employee with a disability unless it can be shown that doing so would impose an undue hardship on the operations of its business. State law is often broader both in definition of a disability and in what constitutes reasonable accommodation. State law should be consulted in this area.

An individual with a disability is a person who (a) has a physical or mental impairment that substantially limits one or more of the major life activities; (b) has a record of such impairment; or (c) is regarded as having such an impairment. Under the ADA, a disability is a physical or mental impairment that substantially limits one or more major life activities. Examples of major life activities are caring for oneself, walking, speaking, breathing, or lifting. An employer is required to provide "reasonable accommodation" to an otherwise qualified individual. This provision is frequently the subject of lawsuits under this law. For example, if a highly qualified candidate has mobility impairment and uses a wheelchair, should the employer be required to install an automatic door opener as a "reasonable accommodation" so that the employee can access the office? If an elevator is essential in order for a school principal to move between floors of a building to "observe teachers in a classroom," should the employer be required to install one for a qualified candidate? If full-time work is an essential function of the job, is making the position part-time reasonable? The courts examine these cases on a case-by-case basis and look at undue hardship; cost; how extensive and substantial the alterations must be to reasonably accommodate the disability; the nature of the disruption to the ordinary operations; and whether the need would fundamentally alter the nature of the position, eliminate an essential function, or change the operation of business. The same standards are applied to a situation where an employee requests "reasonable accommodation" because of the onset of a medical condition or disability while employed.

The Family and Medical Leave Act (FMLA) entitles eligible employees to take up to twelve weeks of unpaid job-protected leave in a twelve-month period for specified family and medical reasons. This applies to employees in private organizations with fifty or more employees. The employer must provide an eligible employee up to a total of twelve work weeks of unpaid leave for the birth and care of a newborn or adopted child, to care for an immediate family member (spouse, child, parent) with a serious health condition, for an employee with a serious health condition that prevents the employee from working, and for a "Qualifying Exigency Leave" arising out of a covered military member on active duty or called to active duty for members of the National Guard or Reserves. Recent changes in this law also provide for up to twenty-six weeks of leave to care for a service member with a serious illness or injury incurred in the line of duty while on active duty. There are many rules that apply to claims under this law, and it is important to note that the request for leave and permission granted must be in writing. At the end or during the intermittent leave, the employee is entitled to be restored to his or her original job or equivalent. Visit www.dol.gov/esa/whd/fmla/index.htm for further information.

Disabilities and Workplace Etiquette

(Also available in reproducible download format at www.avemariapress.com)

- Do not refer to a disability unless it is crucial.

- Do not sensationalize a disability by saying "victim of," "afflicted with," and so on, but rather, "person who has multiple sclerosis," or "people who had polio."

- Avoid using emotional descriptions. Say "uses a wheelchair" rather than "confined to a wheelchair"; "walks with a cane or crutches" rather than "is crippled."

- Avoid labeling people into groups, as in "the disabled," "the deaf," "a paraplegic." Instead say, "persons with disabilities," "people who are deaf," "a man who has paraplegia." (Note especially that the words "disabled" and "handicapped" are adjectives, not nouns.)

- Avoid portraying disabled people who succeed as remarkable or superhuman. This implies that it is unusual for people with disabilities to have talents or skill.

- Avoid using the word "special" in regard to disability, as in "special entrance" or "special transportation." Instead say "accessible entrance" and "lift-equipped buses." The word "special" serves only to segregate rather than to integrate people with disabilities.

- Avoid putting disabilities into a medical context. The overwhelming majority of people with disabilities are not sick. Words like "patient," "case," and "invalid" should not be used. Most current disability issues concern civil rights, education accessibility, and so on.

- Avoid using an over-familiar tone in referring to people with disabilities. A disabled person deserves the same courtesy of address and reference as a nondisabled person. (Disabled people, for example, are often "first-named," whereas nondisabled people in similar contexts are not.) Rather than any label, a person with a disability prefers to be called by his/her name and treated with the same dignity and respect as other employees and volunteers.

Discrimination-Related Harassment

In the past few years, the field of employment relations has been dominated by a proliferation of litigation for "sexual harassment" and other "harassment" cases based on the protected classes in the anti-discrimination laws. Harassment cases can be based on race, color, sex, national origin, religion, age, or disability, as all are protected in civil rights statutes. Sexual harassment cases are most common and have two forms: *quid pro quo* harassment and hostile environment harassment. *Quid pro quo* means "something for something." *Quid pro quo* sexual harassment occurs when a person in an authoritative position places a person subordinate to him or her in a compromising position. In other words, a supervisor conditions a raise, a promotion, or a favorable work assignment on the employee's succumbing to sexual advances. Hostile environment sexual harassment arises when sexual advances or other verbal or physical conduct of a sexual nature are unwelcome and create an intimidating, hostile, or offensive work environment.

The harassment can be one or two serious incidents that affect the person's job, or it can be a pattern or series of smaller incidents that are so "pervasive" or widespread that they cause the victim to have trouble performing her or his job. The victim does not have to be the person being harassed but can be anyone affected by the offensive conduct. The harasser can be either a supervisor or a coworker. In order for the employer to be liable for harassment by a coworker, the supervisor must be made aware of the conduct of the coworker, or the conduct must be so obvious that the supervisor should have been aware of the conduct. Sexual harassment can be words, jokes and/or conduct, or it can be conduct alone (such as unwanted touching or groping). It can be acts of gender-based animosity or sexually charged workplace behavior (such as relating sexual exploits from a weekend date).

The victim must show that "an ordinary, reasonably prudent person in like or similar circumstance" would have been similarly offended. Objectively, the harassment must result in a work environment that a reasonable person would find hostile or abusive, and the employee must actually feel that the work environment is hostile or abusive. It should also be noted that persons of the same gender can harass each other.

Sexual harassment also includes conduct that is criminal in nature, such as rape, sexual assault, stalking, and other similar offenses. If the harassment involves physical touching, coerced physical confinement, or coerced sex acts, the conduct may also constitute a crime, and a police complaint should be filed. Non-work sexual harassment can occur between an employee and a client, parish member, minors, and vendors. Different laws than those that prohibit sexual harassment in the workplace regulate this behavior. These laws are also covered in the legal chapter and are of grave concern to employers because of the doctrine of *respondeat superior*. Because of this, some employers are also adding "anti-fraternization" policies to their employment policies. These policies limit or prohibit intimate relationships between supervisors and workers and between employees or volunteers and consumers (see Exercise 5.7).

Wage and Hour Laws (Fair Labor Standard Act)

Wage and hour issues are frequently a source of legal problems for small employers. Knowing the law in this area is imperative. Because these laws are different state to state, it is important to check with local legal counsel and/or the state government department of labor to determine responsibility as an employer. Under the Federal Fair Labor Standards Act (FLSA) there are three basic types of work classifications and three types of pay (NACPA 2006, 41). The first classification is "hourly" worker, or those subject to the provisions of the FLSA, referred to as "nonexempt." FLSA has established the "salary test" (NACPA 2007, 102) that classifies all employees who earn less than $455 weekly as nonexempt. (See also http://www.dol .gov/esa/whd/regs/compliance/fairpay/main.htm.) Additionally, for employees earning more than $455 weekly, the "duties test" is applied to determine if the employee should be classified "nonexempt." Employees performing administrative, secretarial, receptionist, bookkeeping, maintenance, teacher aid, and similar work fall into this category. For this category, records must be kept of hours.

The workweek is forty hours. If more than forty hours are worked within the established seven consecutive days of the workweek, an overtime rate of time-and-a-half must be paid. Compensating time off (also at time-and-a-half) can be substituted for overtime pay during the same workweek.

The second category is "salaried employees." Employees who perform particular administrative, managerial, and professional duties fit this category and are called "exempt" workers. These employees do not have a standard workweek—the actual workweek may be as long as it takes to get the job done. Overtime compensation is not paid. For the above two categories the employer is responsible for applicable taxes and other deductions and legally required benefits such as social security, workers compensation, unemployment insurance, and family and medical leave (FMLA). State and federal laws should be consulted for mandatory benefits.

The third category of classification is "independent contractor." An independent contractor is not an employee. It is an outside service that a church or agency may hire for the purpose of accomplishing a specific project or tasks. The contractor is paid a fee with no benefits or money withheld for taxes. A federal tax form (1099) must be completed for annual payments exceeding certain limits. Misclassification of employees as independent contractors is an ongoing concern. The IRS looks at the "degree of control" test. The NACPA offers this definition: "An independent business or person who performs work according to their own means and methods with the hiring agent establishing the desired results" (NACPA 2006, 42). A person hired as a bookkeeper to work one day a week in the office, using the computers and software of the agency or church, is usually determined to be a nonexempt employee subject to withholding, not an independent contractor.

Right to Employment

Immigrants

The Immigration Control and Reform Act of 1986 is a federal law that requires all employers to check documents of all employees to determine if it is legally permissible for the individual to have a job in the United States. Every employee must produce two forms of identification to prove citizenship and, if the employee is an immigrant, refugee, or asylee, additional documentation of a legal right to work must be seen by the employer, and the I-9 form must be completed. Failure to have correct immigration forms, such as a "work visa" or proof of "legal permanent resident" status (commonly called a green card), or an employment authorization document (EAD) precludes an employer from a lawful hire. The Church must comply with this neutral law. Failure to have an I-9 form on file for the required three-year period for all workers subjects the employer to fines. While there is no penalty imposed on the worker, deportation is a grave risk if authorities detain the employee as part of the inspection of the workplace.

Termination of Employment

New York State, among several others, is considered to be an "employment at will" state. This means that a private sector employer can hire and fire as he, she, or it pleases, and a discharged employee usually will have no legal recourse even when the discharge is unfair or unreasonable. The discharged employee may seek unemployment compensation if fired without cause. "Employment at will" is limited by union contracts, a written contract of employment, or in some cases an employee manual that creates an *implied contract of employment* entitling an employee to the protections against discharge that are written into the manual. For example, an employee manual might provide that an employee whose performance is below standard shall receive a counseling session and letter designed to address the performance problem before being discharged. Lawsuits involving unlawful discharge generally seek reinstatement and/or lost wages.

There are several exceptions to *employment at will*. "Whistle-blower" laws protect an employee who is fired for reporting to a supervisor or to a public agency a violation of law that creates a danger to public health and safety, or a labor law violation. Retaliation against an employee who alleges discrimination or harassment is also prohibited. An employee cannot be discharged for filing a worker's compensation or disability benefits claim; however, the employer does not have to hold a job until the employee is able to return to work; the employee can be replaced. However, if an employee's leave is under the FMLA, there is an obligation to allow the employee to return to the same or equivalent job.

Also, an employee may not be discharged because of participation in lawful political or recreational activities outside of the scope of employment. However, this may not be the case when an employee brings such political action into the workplace because it may threaten the 501(c)(3) status of a nonprofit organization, or where the employee signs a "moral and ethical clause" as a condition of the employment and such activities violate an employee policy.

An employee who has excessive absences due to illness may be fired, even if such absences are *bona fide*. An employer may change the conditions of employment, including salary, prospectively and fire an employee for failure to accept the new conditions.

Uniformed Services

Employees who take leave for military duty are protected by the Uniformed Services Employment and Reemployment Rights Act of 1994 (USERRA, 38 U.S.C. §§ 4301–4335). This federal law ensures that persons who serve or have served in the U.S. Armed Forces, Reserves, National Guard, or other "uniformed services who have five years or less of cumulative service in the uniformed services while with an employer": (1) are not disadvantaged in their civilian careers because of their service; (2) are promptly reemployed in their civilian jobs upon their return from duty with an honorable discharge; and (3) are not discriminated against in employment based on past, present, or future military service. Employers are entitled to advance written or verbal notice of service and a "timely" return to employment after discharge. This law protects members of the military from discrimination based on military obligation and requires employers to reemploy them in the job that they would have attained had they not been absent for military service (the "escalator" principle), with the same seniority, status, and pay, as well as other rights and benefits determined by seniority. USERRA also requires that reasonable efforts (such as training or retraining) be made to enable returning service members to refresh or upgrade their skills to help them qualify for reemployment. USERRA has provisions that allow an employee to extend health care and pension coverage during leave for up to five years, and there are protections in this act for disabled veterans.

Jury Duty

This is an important obligation of citizens, and in most states is a protected activity. An employer who is notified in advance of a jury duty summons may not fire an employee because of that absence.

Conflict Resolution

As indicated earlier, an employer can discharge an employee for various reasons. Because of the nature of the position, the investment of training in the employee, the morale of the work-force, and sometimes because it is an aberration in an otherwise acceptable employee performance, an employer may wish to avoid termination. A counseling session may be appropriate. There are several steps to counseling that may lead to the rehabilitation or firing of an employee.

1. *Document.* Document the unsatisfactory work behavior in writing. A detailed record should be kept, as well as a log of any conversations with the employee about performance. It is important that these records contain objective facts, not judgments and feelings.

2. *Schedule the counseling session.* The session should be scheduled for a specific time frame and in a private setting. Prepare for the discussion by gathering facts. For example, if it is about absences or lateness, have a record of the absences or lateness. If this has affected deadlines, have a list of the ways this has affected the efficiency of the parish, diocesan, or organizational office. "Because you were late on [month/day/year], when Mrs. B.

called for a hospital visit for her dying husband, it went to voice mail. . . . When we retrieved the message, he had died."

3. *Share concerns about work performance.* Directly address the situation. The supervisor or manager should share her or his concerns. Be specific and behavior-oriented. "You have been late at least once a week for the past month." The concerns need to be limited to what can be seen and observed, not feelings and perceptions. Never say, "You do not seem to care about this job." The conversation may also include observations about how others are affected. Allow the employee to respond to the specific job performance issues that have been raised. Keep going back to the issues. "You have never liked or appreciated me" is a likely response from the employee, but not one of the issues on the table. Keep the focus on the issues.

4. *Define options.* If it appears that the employee is willing to work to correct performance, ask him or her how this will be accomplished, and set time limits for these things to occur. If there are personal reasons and you have an employee assistance program or can refer him or her to community services, make such recommendations.

5. *Reach an agreement and create a document.* The writing can be a summary of the conversation and a plan of correction. This writing must be signed by the employee and the supervisor and witnessed by a third party.

6. *Set up a date and time for an evaluation of improved performance.* This session requires the supervisor to repeat all the above steps or to escort the employee to the exit after collecting all work equipment and keys.

Conflict resolution allows all sides to be heard and can result in improvement in some cases. Care should be taken to avoid ongoing counseling. If the matter is not resolved after the first session, the best resolution may be a dismissal. Workplace morale will suffer if one employee is allowed to underperform while others are required to pick up the slack.

A Concise Guide to Catholic Church Management

Conclusion

As mentioned in the beginning of this chapter, human resources management is about being human. Both managers and employees will learn about and help to develop each other as they carry out the mission of the organization. Neither group will be perfect all of the time, but effective hiring, training, supervision, and assessment will build a successful organization and avoid employment litigation. Care must be taken to treat all employees and volunteers with respect and dignity on an objective and fair basis. All decision-makers and leaders need to be informed about and sensitive to employment issues. Appropriate policies and procedures need to be formulated and applied in a consistent and fair manner. All positions must have appropriate job descriptions that can be evaluated and are outcomes-oriented. Maintain confidential and well-documented employee files, and, finally, seek appropriate advice from other professionals or legal counselors when in doubt.

Exercises

1. Develop a job description for a business manager based on the outline provided in this chapter. Be sure to establish clearly defined relationships of this staff person to others.

2. Draw an organizational chart of your parish or agency. Do the lines follow functions or the priorities in your organization's mission statement? Check the lines of direct reports and reporting responsibilities. The span of control of any supervisor should not exceed five subordinates. Note comparative salary scales across organizational levels.

3. With a peer, role-play an annual evaluation session based on the following scenario. Use the "Employee Performance Assessment" form available at www.avemariapress.com.

   The social ministry coordinator (SMC) has been at the parish for two years. He has maintained most of the activities from the predecessor, such as the annual blood drive and food drive. The SMC always complains about how busy the job is. When you ask for specifics, the response is vague. The coordinator is frequently at community meetings about "some issue" when you contact the office. The ministry is the least visible to parishioners, there are diminishing numbers of volunteers, and you are becoming concerned.

4. Develop a strategy based on the following case study.

You are pastor for about six months. Gloria Hartful is a long-term employee and parishioner of the parish. She is active in many ministries, and she has worked part-time in the rectory for over twenty years. She raised her family in the parish, and her three children are parishioners who are raising their families in the parish. She is recently widowed. She considers herself the "right hand of the pastor." One of her "qualities" is that she always knows what is going on. She keeps abreast of everyone's schedule and always wants to know people's whereabouts.

A school board member had a complaint from one of the parents that Gloria personally reminded the parent "he was late paying his school tuition." Church member "A" told you that her friend heard from Gloria that "A" was seeing one of the priests for counseling. What are your options in resolving this issue? Which option would you choose? Why?

5. Listed below are seven human resources problems that have been cited in this chapter. Read the first paragraph carefully, and formulate a response. Compare your solution to the prepared response that follows at the end of the chapter for each case study.

5.1 A very large parish determines that it wants to create a paid position for a part-time youth minister. Tabitha Smith applies for the position. She has spent several years in youth organizing with the city youth administration. Her achievements are noteworthy, and her references are very impressive. She wishes to dedicate her career to working with youth and is seeking this part-time position because she is returning to school to secure an advanced degree in social work. She assures you that she can work out the schedule to meet the time needs of the ministry. There is no indication of religious affiliation on her resume or list of activities. When presented with the mission statement and the moral and ethical dimensions of the position of the Church, she indicates that she does not have any problem with upholding and acting within the values. How effective will she be in advancing the mission with youth and collaborating with other mission-driven members of the team?

5.2 Choir director Mr. Leonardo has choir practice for the children's choir in the choir loft. It is a standard policy and practice that at every practice a parent volunteer assists the director as a monitor. At this particular practice, the parent does not show up. During the practice, the director receives a phone call and goes into a stairwell adjacent to the loft to take the call. Several of the children become restless in the two minutes he is gone and begin pushing each other. One child bumps into a music stand that falls from the loft and injures a man who has entered the church to pray. He files a lawsuit against the parish, the choir director, and the young man's parents for his severe head injuries. Will he prevail? How should the director or parish deal with the parent volunteer?

5.3 Adam worked for ABC Non Profits in a supervisory position. He did not get along with Bill, one of his subordinates. Adam and Bill became involved in a heated argument that led to a physical altercation. Adam stated that Bill threw the first punch. ABC conducted a complete investigation. The investigation determined that Bill's actions were inappropriate, but there was insufficient evidence for formal disciplinary action. Both employees received informal warnings, and Bill transferred to a new department. No other incidents followed. Adam was later promoted and subsequently left the company. Recently, ABC received a request from XYZ for employment verification for Adam. The form asked: Is this person eligible for rehire?

    a. Should ABC answer the question about rehiring?

    b. Should they reveal that Adam was involved in an altercation?

5.4 A vice principal was accused of sexual misconduct three times. He was forced to resign from two schools because of sexual misconduct allegations (not adjudicated). Both schools provided positive recommendations to a third school. At the third school he molested a thirteen-year-old. Are the previous employers liable to this student in the third school?

5.5 Martin Levy retired as a teacher in the public schools and took a position in a Muslim high school. He is an excellent math teacher and has increased the student's scores on state standardized tests, SATs, and Regents exams. He is not a tenured teacher, as this is his first year at the school. He has a renewable one-year contract to develop the math curriculum, chair the department, and teach several grades. He has excellent evaluations from the students, the principal, and the parents.

The board of the school has established a new policy that states: "It is the policy of the Muslim High School that only Muslims may teach in the school. No exceptions." The policy will go into effect in the next academic year. The principal fires Mr. Levy because he is an Orthodox Jew. He sues, stating that he was discriminated against on the basis of religion, and that in no way is the teaching of math related to the religious nature of the school. He also states a cause of action based on age and sex discrimination and breach of contract. Can he save his job?

5.6 Thérèse is the French teacher in a Catholic middle school. It became common knowledge after she gave birth to twins weighing only two pounds each that she used in vitro fertilization to conceive. She was fired because according to school administrators she violated a "morals clause" in her contract to "teach and act in accordance with Catholic doctrine and Catholic moral and social teaching." She argued that a male teacher whose wife gave birth after in vitro fertilization had not been similarly disciplined. She went to the state Equal Rights Division and argued that the case was based on "selective enforcement of the rules and pregnancy discrimination."

5.7 Father Patel and Deacon Bob Polishman enjoy exchanging ethnic jokes, each having a keen sense of humor and an extensive repertoire of jokes about South Asian and Polish people. For the past two years they have had quite a few laughs in the parish offices. Mrs. Kucich has been the parish receptionist for over twenty-six years. She has refused to learn the computer and the new phone messaging system installed this year. Pastor O'Toole decides it is time for Mrs. Kucich to retire. He advises her that at the end of the month, the parish will celebrate her retirement. She brings an employment discrimination action claiming age discrimination and ethnic "harassment" because of the constant barrage of "Polish" jokes that have been exchanged in the rectory in the last two years. Will the charges enable her to get a civil rights hearing?

Prepared Responses to the Case Studies

5.1 This is a decision based largely on the scope of the position and the mission leadership that supports this position. As a general rule, mission formation is very important in youth ministry. Citing a video about Apple, Inc., J. Patrick Murphy, C.M., explained, "If they said, 'that's a nice computer,' we didn't want them. We wanted their eyes to light up and sirens to go off!" Murphy concluded that candidates should be excited about the mission. Citing Kouzes and Posner, he explains that "leadership begins with something that grabs hold and won't let go." He further cautions that "You cannot lead through someone else's values, someone else's words" (Murphy 1–8).

5.2 Yes, the injured man will prevail. The choir director violated a standard practice of having a monitor and was negligent in leaving the room. Both these acts will be imputed to the employer. Since there was no intentionality on the part of the ten-year-old (he was pushed), he is probably neither criminally or negligently liable under his parents' liability policy. The parish's insurance will defend and pay the judgment or settlement from the proceeds of the liability policy on behalf of the parish and the choir director.

5.3 No to both questions. There is no obligation to answer any question other than the dates of employment. The investigation did not provide evidence of formal disciplinary action. Adam was later promoted. He does not have a record of misbehavior that could be a danger in future workplaces.

5.4 The schools providing the references were liable. The court looked at misleading representation versus mere nondisclosure.

5.5 No, the teacher cannot save his job. Both federal and state civil rights legislation protect the right of religious entities to "discriminate or state a preference" on the basis of religion. However, without Mr. Levy's allegation of religious discrimination, the courts would pursue the other causes of action based on the other protected classes and determine his right to save his job.

5.6 This example is drawn from a case brought in Wisconsin. At the state's administrative hearing the judge found probable cause for pregnancy discrimination. The case was settled out of court. Policies must be firm and applied fairly to all employees. In this case, trying to argue that the policy does not apply to the husband is going to fall into possible sex or pregnancy discrimination. A second issue is the basis of this knowledge. If this information was part of a medical claim for health insurance benefits, in some states that information cannot be used against the employee. However, the facts in this case lead us to believe that there was "common" or community knowledge that both employees used "reproductive technologies" in violation of the morals clauses in their employment contracts.

5.7 Yes, she will be entitled to a hearing based on age if she shows that she was replaced with a younger worker. However, since she may not be able to show competence in the position—no skills with the computer or telephone answering system—she may not prevail. She may have an administrative or a civil remedy if she can scrape together the burden of proving harassment. However, she will have to prove that either Fr. Patel or Deacon Bob has authority to affect her working conditions and/or that the pastor knew or should have known of the hostile work environment. Because of her failure to object to the behavior of either superiors or coworkers, she will also have to overcome a presumption that she did not consider the bantering and ethnic jokes harassment that created a hostile work environment.

BIBLIOGRAPHY

Brough, Michael. "Raising Expectations in the Ministerial Workplace." *Origins,* September 6, 2007, 203-207.

Dart, John. "Taking Care of Business." *The Christian Century* 122, 2005, 8–9.

Hiesberger, Jean Marie. *Fostering Leadership Skills in Ministry.* Liguori, MO: Liguori Publications, 2003.

Kress, Robert. "The Priest-Pastor as CEO." *America,* March 11, 2002, 8–11.

Lundholm-Eades, Jim. "Best Practices in Church Management." *America,* December 12, 2005, 13–16.

Miller, Robert. "Enhancing and Supporting the People Who Work in Parishes." In *The Parish Management Handbook,* edited by Charles E. Zech. Mystic, CT: Twenty-Third Publications, 2003, 63–89.

Murphy, C.M., J. Patrick. *We Want the Best: Hiring and Keeping an Excellent Church Workforce.* Cincinnati, OH: NACPA, 2007.

Murphy, Thomas P. "Disabilities Discrimination Under the Americans with Disabilities Act." *Catholic Lawyer* 36, 1995, 13–36.

NACPA. See National Association of Church Personnel Administrators.

National Association of Church Personnel Administrators. *Church Human Resources Administration.* 3rd ed. Cincinnati, OH: NACPA, 2007.

———. *Parish Personnel Administration.* Cincinnati, OH: NACPA, 2006.

Priests of Wilmington, Delaware. "Diocesan Presbyterate Examines Its Roles." *Origins* 36, February 15, 2007, 549–553.

USCCB. *Co-workers in the Vineyard of the Lord: A Resource for Guiding the Development of Lay Ecclesial Ministry.* Washington, D.C., 2005.

CHAPTER 11

Legal Principles and Pastoral Issues

Mary Ann Dantuono, JD

You pay tithes . . . and have neglected the weightier
things of the law: judgment and mercy and fidelity.
—Matthew 23:23

Key Concepts

1. The law is a complex body of case law, statutes, and regulations.

2. The law is constantly changing and evolving. Managers are
   expected to know, adapt to, and implement new laws and
   regulations.

3. Consulting with lawyers is a standard practice in the management of organizations.

4. Understanding basic principles of law in the areas of contracts, negligence, employment, and corporations helps avoid
   litigation.

5. Legal terms and concepts have very clear meanings within the
   law but are frequently misused outside of legal understanding.
   It is necessary to clarify and define terms before use.

6. "Separation of church and state" is helpful as a metaphor for
   allowing religious practice to flourish.

7. Behavior that follows the golden rule, "Do unto others . . ."
   when dealing with parishioners, clients, employees, vendors,
   or contractors, will generally fall well within the standards
   required by the law.

8. Because an appearance of impropriety can be as damaging as an actual impropriety, standardizing policies and practices within the organization is a safeguard against both.

9. Many "pastoral" activities, such as counseling parishioners, advising on death and dying, sponsoring fundraisers, and serving on community boards, involve legal duties with implications for the individuals and Church organizations involved.

Introduction

This learning segment presents the basic structure and principles of American jurisprudence. The topics have been chosen to give a broad overview of the law and to identify some particular issues encountered in areas where managerial and pastoral issues intersect the law. New York law is used as an example of state law, but the rule of law discussed will apply to most states, since it is illustrative of general principles of law. However, further research within certain states may be necessary. The goal of this chapter is to provide a framework for Church and organizational decision-making that will not contravene the law and will assist Church leadership to know when to consult a lawyer.

The most important concept in this chapter is "don't hesitate to ask a lawyer." Many dioceses have counsel on retainer to the diocese and the parish. In addition, getting to know a trusted attorney who is familiar with the parish or other institution may be reassuring since the scope of legal issues is daunting and growing each day. "Ignorance of the law is no excuse," and never a defense in litigation. This presentation is an attempt to offer some of the broadest parameters of the civil and criminal laws that will affect Church ministry, especially at the parish level. This chapter does not cover issues of canon law, although the Code of Canon Law certainly does impact decision-making in ministry. Two other books in this series, *A Concise Guide to Canon Law* and *A Concise Guide to Your Rights in the Catholic Church*, both by Rev. Kevin E.

McKenna, provide excellent presentations of the many pastoral issues affected by the law of the Church.

In the United States, some believe that a government is best that governs least, and that ours is a "government of the people, by the people, for the people." Oliver Wendell Holmes once wrote that he thought of the law as the "predictable behavior of judges," thus indicating that "a large part of the law is the predictable behavior of power: power held by legislatures, by the administration, by the judges" (Overton and Frey 210). After this review of laws as well as the general principles of law, you may decide which philosophy prevails. Or, as our entertainment shows challenge: "You be the judge!"

The Constitution is the source document that created the system of laws and government in the United States. Signed in 1787, it became a model for many nations. It set up the system of the federal government and the "checks and balances" that exist between the three branches of government—legislative, executive, and judicial. In addition, the Bill of Rights, which amended the Constitution, set forth individual freedoms that are the hallmark of American jurisprudence. All powers not reserved to the federal government reside in the state governments. Each state also has a constitution modeled after the federal constitution. All the branches of the federal government make laws. The chief executive (the president) must sign all bills that the legislature passes to become a law. The executive branch, through its administrative agencies, makes administrative laws and regulations such as tax codes and regulations. The legislative branch (Congress) creates statutory laws that are "codified" by topics. The judiciary branch (the courts) make what is known as the "common law" or case law. This law is created by deciding disputes between parties and used as a precedent for future disputes. It should also be noted that states, cities, counties, towns, and villages have capacities to make laws.

Categories of Law and Types of Laws

There are two categories of law: (1) *Substantive*—do you as an individual or corporation have a right or an obligation? And (2) *Procedural*—how does the system of justice allow you to enforce that right or require performance of an obligation? The system of justice is divided into *civil* and *criminal* matters. A civil case is one in which a person is suing for monetary damages or equitable relief, asking some action of the defendant. Examples of civil cases are auto accidents, medical malpractice, products liability, slips and falls, or disputes involving contracts. For example, Mrs. Walker slips on the church steps on the way out of the 6:30 a.m. weekday Mass. She suffers a broken hip and sues the parish for negligence in maintaining the steps and sidewalk. Generally, insurance is involved in these types of cases. The insurance policy/company provides the defense of the parish or other institution and payment of the "judgment" if the case is resolved in court, or will pay a "settlement" if the case is resolved by the parties out of court, up to the limits of the policy. A criminal case involves the state representing the "people" and bringing action against a person because of behavior that is a violation of a law. The penalty in a criminal case may result in a prison sentence or fine and in certain matters may call for restitution.

First Amendment Principles: Church-State Relationships

The "wall of separation" between church and state in the United States is a frequently quoted phrase and even more frequently misapplied. It is helpful to review its meaning. This is an arena of the law where there is currently much activity. The United States Supreme Court has final jurisdiction to resolve such Constitutional issues.

The fundamental legal basis of church-state relationships is the First Amendment to the Constitution, which states, *"Congress shall make no law respecting an establishment of religion, or prohibiting the free exercise thereof."* These two phrases, commonly called "the establishment clause" and "the free exercise clause," are the core of the debates and court decisions about church-state relationships. It is interesting to note that from the time of the ratification of the Constitution until the end of World War II there was little case law relating to this issue. In the 1899 case of *Bradfield v. Roberts,* the United States Supreme Court ruled that public support to a religiously sponsored hospital, incorporated under the civil laws with a board of directors made up entirely of the members of a religious congregation, did not constitute establishment or advancement of religion. Cases relating to education began to appear in the 1960s and 1970s. In 1988, the *Kendrick* decision (*Bowen v. Kendrick*) analyzed the entanglement of religion in the provision of health and human services under the Family Life Act, which authorized federal grants to public or nonprofit private organizations or agencies for services and research in the area of premarital adolescent sexual relations and pregnancy. While following the thinking of the Supreme Court in *Bradfield,* this case began a more complex analysis known as the *Lemon* test, which we will discuss later in this section.

As a religious people in a pluralistic society, it is helpful to reflect on the thoughts of such leaders as Bishop Howard Hubbard of Albany, who stated at the St. John's University Founder's Convocation (1998), "Our founding fathers established the separation clause not to silence the religious voice but to strengthen it, not to fetter religious communities but to free them to contribute to the public life of our nation." More recently, in an article entitled "The Metaphorical Wall of Separation," the Hon. Edward F. Harrington, U.S. senior district judge for the District of Massachusetts, emphasized that the term "separation of church and state" was first coined by Roger Williams in the seventeenth century and used again by Thomas Jefferson in an 1802 letter to Baptists, and was meant to protect religious liberty and freedom of conscience—both "sacred individual liberties." Judge Harrington argues that the "wall of separation" permits maximum freedom of religious ideas and expression. Ministers of religion of every creed and sect can freely engage in public debate in an endeavor to influence governmental policy. "Religion shall have the power to persuade; government shall lack the power to compel." Further, a vibrant public policy can endure only if grounded on such fundamental moral values as equality, fairness, freedom, love of neighbor, and compassion for the poor, the sick, and the aged.

Establishment Clause

The establishment clause, "Congress shall make no law regarding the establishment of religion," prevents the state from maintaining a preference for any denomination or religious belief or practice, or in any way endorsing such practices. It precludes laws or regulations that support one theological view or religion and also serves as a principle to prohibit or limit government aid to religious groups.

Education cases demonstrate the Supreme Court's thinking on whether or not action by the state, primarily funding, will benefit or endorse a particular religious belief. The courts have reasoned that primary and secondary schools operated by churches are by their very nature pervasively sectarian and have the effect of advancing religious doctrine. The courts found that such schools are an integral part of a church system, that children in elementary and secondary schools are at an impressionable age, and that dedicated religious persons teaching in such a setting will inevitably breach the separation between secular teaching and religious doctrine. While the government will certify such schools as satisfying educational requirements (*Pierce v. Society of Sisters*, 1925) if they meet standards, government support is limited to nonsectarian assistance.

A landmark case relating to nonpublic education is *Lemon v. Kurtzman*, which was decided in 1971. This case dealt with acts of the Pennsylvania and Rhode Island legislatures to supplement the salaries of nonpublic schoolteachers and for providing other subsidies to private elementary and secondary schools. The Supreme Court's reasoning led to a standard for determining the constitutionality of state funding that is now known as the *Lemon* test. This test has been applied to social and health services as well. The three requirements of the *Lemon* test are:

1. The state's involvement must have a secular or public purpose.

2. It cannot have the primary effect of advancing or promoting a particular religion.

3. It may not result in excessive entanglement between church and state. If a program, by its nature, requires so many safeguards to ensure that the first two standards set forth above are met, the result itself is government intrusion in church affairs.

When applying the *Lemon* test, the court first asks, "Is the law neutral on its face, or does it say something that seems to encourage people to support religion?" The second question for the court is, "When aid is given to a religious entity, does the government give that aid, or is it the product of independent choice by private people?" From this line of cases (see *Mitchell v. Helms*, 2000), we allow government funding of school lunch programs for children living in poverty, textbooks (*Board of Education v. Allen*, 1968), a signer for the deaf (*Zobrest v. Catalina Foothills School District*, 1993), aides for children with disabilities (*Agostini v. Felton*, 1997), and district-funded transportation for Catholic schools, as well as release time for religious education.

Following the *Lemon* test the Court extended its rationale and added two more tests: The "coercion test" (*Lee v. Weisman*, 1992), and the "endorsement test" (*Santa Fe Independent School District v. Doe*, 2000). In the coercion test the court asks whether the action of a state agent is causing a pressure or "coercion" on an individual to support or condone a religious practice or belief. The endorsement test asks whether an objective observer would perceive the policy or its implementation as a state "endorsement" of religion. These last two tests have been a major part of the discourse on prayer in public schools. Today, prayer in public schools is not allowed (*Engel v. Vitale*, 1962). A moment of silence is constitutional. A moment of silent prayer is not constitutional. Prayer is also not allowed at public school functions (*Lee v. Weisman*, 1992). An example of a violation of the establishment clause is *Board of Education of Kiryas Joel Village School District v. Grumet*, 1994. This New York case held that a state statute creating a special school district following village lines, when that village had been incorporated in the first place to exclude all but members of a religious enclave, violated the establishment clause of the First Amendment. Vouchers and charter schools will present new challenges to this line of cases. Parents of children attending Catholic schools shoulder the double burden of paying taxes to support the public school system and paying tuition to support the Catholic schools. Creative as well as Constitutional sources of funding will need to be developed as costs continue to escalate for both systems.

Free Exercise Clause

The Constitution also assures each person the individual freedom to believe and practice one's faith unless it is deemed to be against public policy or such practice is deemed to conflict with "a compelling state interest." This line of cases historically resulted in a *laissez faire* stance of government to any practice held by an individual to be part of the practice of their faith. Lawyers can wear a *yarmulke* in the courtroom, priests can wear *collars*, and religious can wear *habits* when testifying as a witness or serving on jury duty. There are some cases limiting these rights in criminal jury trials. Prisoners must be granted the right to wear a *fez* along with prison uniforms unless the prison can show it is a threat to the safety of others in the prison. However, more recently the thinking of the courts has begun to change. In 1990, in the landmark case of *Employment Division v. Smith,* the court defined a new standard stating that "the right of free exercise does not relieve an individual of the obligation to comply with a valid and neutral law of general applicability on the ground that the law proscribes (or prescribes) conduct that his religion prescribes (or proscribes)."

Following this line of cases, the Court has applied the principle that "free exercise" can be limited by a law that appears on its face to be neutral as to the practice of religion. The thinking in *Smith* has been applied in cases involving zoning and may be an area of concern as we as we look at new and different needs of the Church in the new millennium. Buildings presently zoned for religious use may need to comply with local zoning, traffic, and environmental regulations prior to renovation. Churches seeking to be built or expanded will benefit from a review of case law as well as local zoning regulations. The Religious Land Use and Institutionalized Persons Act of 2000 prohibits localities from adopting zoning that "imposes a substantial burden" on people's ability to practice their religion unless there is a compelling governmental reason. The law also requires that religious and nonreligious institutions be treated the same.

Another concern in this area is known as "conscience clauses." These clauses exempt a church-related entity and individuals from having to comply with provisions of laws that would require the religious entity or individual to violate religious beliefs, e.g., provide abortions, counsel divorce in family therapy, provide contraceptive coverage for employees in health insurance benefit packages, or allow coverage for domestic partners in employee benefit plans. The courts, legislation, and various regulations carved out exceptions for religious entities and individuals with the rationalization of the protection of the "free exercise" clause of the First Amendment. The "conscience clause" has become a "political seesaw by using executive regulations to provide or eliminate this constitutional protection. As we begin the twenty-first century, cases are presently in the courts and are producing serious concerns for Catholic as well as other religious entities (see *Catholic Charities of Maine, Inc. v. City of Portland*, 2004; *City Council of NY v. Bloomberg*, 2006). (See Exercise 1.)

A recent attack on the structure of the Catholic Church was launched in the state of Connecticut. The Connecticut legislature is considering a bill (1098) that would revise the corporate governance provisions of the Connecticut Statutes applicable to the Roman Catholic Church. The proposed bill would restructure the parish from a nonprofit corporation directed by a board including the bishop, two clergy, and two lay people to an organization operated by a board of seven to thirteen elected lay people. This bill has not passed but is a potential transgression of the "free exercise clause" as well as the "establishment clause."

Political Activities

In addition to constitutional issues, another area where church and state relations intersect is political activities. The regulations governing this issue are part of the Internal Revenue Code and are linked to the nonprofit corporation status of churches and sectarian organizations. These rules apply to all nonprofit corporations as well as religious corporations. Although nonprofit corporations and churches have a different source in statutory law, their tax exemption status is shared and found in Section 501(c) of the Federal Internal Revenue Code. Tax-exempt status may be obtained as an individual corporation or as an auxiliary of a larger entity. The Catholic Church obtains the proof of its tax-exempt status for all of its dioceses, parishes, and agencies through a listing in the *Official Catholic Directory* ("Kenedy Directory") which issues a "Group Ruling Letter" certifying the tax-exempt status of all entities listed. The IRS regulations prohibit nonprofit corporations from "political lobbying or endorsing a candidate for public office." The United States Conference of Catholic Bishops (USCCB) issues guidelines for use in the Church every four years to coincide with the

---

**IRC §501(c)(3)
Political Activities**

The regulations governing the Internal Revenue Code §501(c)(3) of the United States tax code provides that an organization incorporated and claiming tax-exempt status under this section of the code may not "participate in or intervene in any political campaign on behalf of any candidate for public office." The IRS considers the following five types of activity a form of participation or intervention and therefore inappropriate:

- Endorsement of candidates
- Donations to a candidate's campaign
- Fund-raising for a candidate
- Distributing statements relating to specific candidates
- Involvement in other activities that may be beneficial or detrimental to a candidate

---

presidential election. The basic rule is twofold. First, churches can inform parishioners about the issues of the election and encourage as well as assist parishioners to register to vote. Second, the Church or Church leaders cannot use the Church as a "podium" speaking for or against any candidate for public office (see Exercise 2).

Corporations

In New York, as in many states, churches are civil corporations organized under the Religious Corporation Laws of the State. As a legal entity (artificial person) it is recognized by the legal system as having rights and responsibilities. A corporation can enter into contracts, buy land, borrow money, and have bank accounts in its own name. The courts will not interfere with matters of religious laws, and both canon law and civil law respect the jurisdiction of the other. For example, in the matter of the sale of real estate, a Catholic parish is required by canon law to have the written approval of the local ordinary for the alienation of certain property. Failure to secure that approval will result in a civil court's refusal to enforce the contract (see Exercise 3).

In addition to being a corporation, churches are forced to deal with corporate entities frequently and may also consider creating a corporation for some aspect of church ministry. In addition, pastoral leaders are frequently asked to serve on boards of trustees or directors for community-based nonprofit corporations. For these reasons, the following overview of corporations law is presented.

Two General Types of Corporations
1. **Business Corporation (for-profit)**: In this type of corporation, shareholders own the corporation and elect the board of directors. Boards of directors are responsible for governance, policy, and management.

2. **Nonprofit Corporations**: There are generally three classifications of nonprofit corporations:

a. Public benefit corporations. These operate for public or charitable purposes.

b. Mutual benefit corporations. These operate for the benefit of their members.

c. Religious corporations. These operate to advance or maintain the religion motivating their members or directors.

From the beginning of the creation of this special class of nonprofit corporations, the beneficiaries had no direct power over the directors or trustees. Therefore, while the state created special advantages for such corporations, they also created accountability to the state. This is usually the office of the State Attorney General. The State Attorney General is generally deemed to speak for the beneficiaries of any entity, which has assets that are donated to the corporation to be used for the mission or purpose of the nonprofit corporation, whether it is a public benefit, mutual benefit, or religious corporation.

Advantages of a Nonprofit Corporation

The nonprofit corporation has a special status as mentioned above. Some of the ways these corporations are assisted in their "public benefit" are as follows:

- Mission and culture are the key to governance of the organization and place emphasis on value-based goals and objectives.

- A nonprofit corporation will qualify for tax exemptions under the Internal Revenue code, Section 501(c)(3) and under most state tax laws, relieving them of real estate, sales, and income tax burdens.

- Nonprofits can receive public funds and private tax-deductible donations. In addition, most private foundations will only fund nonprofit corporations with 501(c)(3) status.

- While the notion of "charitable immunity" has been eliminated in most states, nonprofit corporation laws in most states limit liability for members and directors unless there is proven fraud or malfeasance. There are exceptions for personal guarantees and tax obligations. Directors' and officers' liability insurance policies are available for this insurable risk.

- A nonprofit corporation, like a for-profit corporation, is an entity with a perpetual or time-limited existence that is not dependent on a particular person or group of persons to continue its work. Its structure allows for the continuance of the public benefit through a self-perpetuating board.

- Creation of a corporation segments assets and liabilities from the founding organization or individuals.

- Nonprofits qualify for lower postal rates on bulk mail and discounted advertising. They also qualify for public service announcements to reach out to the community served and to communicate community benefit messages.

Becoming a Nonprofit Corporation

As with any benefit there is required duty. In addition to the oversight by a State Attorney General's office, there are specific requirements that a nonprofit board must fulfill.

To become a nonprofit corporation, the first task is to prepare and file with a state entity a document known as the "Articles of Incorporation." Approvals (licenses) for certain types of activities must be obtained from appropriate state government departments. Registration is required with appropriate state and local agencies, e.g., "Charities Bureau," and finally, minutes of meetings and corporate documents must be maintained. Federal and state tax exemptions must be filed, and formal meetings of the board of directors must be held. A nonprofit corporation must establish and follow its bylaws, which are basic governing rules a nonprofit corporation will follow. If these are not created, then the applicable state law will apply.

Acting as a Nonprofit Corporation

The board of directors or trustees has a mandate for the stewardship of the corporation. They oversee and must operate independently of management. Directors must know and abide by the corporate documents, statutes, regulation, and case law. The size of the board is based on the size of the corporation, its purpose, and various regulations. Orientation should be conducted for new members, and the board must have a process to evaluate its own effectiveness.

In general, boards are responsible to determine and oversee the implementation of the organization's mission and purpose; elect the officers of the corporation; and select and evaluate the chief executive. Additionally, members of the board of directors must ensure that there are adequate resources and organizational planning. Regardless of the size of the organization, the law has established certain duties of directors. A director is a *fiduciary*. This legal relationship involves a duty to act for the good of others rather than for one's own benefit (Oleck, p. 746).

There are three legal duties that the directors of nonprofit corporations assume: a duty of care, a duty of loyalty, and a duty of obedience. These are the common terms for the standards that guide all actions a director takes. The "duty of care" calls upon a director to act in a *reasonable* and *informed* manner when participating in the board's decisions and its oversight of the corporation's management. It requires that a director be informed, and second, that a director discharge his or her duties in good faith, with the care that an ordinarily prudent person in a like position would reasonably believe appropriate under similar circumstances. A director carries out this duty by attending meetings, exercising independent judgment, and, particularly, judging what is in the corporation's best interest, even if he or she represents a particular constituency within the corporation. In order to exercise this duty of care, a director must have proper information, such as financial, legal, and programmatic information. While a director may act in reliance on information and reports received from regular sources (auditors, officers, or employees of the corporation as well as other board committees or, if a religious corporation, by religious authorities), he or she is required to pass an independent informed vote. However, a director having knowledge that brings into question the reliability of any information presented to the board may have a duty to share such knowledge with the other board members. A general rule to observe is that a director must oversee but not directly engage in the corporation's day-to-day operations.

The "duty of loyalty" requires directors to exercise their powers in good faith and in the best interests of the corporation, rather than in their own interests or the interests of another entity or person. The director shall never use a corporate position for individual personal advantage. The duty of loyalty primarily relates to conflicts of interest, corporate opportunity, and confidentiality. There is much scrutiny of the law in this area, and "conflict of interest" policies in most nonprofit corporations require all directors to sign such statements of disclosure annually. In general, a corporation and the director may avoid a violation of this duty if the transaction that involves a personal interest or benefit was approved by a disinterested majority of the board or, in some cases, by a board committee after full disclosure by the affected director of the material facts regarding the transaction and the director's interest. It must also be shown that the transaction was fair to the corporation at the time it was entered into.

In addition to the duty to disclose personal interests in the nonprofit corporation's transactions, a director should not disclose information about the corporation's legitimate activities. A director is not a spokesperson for the corporation, and unless such information is a matter of public record or common knowledge, this presumption of confidential treatment should apply to all current information about legitimate board or corporate activities.

The "duty of obedience" is the duty to carry out the corporation's mission in accord with the law. A director must require actions in accord with the organization's mission, its charter, and its donor intent. The directors must determine that all acts of the corporation are within its lawful purpose and that the corporation does not engage in unauthorized activities. Further, this duty imposes on the board the responsibility to determine that the corporation comply with all appropriate laws, including registration and reporting laws in all states in which it conducts activities and/or solicits contributions, and with the provisions of the Internal Revenue Code.

Religious Civil Corporations and Sponsorship

Dioceses and parishes have been incorporated in civil law. Parishes have both ordained and lay trustees. In the past, some dioceses have used a two-tier structure known as membership corporation, with the members holding certain reserved powers. In addition, in the 1980s and 1990s many sectarian nonprofit corporations, such as schools, hospitals, and service agencies sponsored by religious orders and dioceses, adopted the "membership corporation" as a means to permeate a corporation with the mission and culture of the sponsoring organization. However, that is changing as members seek to divest themselves of corporations where they no longer have personnel to serve as members or on boards. There is an option in canon law that may be explored here. "Private Lay Association of the Faithful with Charitable Purposes" (§ 299-S.1) may be the next phase of "sectarian" corporations. Under this provision of the Code of Canon Law, Christian faithful—clergy, and/or laity—can privately agree to engage in efforts such as the perfection of life, public worship, and apostolic work and can become a "public juridic person." This requires a formal written decree of the bishop of the diocese. Some healthcare systems have adopted this approach.

Hypothetical
Evolution of a Nonprofit Corporation

a. A parish social ministry committee started a soup kitchen several years ago. An advisory board was established.

b. The board determines that the soup kitchen could access funding and expand services if they were separately incorporated from the parish. Pastor agrees. After consultation with the chancellor, diocesan attorney, a membership corporation was established. Pastor, associate pastor and one other person appointed by the pastor constitute the membership. They elect the board. New funding has been infused into the program. The associate pastor is transferred, and two lay people with the pastor constitute the membership. Both lay people are active with the soup kitchen but have no other responsibilities in the parish.

c. The board decides that the program will be more accessible to people in need if it is moved from the parish property to a storefront near the train station. The decision is made to move off the parish property. The operation is very successful. More private and government funding is realized. The pastor is transferred.

d. The new pastor in his review of the parish operations does not see the connection to the parish. All of the funding for the soup kitchen comes from sources other than the parish, and there is little if any connection other than his role as a member. The board feels like it is capable of generating the interest of new board members without parish support, as the soup kitchen has become an integral part of the municipal community. They want to eliminate the membership structure. Issues that are raised concern sectarian/non-sectarian, tax-exempt status. The options are researched. The following are possible plans from this research:

    1. Create an independent, self-electing board with its own tax-exempt status that has no sectarian basis. It will be a private nonprofit non-sectarian agency.

    2. Create an independent, self-electing board that is listed in the *Official Catholic Directory* (OCD-Kenedy's) and maintains its Catholic identity through its statement of mission and vision but eliminates the membership structure. (This option generally requires diocesan approval, and the chancellor may have other requirements.)

    3. Create a Private Lay Association of the Faithful with Charitable Purposes (Cannon 299-s.1.) Christian faithful, clergy and/or laity privately agree to engage in efforts: perfection of life, public worship and apostolic work, can become a public juridic person with a formal written decree of Bishop of the Diocese.

Judiciary Law: Jury Duty

Under the federal and state constitutions a person is entitled to a jury trial in criminal cases and many types of civil cases. State judiciary laws require that litigants have juries selected from a fair cross-section of the community and that all eligible citizens have both the opportunity and obligation to serve on juries. In general, the juror selection process is random; names are obtained from lists of registered voters, state taxpayers, licensed drivers, and recipients of public assistance benefits and state unemployment compensation. In general, to qualify a person must be a U.S. citizen and a county resident, at least eighteen years of age with no felony convictions, and able to understand and communicate in English. Employers are required to allow an individual time off work to serve on a jury.

A prospective juror who has received a jury summons may apply to be excused from jury service by submitting a written application for excusal to the commissioner. The conditions for excusal are very limited. For example, in New York, an application for excusal may be granted only if the prospective juror has demonstrated satisfactorily that (1) he or she has a mental or physical condition that renders him or her incapable of performing jury service, or that jury service would cause undue hardship or extreme inconvenience to the prospective juror, a person under his or her care or supervision, or the public; and (2) he or she will be unable to serve as a juror on a date certain within the time restrictions applicable to postponements (six months).

In 1995, New York State passed legislation eliminating the exemption for priests and religious as part of an overall effort to eliminate many existing exemptions. Therefore, priests and religious receive a qualifying questionnaire and summons to report for jury duty. Due to pastoral sensitivities, each chancery has worked with the Commissioner of Jurors to accommodate the balance of citizen and pastoral responsibilities. If a priest or religious receives a summons and qualification form, then he or she should contact

A Concise Guide to Catholic Church Management

the vicar general or office of religious personnel to determine if there is a policy in place to address his or her situation.

𝒯ort 𝒫rinciples

Torts are civil wrongs recognized by law. These wrongs result in an injury or harm constituting the basis for a claim by the injured party. While some acts may be both a tort and a crime punishable with imprisonment, the primary aim of tort law is to provide relief for the damages incurred and deter others from committing the same harms. The injured person may sue for an injunction to prevent the continuation of the tortuous conduct or for monetary damages. The goal of the remedy is to make the injured person whole, to the extent that money can do that.

The source of this law is the common law created by the courts, supplemented by state statutes. The basic elements of a "tort" are a duty between two persons, a violation of the duty of care, the act must be the proximate cause of the injury, and the injured party must sustain actual loss or damages. Liability insurance provides the main source of compensation for judgments rendered in tort actions by the court.

There are several doctrines that have developed to protect the "ordinary" person in society. An example of such a doctrine is one of vicarious liability, or *respondeat superior*. The doctrine requires that the principal answer for the acts of the subordinate, such as in employer-employee relationships. If an injury is caused by a subordinate, then the principal may be liable. As such, parishes, schools, and other Church institutions are required to provide adequate supervision of employees and volunteers so that they are properly screened, oriented, instructed in their tasks, and evaluated in their positions. Additionally, it is important when hiring or recruiting volunteers to work in ministries that the "superior" have some knowledge that the person is competent to perform the task so as to avoid injury to third parties. A volunteer application should be an important record of a volunteer's work history and educational background. For additional discussion of the relationship and legal issues in employment law, refer to chapter 10, "Human Resources: The Spine of an Organization."

Injury or damage caused by negligent conduct is generally covered by insurance with general or specific liability coverage. However, such coverage has exceptions and exclusions. Invoked frequently are the exclusions for intentional or criminal acts (see Exercise 4).

Principles of Contract Law

A contract is a promise or a set of promises between two persons (and either or both of those persons can be a corporation) that the law recognizes as mutually enforceable. The law provides remedies if a promise is breached or recognizes the performance of a promise as a duty. To be legally binding as a contract, a promise must be exchanged for adequate consideration. Adequate consideration is a benefit or detriment that a party receives that reasonably and fairly induces him or her to make the promise or contract. For example, promises that are purely gifts are not considered enforceable because the personal satisfaction the grantor of the promise may receive from the act of giving is normally not considered adequate consideration. Certain promises that are not considered contracts may, in limited circumstances, be enforced if one party has relied to his detriment on the assurances of the other party. Another condition that is required for a contract to be binding in law is that it must be "lawful," e.g., gambling contracts are not legal, therefore not enforceable. There must be an "offer" and an "acceptance" of that offer (terms must be understood between the parties), and all parties to the contract must have legal capacity (age and mental capacity).

Contracts are mainly governed by state statutory law, case law, and private law. Private law principally includes the terms of the agreement between the parties who are exchanging promises. Statutory law may require some contracts be put in writing and executed with particular formalities (see Exercise 5).

Privileged Communications

Conversation that takes place within the context of a protected relationship, such as that between an attorney and client, a husband and wife, a priest and penitent, or a doctor and patient, is known as "privileged communications." In a few states, the above-mentioned privileged conversations extend to a psychotherapist and client and to a reporter and his or her source. The law protects against disclosure of such conversations. However, there are exceptions that can invalidate a privileged communication, and there are various circumstances where it can be waived, either purposefully or unintentionally. In judicial proceedings, the law allows people to refuse to disclose the contents of certain privileged conversations and writings. To qualify for privileged status, communications must generally be made in a private setting (that is, in a context where confidentiality could reasonably be expected). The privilege is lost (waived) when all or part of the communication is disclosed to a third person (see Exercise 6).

Children and Families

In the Catholic Church we consider the family the "domestic Church," or the smallest unit of Church. The law looks at the family as a distinctive entity in which parents have autonomy and children should be within their care, custody, and control without interference from the state. However, as parental flaws have become social problems, the law has intervened to protect its most vulnerable citizens.

In Loco Parentis

Parents are the legal guardians of their children. A minor child does not have legal status as a person. As such she or he can not legally contract or consent to any practice. Therefore, in order for a child to receive healthcare treatment (nonemergency) or for a teacher to discuss a child's options or behavior, the permission or conversation must be with the parent or legal guardian. If parents are going to be out of the country for a period of time and leave children in the care of others, they are advised to give written consent and authority to the adults with whom they are leaving their children. The writing should state the period of time the child will be in the care of the adult and specifically state that the person may act *in loco parentis* or "in place of the parent." This gives the temporary guardian of the child the ability to make all decisions as they (the parent[s]) could do. It is a good practice for the parent to give this permission in writing to avoid any issues of neglect. It is a good practice on the part of schools or childcare agencies to have a policy in place that clarifies the authority of a caregiving adult. Schools now regularly require parents to designate caregivers and emergency contacts in writing and maintain these instructions as part of the records of each child.

Adoptions

State and federal laws regulate adoptions. In general, there are two kinds of adoptions: private placement adoptions and agency adoptions. Private adoptions are arranged by a couple with the birth mother or her representative and approved by the court. Agencies that are "private" but are licensed by the government, for example, Catholic Charities, or an agency of the government, such as an office of Children's Services, facilitate adoptions. All legal adoptions must be completed through one system or the other. This will allow proper protections for all the parties involved in the adoption: the birth parents who wish to place their children for adoption, the adoptive parents, and the child. The procedures in a legal adoption require that the birth parents exercise informed consent in terminating their parental rights and that the adoptive parent is appropriately screened and prepared for parenting. All of these protections are based in public policy to protect the "best interests" of the child.

Reporting Abuse

Child abuse is a very serious social problem and a crime in the United States. It has become a very sensitive issue for churches. In general, child protective laws require professionals and officials to report when they have reasonable cause to suspect that a child coming before them in their professional or official capacity has been abused or maltreated. Additionally, reports are required where the parent, guardian, custodian, or other person legally responsible for such child comes before them in their professional or official capacity and states from personal knowledge facts, conditions, or circumstances that, if correct, would render the child an abused or maltreated child. The Federal Child Abuse Prevention and Treatment Act (CAPTA) defines child abuse and neglect as, at minimum:

- any recent act or failure to act on the part of a parent or caretaker that results in death, serious physical or emotional harm, sexual abuse, or exploitation;
- an act or failure to act that presents an imminent risk of serious harm.

If a person suspects that a child is being abused or neglected, the Child Protective Services (CPS) agency in the state in which the child resides or in which the abuse occurred is notified. Each state has jurisdiction over these matters and has specific laws and procedures for reporting and investigating. In some states, all citizens are "mandated reporters" by state law and must report any suspicion of child abuse or neglect. In other states, specific classes of people are mandated reporters, such as physicians, educators, childcare workers, and law enforcement officers. It is necessary to become familiar with both your state and diocesan policy and laws. Subsequent to the Catholic Church's sex abuse scandals, many states have expanded mandatory reporters to include clergy and have expanded the statute of limitations for victims to bring criminal and civil suits. They have also expanded the criminal liability for failure to report cases of abuse. From 2001 to date, there have been many changes in these laws that affect churches and church professionals. Care and consultation with legal counsel is recommended.

Adult abuse of the elderly and disabled is an equally serious issue. This abuse can take many forms: physical, sexual, or emotional maltreatment; financial exploitation; and active as well as passive neglect. It can also be an issue of self-neglect—an adult's inability, due to physical and/or intellectual impairment, to perform tasks essential to caring for him- or herself. While the reporting requirements are not as stringent, morally and legally, it is important to be informed of the problem of adult abuse and also of what can be done to alleviate dangerous situations for vulnerable adults. For example, a young woman lived in an apartment next to an elderly couple. She knew that the couple was to be home when she was away. However, when she returned from a short vacation, she did not see any activity. She knocked on the door and discovered that the man had fallen and needed medical attention and that his wife was confused and disoriented. She called Adult Protective Services, who assigned a caseworker and engaged services for the man and woman. A local Catholic Charities agency may also be a resource to intervene in cases like the example.

Abandoned Infant and Safe Haven Laws

Abandoned Infant and Safe Haven Laws exist in forty-seven states. These laws are enacted in response to parental abandonment of a newborn child in places that may result in injury or even death. These laws decriminalize the otherwise criminal act of the abandonment of a child. Pursuant to these laws, municipalities create "safe havens" in partnership with local hospitals, emergency medical services, fire stations and other human service agencies, churches, and other places of worship. Parents in dire need can leave a child in the care of responsible persons via these havens and face no criminal action in most states. County district attorneys have the power to define a "safe haven" within their counties. Although these laws are designed to facilitate the safe placement of children who cannot be properly cared for, they create no new procedural methods for adoption and do not automatically terminate parental rights.

Laws Related to Illness and Dying

Laws related to illness and dying have been passed as advances in medical technology have increased the complexity of life-and-death situations for the ill or injured person. There are four different legal terms that will help you or someone you minister to "put their affairs in order." A brief outline of some legal definitions and legal applicability follow.

Healthcare Surrogate Decision-Making

The laws allowing adults to delegate their God-given, legally recognized right to make healthcare decisions to a designated and trusted agent are intended to allow consent to medical treatment when an individual lacks capacity to legally consent to or to withhold treatment. The law does not encourage or discourage any particular healthcare treatment. The healthcare "proxy" or "surrogate decision-maker" or "durable powers of attorney for healthcare" laws allow any competent adult to designate an "agent," such as a family member or close friend, to make health care decisions if the person loses the ability to decide for himself or herself in the future. (Some hospitals require the execution of this proxy form upon admission.) The proxy or power is put on file with medical treatment providers of the individual. In order for an "advance directive" to be legally binding it must be in the statutory form required by the particular state. In most states an individual can execute it. A person does not need an attorney, but an attorney will be willing to provide such an instrument and assist in the execution. The correct form can be located on state legislative and administrative websites.

Many state Catholic Conferences provide the Catholic perspective on advance directives and offer their state's legal forms. For example, the New York State Catholic Conference has a guide for Catholics who wish to consider Catholic teaching in the completion of the Health Care Proxy form (see www.nyscatholic.org). For additional resources visit the National Catholic Bioethics Center at www.ncbcenter.org/eol.asp. The Center has an online publication, "A Catholic Guide to End-of-Life Decisions," that is very helpful.

Living Will

A *living will* is a written document in which an adult who is competent can express his/her wishes regarding future health care in the event that he or she is unable to make health care decisions. This statement of preferences and desires regarding medical treatment can provide a useful resource for treatment providers as well as for a person's "proxy" or surrogate decision-maker, even though the writer cannot anticipate future treatment options. It differs from a health care proxy in that it actually expresses wishes as to treatment options the writer seeks to have, or to have withheld, in certain medical situations. The health care proxy allows greater flexibility in that an agent is appointed who will act and decide. Some states recognize "living wills," and others may consider it as evidence of the patient's wishes in an end-of-life ethics situation but are not bound by the document.

Durable Power of Attorney

A *durable power of attorney* is an instrument by which a person can appoint an agent to handle property and other monetary and contractual affairs. It is good only for the time of appointment and can be revoked at any time. The power of attorney is based in the law of agency, so only the rights of the principal can be delegated. If a person becomes "incompetent" as a matter of law, then the agent is "incompetent." In order to overcome this deficit, the law allows for a "durable" power of attorney. This is a special designation and should be carefully considered. It can be a substitute for guardianship or having a committee appointed for a person who becomes incompetent. There are very specific requirements for a *durable power of attorney* and a *general power of attorney* to be valid. These legal instruments must be carefully executed and witnessed.

Last Will and Testament

A *last will and testament* is a legal instrument that provides for the distribution of personal and real property after death. If a person fails to execute such a legal document, his or her "estate" will be distributed according to intestacy law. Most states will accept a will executed according to the laws of another state if the will would be deemed valid in that state. It is always recommended that an individual execute a last will and testament. Most states require that this instrument be in writing, and there are very specific instructions for the execution of this document. The person must be of sound mind and not under duress. Dying people will sometimes choose to change their will. Changes to a will are put in an instrument called a *codicil*. This document must be in writing also and specifically state that it is the purpose of the writing to revoke previous provisions in the will and replace them with the present writing. The execution of this document requires the same formality as the execution of a will.

People at the end of life become very grateful for the people who care for them or minister to them. Occasionally, a recipient of such care may wish to change his or her will to leave a part of his or her estate to a parish or to the organization/agency/institution that ministered to him or her, or in some cases to the individual minister. A representative of a church or agency should not be named in a will or agree to be an executor of a will. Rather, provide the attorney for the dying person a contact with an appropriate counsel for the parish or agency if faced with such a request. In that way, a minister (lay or ordained) will avoid impropriety or even the appearance of it. This is also a principle that should be applied when asked to be an *attorney in fact* on a durable power of attorney.

Fundraising Issues

Fundraising is implicit in job descriptions of Church leaders as well as in the nonprofit sector. It is an activity that is fraught with peril yet can be negotiated with great care. In some cases the people who want to contribute also want control over how their donations are used, or they may be filled with great ideas about investment strategies and additional fundraising strategies. They can sometimes disrupt existing structures for decision-making in the parish, institution, or agency even when well-intentioned. It is important to be appreciative but firm and clear in these kinds of dealings. Additionally, it is necessary to establish and to be familiar with policies and procedures of the finance committee of the parish or agency board about gifts. The finance committee needs to be part of the decision-making process on all fundraising and investments of funds. Clear policies and practices contribute to transparency and accountability for both donors and recipients. Case-by-case decision-making is fraught with peril.

Institutional Development

Because the best advice is *caveat emptor* ("let the buyer beware"), it is imperative to research the firms bidding for the position of running fundraising campaigns. When beginning the process, establish clear criteria on which to evaluate firms: familiarity with the nature of the nonprofit or church culture; how they will charge the parish for their services; the length of time they feel it will take to reach the established goal; the source of their projections; and the sources of data on which they base their projections. It is reasonable to ask a fundraising firm to produce several examples of successes as well as success rates and the names of parishes and other organizations where they conducted campaigns. This allows the fundraising committee or finance council to check with leaders about their experiences with the professional fundraisers.

Compensation for fundraising activities should be based on general performance and commensurate with the time and effort expended. A charitable organization should not compensate internal or external fundraisers based on a commission or a percentage of the amount raised. It is important for fundraisers to reflect the organization's core values and to comply with all legal requirements of the state.

Written policies concerning fundraising for your parish or other Church organization should be developed and easily accessible to key stakeholders in the process, including any outside firms with whom you might work. A written contract with such a firm, defining the responsibilities of all involved parties, should be proposed and reviewed by your board and finance committee prior to signing. A good professional fundraiser can help your organization in many ways, building a sense of community and ownership of the project. Other church leaders can be a helpful resource in establishing policies for fundraisers.

Charitable Subscriptions, Funds, Endowments, and Restrictive Gifts

All of the above are legal terms that are frequently misapplied. When such terms are used in any documents, it is important to seek professional help to determine your responsibilities as either the solicitor or the recipient of such assets. Your state attorney general's office may be helpful in outlining the highly regulated activities and legal issues involved in this area of financial management. *A promise to make a gift is not legally enforceable.* If someone promises or pledges to make a gift, do not rely on that gift until the money is in your account. There is a normal discrepancy between the amounts pledged in a charitable auction, fundraising campaign, or even a friendly whisper (" I will gladly donate the money for . . .") and the amounts that are actually received. Rarely, but it can and does happen, a donor will ask for his or her money back because he or she is disenchanted with the organization. Prudence, not law, is the best prompter of the correct response. See chapter 12, "Stewardship: Financial Control and Accountability" for more suggested practices and policies.

Restrictive gifts need to be honored and therefore communicated to the parish finance committee and to the administrator or accountant who creates the appropriate fund accounts and budgets. Tracking such gifts is more an accounting issue than a fundraising issue, but it can influence future efforts.

Tax-Deductible Donations

All donations to a church or nonprofit are tax-deductible for a donor. However, in order for the donors to claim the deduction on their tax return for amounts over $250, they must have a receipt for the donation. Maintaining accurate records of donations should be a priority fundraising strategy, as noted in the parishioner satisfaction chapter. Many parishes issue one statement a year to registered members with the full amount of their contributions. This is an excellent way for donors to keep track of their stewardship. However, thank-you letters for special donations are always recommended.

Organizers of a fundraising campaign or event must also be aware of the requirement for "deductibility of contributions." An event must be advertised with carefully delineated costs. If the event is a gala dinner dance to benefit the school, the cost of the event (dinner and reception) and the amount of the donation must be indicated on the solicitation for the event. Any receipt for the donation will only indicate the amount that is credited to the donation. For example if you are holding a $500 per person dinner, the $100 cost of the dinner is deducted from the acknowledgment of the donation. These rules are subject to change, and auditors and accountants who keep up-to-date information should be consulted.

Games of Chance

Raffles, bingo, "Las Vegas nights," carnivals, and the like are considered "games of chance" for charity and may require a license from a local municipality. Accompanying the license will be the local municipality's regulations for the event. From the hours of operation to the amounts that can be raised, these are highly regulated fundraising events. There are some exceptions. For example, in New York, raffles are exempt from licensing requirements of the general municipal law if the raffle involves prizes with a value of less than $5,000. It is important to encourage any fundraising committee to research the local laws and regulations early in the planning for the event. It is also important to be familiar with your diocesan policy concerning parish sponsorship of such activities.

Music, Art, and Copyright Concerns

Copyright is the body of laws that ensure that people who work in the creative arts—composing and performing music, writing texts, and creating works of visual art—are compensated for the "fruit of their work." The basic foundation of copyright law is that the owner of a copyrighted work has the exclusive right to grant others permission to use (i.e. perform) and copy (i.e., photograph or record) the work. While U.S. copyright law contains an exception for music and songs performed in a place of worship or other religious assembly, this exception does not allow reprinting the music and/or words of a song in a program booklet or worship aid and does not allow a recording of the performance. Reprinting and recording the music and songs require a license, which may include a request for a royalty payment from the owner. Recording also requires the permission of the performers. Most churches are familiar with the need to secure a license to reprint words and music in programs or booklets and purchase annual reprint licenses from publishers of church music. It should be noted that the exception for music and songs does not extend to literature. Poems, prayers, and texts of literary words, if they are recited and/or printed in worship aids, require a license to recite and or print.

Additionally, the copyright law permits a photographer or videographer to photograph images of the church building, but care should be taken if sculptures, statuary, stained glass, paintings, frescos, and other works of visual arts are acquired separately. When receiving such art, parishes should be clear on permission to photograph and reproduce or how to secure such permission from the artists if necessary.

In this digital age, churches should check that contracts with musicians and cantors give a blanket permission to record their performance and publish on the parish website. Anyone who does videography and photography at weddings and other occasions should also check that they have the appropriate permissions, in writing, if the video contains musical performances and art work at the church or if photographs are to be published.

Conclusion

While we have covered many issues in this brief segment on legal issues, there are probably seventy times seven more that one could include. This chapter is offered only as an introduction to the system of law and various principles that will be applied and is not intended to be a legal service or legal advice. This approach is intended to illustrate the ways that our complex legal system helps to determine rights and responsibilities of individuals, groups, and corporations. It is important to be prevention-wise and seek to avoid potential legal liability by following approved policy and regulations. Additionally, maintain adequate insurance for legal liability and property risks. If faced with a difficult situation or an actual case, seek counsel promptly. Your lawyer will be glad you did!

Exercises

Read the six case studies detailed below and use the information presented in this chapter to answer the question(s) that is posed for each. Answers appear at the end of the case studies.

1. Father Timothy Mockaitis is a Catholic priest who regularly visited the inmates of the county jail. On one occasion he heard a confession of a prisoner. He later learned that the district attorney purposely taped the confession to obtain evidence of a crime. The tape was transcribed. The priest and his bishop brought an action in federal court to prohibit the use of the tape and to request its destruction. The case was brought under the First Amendment of the U.S. Constitution. What did the court hold?

2. Father Bradford is the pastor of Our Lady of Perpetual Help, which publishes a monthly newsletter that is distributed to all

parish households. In each issue, he has a column titled "My Views." The month before the election, Father Bradford states in the "My Views" column, "It is my personal opinion that Candidate K. should be elected." For that one issue, Father Bradford pays for the portion of the newsletter attributed to the "My Views" column from his personal funds. Does this constitute endorsement of a candidate for political office by a nonprofit religious organization?

3. The pastor of a very large parish agreed to rent a house adjacent to the church parking lot to a local attorney, McCarthy. At one time, the house was occupied by the sacristan of the parish and his wife. The attorney drafted the lease for an initial term of ten years, with two five-year renewal options, which provided for minimal rent increases. Three years later, the press reported that the diocese was not paying taxes on the building. The taxes were more than the lease amount. The diocese tried to renegotiate the lease with McCarthy to increase the rent, but the tenant refused to modify the terms of the lease. The diocese went to court to have the lease declared void, to evict the tenant, and to be compensated for the fair rental value of the premises with the taxes. Who will prevail and why?

4. A pastor asks the parish liturgy director to gather information on the costs of new candlesticks for the sanctuary. The liturgy director goes to a local religious supply store and asks to see candlesticks. The saleswoman/owner informs her that she is very lucky because a $2,000 set of candlesticks is the last one in stock and that if she buys the set today, she will sell it for $1,000. The owner further tells the liturgy director that the sale would be final.

   The liturgy director agrees to purchase the set of candlesticks, and they use a tax-exempt number that the store had on file. The director drives back to the church and is somewhat distracted wondering if she did the right thing. She fails to stop at a red light and collides with a car driven by an eighty-three-year-old woman, who is tragically killed in the crash.

The spouse of the elderly woman sues the parish, the pastor, and the liturgy director for the wrongful death. The pastor tells the liturgy director to return the candlesticks, and he refuses to pay the bill. The store refuses the return and sues the parish for the $1,000.

    a. Does the pastor have to purchase the candlesticks?

    b. Are the parish, pastor, and liturgy director liable in the wrongful death action brought by the spouse of the woman who died?

5. A pastor puts this notice in the bulletin: "Painters needed for parish clean-up day, Saturday June 9." Harry Painter shows up on that day. The parish hall needs a fresh coat of paint, so Harry proceeds to lay down drop cloths and go to work. There are many people around working in various areas. He asks Mrs. Organizer, "What color?" She responds, "White on the walls." He paints the entire day and completes the room. On Monday, the pastor finds a bill from "Harry Painter, Inc." on his desk for $1,500 for painting the parish hall, paint and labor included. Does the pastor owe the money?

6. A parishioner calls his friend and tells him he is in some business trouble and is anticipating arrest. He asks his friend, who is a priest, to communicate some information to a third person—a mutual friend from high school and a business associate—in order to evaluate his options. The priest complies with the request. In addition to being the parish priest he is also his friend's informal spiritual director/counselor.

    The parishioner becomes the defendant in a criminal lawsuit involving white-collar crime. The priest is subpoenaed as a witness against the parishioner. The parishioner's attorney claims the communication was privileged. Will the priest be forced to testify as to the contents of the phone call?

Answers:

1. *Unconstitutional.* The court ruled this a violation of the free exercise clause of the U.S. Constitution. Although the district attorney had a warrant to tape all conversations, priest-penitent confidentiality must be observed as a constitutional right and statutory right (Mockaitis v. Harcleroad, 1997).

2. *Yes.* The use of the Church as a podium to promote a candidate for election is not affected by who pays. (See: *"Political Activity Guidelines for Catholic Organizations,"* Office of General Counsel, USCCB, March 15, 2004.)

3. *The diocese.* The pastor did not have authority to enter into a lease agreement on behalf of the diocese. The bishop is required to ratify contracts for the alienation of property by special act of the state legislature that incorporated the parish and by canon law. Since he did not, the lease is null and void. Because everyone is legally required to know the law, the diocese cannot use ignorance on the part of the pastor as an excuse. The court ruled that the tenant paid reasonable rent and that the diocese is not entitled to additional amounts from the tenant. It is entitled to the nullification of the lease and eviction because the pastor did not have authority to enter into the contract. The diocese is liable for the taxes as the property was not used "for religious purposes." (*Diocese of Buffalo v. McCarthy*, 1983. See also *Soho Center for Arts & Education v. The Church of St. Anthony of Padua*, 1989.)

4a. *No.* The principal (pastor) is not liable for the acts of an agent (liturgy director) where the agent acts outside of the scope of his or her authority.

4b. *Yes.* Under the doctrine of *respondeat superior,* the parish can be sued for the negligence of its employees while carrying out the duties and responsibilities of their jobs.

5. *Possibly.* Under the law of contracts, even where there is a misunderstanding of the parties as to whether or not there is an agreement to perform, the courts may award the painter

the reasonable value of his service under the theory of "unjust enrichment."

6. *Yes.* The clergy-communicant or priest-penitent privilege is statutory in most cases. Disclosure to a third party will void the privilege unless it is in furtherance of the communication. The communication must have been made with the purpose of seeking religious counsel, advice, solace, absolution, or ministration within the context of a confidential relationship recognized by the law.

BIBLIOGRAPHY

Gagliano, Esq., Joseph. "Proposed Diocesan Guidelines on Copyright Concerns." 2009, unpublished, used with permission.

Harrington, Edward F. "The Metaphorical Wall." *America,* January 17, 2005.

Hubbard, Howerd J. "Charity and Justice within the Gospel and the Church's Social Teaching," *Vincentian Chair of Social Justice Presentations.* New York, 1998. http://www.vincenter.org/98/Hubbard/html.

Ingram, Richard T. *Ten Basic Responsibilities of Nonprofit Boards.* Washington DC: BoardSource, 2003.

Levy, Jamie D. *Handbook on Being a Board Member.* JD Levy & Associates, 2008.

Levy, Jamie D. *Philanthropic Sustainability.* JD Levy & Associates, 2008.

McKenna, Kevin E. *A Concise Guide to Canon Law.* Notre Dame, IN: Ave Maria Press, 2000.

———. *A Concise Guide to Your Rights in the Catholic Church.* Notre Dame, IN: Ave Maria Press, 2000.

National Catholic Bioethics Center. "A Catholic Guide to End-of-life Decisions: An Explanation of Church Teaching on Advance Directives, Euthanasia, and Physician Assisted Suicide." www.ncbcenter.org/eol.asp.

New York State Office of the Attorney General. www.oag.state.ny.us/bureaus/charities/guides_advice.html.

Oleck, Howard L. *Nonprofit Corporations Organizations & Associations Fifth Edition.* NJ: Prentice Hall, 1998. Cumulative Supplement, NJ: Prentice Hall, 1993.

Staff of Committee on Nonprofit Corporations, American Bar Association, George W. Overton, and Jeannie Carmedelle Frey, eds. *Guidebook for Directors of Nonprofit Corporations.* 2nd ed. Chicago: American Bar Association, 2002.

———. *The Principles Workbook: Steering Your Board Toward Good Governance and Ethical Practice.* Independent Sector and BoardSource, 2009.

USCCB. *Stewardship: A Disciple's Response* 10th Anniversary Edition. Washington DC, 2002.

CHAPTER 12

Stewardship:
Financial Control and Accountability

James W. Thompson, EdD, CPA

Prepare a full account of your stewardship.
> —Luke 16:2

Now it is of course required of stewards that they be found trustworthy.
> —1 Corinthians 4:2

Key Concepts

1. To fulfill their stewardship responsibilities, Church managers must be familiar with the vocabulary and functions of accounting, audits, and budgeting.

2. Financial wrongdoing in faith-based ministries causes "reputational risk" with far-reaching implications for the ministry.

3. The budget is a moral as well as a financial document as it reveals the values and priorities of the organization.

4. The principal financial statements of an organization are the balance sheet, the statement of activities (operations), and the statement of cash flow.

5. Internal control systems are a means to safeguard the assets and support the operation of the organization. They must be a major focus in both the profit and nonprofit arenas.

6. Church managers hold the responsibility for identification, implementation, and validation of internal control systems.

7. "Prevention" by policy and procedure is the key to responsible and accountable financial stewardship.

8. The processing of collections offers a good test of internal controls, the principles of which can be applied to other areas of parish or agency management.

Introduction

When a Church administrator talks with an accountant or financial advisor, the administrator frequently hears unfamiliar terms and concepts that are not easily grasped. Despite the specific and sometimes unfamiliar vocabulary, managers—whether they are in a religious or secular setting—must be financially literate to be effective stewards and to make ongoing use of the information accountants and others provide. Furthermore, Church managers must understand the use of internal control systems in a religious setting because a lack of proper controls, both financial and operational, can cause the loss of valuable assets and harm the reputation and credibility of the Church itself. These two topics as well as budgets are presented here as foundational to effective management.

Financial Reports and Systems

The reports and systems required in a nonprofit organization are closely related to those found in a for-profit business. Two basic questions in both organizations are: "Can this expenditure be justified?" and "How does it advance the mission of the organization?" This approach of controlling expenditures, along with developing assets, is the foundation for financial success. Effective and efficient financial systems are foundational for viability and are the vehicles for stewardship. As the United States Conference of Catholic Bishops in *Stewardship: A Disciple's Response* states, "Sound business practice is a fundamental of good stewardship, and stewardship as it relates to Church finances must include the most stringent ethical, legal, and fiscal standards."

It may seem to some that a parish, religious order, or service provider could function if someone would add up the collections, contributions, and other revenues, and deposit them in the local bank. This same person could collect the bills and write the checks to pay the expenses. The bank would send a month-end statement and, based on the balance indicated, the reader would know the amount of money available. After all, logic would seem to say, a parish, homeless shelter, or even a religious order is not General Motors, so why must we go to all the trouble and expense of preparing a full set of reports and implementing a sophisticated system of internal controls?

As stated earlier, the answer is found in the need for accountability and transparency in all forms of religious organizations. Despite their higher purposes, religious organizations are, in fact, businesses responsible to internal and external bodies. Parishes, dioceses, service agencies, and orders of priests, brothers, and sisters are now held to a level of accountability never before found in the Church. The pastor or bishop no longer finds that he must report only to his superiors. Today, financial councils and committees, required or recommended by canon law, are active in parishes, dioceses, educational institutions, and service agencies. Nonprofit boards generally have both a finance committee and an audit committee with separate memberships that each require at least some "independent" members. Councils and boards are responsible to see that systems are in place to assure that necessary state and federal financial statements are filed accurately and in a timely fashion. Financial information and transparency are the order of the day, and it is a major responsibility of the pastors (parish CEOs), bishops (diocesan CEOs), treasurers of religious orders, and agency administrators to make sure the proper information is available, correct, and understandable. The practice of simply making deposits and reviewing the month-end bank balance may have worked in the past, but it is no longer adequate.

Financial Statements

It is helpful to begin with foundational vocabulary and a basic explanation of key financial documents. A glossary of terms and sample financial statements are appended to this chapter. The three basic financial documents are the balance sheet, statement of activities or operations, and the cash flow statement. These financial statements present the financial status and results of operations. A manager's financial literacy necessarily begins with an understanding of the information provided by these statements.

The Balance Sheet

The *balance sheet* shows where the organization is financially at a particular point in time. This tool is sometimes called a "statement of financial position" or, in the nonprofit world, a "statement of assets, liabilities, and fund balances (or net assets)." It is a snapshot taken at a very specific date. The balance sheet is commonly prepared at the end of the fiscal year. The end of the fiscal year does not have to be December 31 and often is not. An organization may designate June 30, or any other date, as the end of the fiscal year. Frequently, the state or the diocese determines this date. What is important, however, is that once this period is chosen, it will not be changed without a very substantial reason. In practical application this means that the organization may not use June 30 this year and September 30 the next year and yet another date the following. The consistency provides for comparability over a period of years and provides helpful annual trending information.

The balance sheet lists the organization's *assets* (the things of value that are owned), its *liabilities* (the amounts that are owed), and the organization's *fund balance* (the original investment, plus profits, less losses since inception). It is prepared in *liquidity* (assets readily available) format or rank—going from cash down through receivables, and then to tangible assets (land, buildings, and equipment).

In a similar fashion, liabilities are listed in two categories. First, the more current amounts due, including accounts payable (amounts due vendors and due to the government for taxes withheld from employees), are shown. Next, the noncurrent liabilities are presented (amounts due on building mortgages and on notes payable with due dates beyond one year).

Balance sheets must "balance." This means that the assets must equal the total of the liabilities plus the fund balance. The accountant may also speak of "debits" and "credits." In using these terms the accountant is saying that the balance sheet must balance and that debits and credits are the method that the accountant uses to enter data. The accountant must make sure that if one item (account) on the financial statements changes, a second account must also change. If these offsetting changes do not occur, the balance sheet will not be in balance.

The Statement of Activities

The second financial statement is the *statement of activities.* The business equivalent to the statement of activities is the *income statement,* but the terms are used interchangeably. This details the sources of the operating monies generated by the organization and the manner in which money was spent. As with balance sheets, the time period of an activity statement is extremely important. While a balance sheet identifies the status of the organization at one point in time, activity statements detail revenues and expenditures over a period of time. For example, if the balance sheet date was June 30, then the activity statement presents the reader with revenue and expense information from July 1 of last year through June 30 of this year.

The accounts (sources of revenue and expense) depend on the type of organization, but each organization has a listing (chart of accounts) that includes account number and category for all revenue and expenses. A parish would have revenue from weekly collections, capital campaigns, or other special sources (e.g. diocesan collections, school tuition, fundraising). Parish expenses would include salaries, payroll taxes, ordinary repairs, insurance, utilities, etc. Social service agencies generally have multiple public revenue streams and require more detailed charts to ensure appropriate records. It is necessary for presentation purposes to consolidate many smaller but related accounts to prevent presentation of too much detail. The same account consolidation process should also take place on the balance sheet.

There are some key indicators to focus on when reading the balance sheet and the activity statement. The cash balance on the balance sheet shows if there is money currently available to pay bills as they come due. The difference between the revenues and expenses on the activity statement is critical. Obviously, if revenues exceed expenditures year after year, the organization is becoming stronger fiscally. The opposite is also true. It is important to note here that the term "nonprofit," whether in the context of a religious organization or a public charity, does not mean the entity cannot make a profit. It indicates that a public service is the purpose of the organization or institution. For example, individuals, unlike shareholders in a for-profit, cannot gain financially from the corporation. Growth and survival mandate that revenues exceed expenses. While it is true that expenses may exceed revenues in some years, this situation, if not corrected, will eventually lead to a financial crisis in a faith-based organization just as it will in a business organization.

The Cash Flow Statement

Along with a balance sheet and a statement of activities (income statement), a *cash flow statement* is included as part of a complete package of financial documents. Notes to these financial statements are also required. The purpose of these notes is to detail the accounting procedures employed in preparing the statements.

Cash flow statements are divided into three components: cash flows from operations, cash flows from investing activities, and cash flows from financing activities. The purpose of the cash flow statement is to present information concerning the *sources* of cash and the *uses* of cash. An income statement is not a substitute for the cash flow statement. There are two reasons for this. First, when accountants prepare income statements (activity statements), they employ a procedure called "accrual" accounting. Essentially, an item flows through the income statement *when it is earned* (for a revenue item), or *when it is incurred* (for an expense). For instance, a donor may sign a pledge card to give a thousand dollars over five years. Under accrual accounting the full amount would be recorded as revenue in the period the pledge was made (assuming there were no conditions attached to the pledge), not when the cash is received, even though for various reasons the actual amount ultimately collected may not match the pledged amount.

The second reason that the cash flow statement differs from the income statement is that some sources and uses of cash do not arise from operations. For instance, money could be borrowed from a bank in order to construct a parish hall. The income statement would not grasp this transaction. However, the cash flow statement would present the money spent on the parish hall as an investing activity and the money borrowed as a financing activity.

The Three Sections of a Cash Flow Statement	
Cash Flow from Operations:	These amounts involve cash flows from the normal day-to-day operation of the not-for-profit organization. These are the cash effects of the items found on the income statement; for example, the amounts paid for salaries or expenses and amounts received from contributions.
Cash Flow Used in (i.e. a cash outflow) or Provided by (i.e. a cash inflow) Investing Activities	This category involves cash outflows for the purchases of assets such as equipment, construction, and investments. The opposite side of these transactions, for example, the proceeds received from the sale of these assets, are shown here as cash provided by investing activities.
Cash Flow Provided by (i.e. a cash inflow) or Used in (i.e. a cash outflow) Financing Activities	This category involves the cash received from borrowings. It includes cash received on mortgage loans to finance construction and short-term borrowings to meet payrolls. The opposite side of these transactions is reflected here also, that is, the repayment of the borrowings.

The Financial Team:
Bookkeepers, Accountants, and Independent Auditors

There are three distinct types of financial team members: book-keepers, accountants, and independent auditors.

Bookkeepers can be nondegreed persons who have special training or satisfactory experience in financial operations. Because this position sometimes includes other tasks, it is very important that internal controls are in place. These are discussed later in this chapter.

Accountants are individuals with either a bachelor's or master's degree in accountancy. Not all accountants are certified public accountants (see description below). If the parish or other religious organization requires the preparation of financial statements, a non-CPA with a baccalaureate accounting degree should be up to the task. This compilation of financial data in the form of financial statements is a permitted activity of a noncertified accountant. In many instances, for example, a parish loan from a local bank, these compilation statements are sufficient and adequate. However, they do not provide the level of assurance to the lender that reviewed or audited statements provide.

An *independent auditor* must be a certified public accountant (CPA) who has completed a required degree program, passed a rigorous licensing exam, and worked for a period of time performing certified audits under the supervision of a CPA. This individual has a license to practice accounting granted by the state and must complete mandatory continuing education courses each year. In addition, his or her accounting practice is subject to peer review by a different CPA firm.

A CPA license is required in order to perform a review or a certified audit of the financial statements. Certified financial statements present the highest level of assurance that the information presented in the financial statements and the footnotes fairly represents the financial position and results of operation of the audited organization. Although an organization's certified statements still may later be found to be in error or fraudulent (e.g., Enron), a certified statement is the highest assurance that the statements are free of error. Compared to a compilation done by a noncertified public accountant, certified statements (external independent audit) present greater assurance that the financial results may be relied on by users (Kelly and Anderson). A review conducted by a CPA falls in the middle of the range of level of assurance. Greater reliance may be placed on the review compared with a compilation, but less than a certification.

It is certainly advisable for all new administrators, especially pastors and agency CEOs, to insist that a certified independent audit be completed prior to accepting the assignment. Consider the following possibility if an audit is not completed: A pastor could function for one, two, or more years believing that his parish was on a sound financial footing. Then, a major past defalcation (an embezzlement; to *embezzle assets*: misuse something, especially money or property, that belongs to somebody else and is held in trust) could be discovered. It would be extremely difficult for him to escape blame for the fact that funds were missing and prove that all this occurred years ago. It is better to incur the costs of a thorough audit than to be subject to the possibility of suspicion and even scandal. Some dioceses have this audit requirement in place now, and many agency boards recommend an audit take place at the time of a change in leadership. Because of expense, smaller agencies sometimes avoid a certified audit, but some type of external review is essential.

Internal Control Systems

While financial statements are the means that organizations employ to present financial information resulting from past transactions and events, internal controls safeguard an organization's assets and integrity. They are as integral to effective accounting as financial statements are to the organization's planning and operations. Simply stated, internal control deals with safeguarding assets, both plant assets (the buildings and equipment) and monetary assets (cash and investments). A more formal defini-tion would identify internal controls as a system of policies and procedures that protects the assets of an organization, creates reliable financial reporting, promotes compliance with laws and regulations, and achieves effective and efficient operations. These systems of control are not only related to accounting and reporting, but they also relate to the organization's communication processes, internally and externally. Internal control procedures are required in a well-run organization (whether for-profit or nonprofit) in each of the following areas.

Control Activities

- Handling funds received and expended by the organization
- Preparing appropriate and timely financial reporting to board members and officers
- Conducting the annual audit of the organization's financial statements
- Evaluating staff and programs
- Maintaining inventory records of real and personal property and their whereabouts
- Implementing personnel and conflicts of interest policies

Internal control is not just about preventing fraud, as important as that is. Internal control goes to the entire day-to-day operation and performance of the parish, diocese, school, or social service agency. The key to an effective system is to engage honest, capable employees and to employ commonsense procedures.

Control and Church Collections

A review of the more obvious areas in which internal control failures occur is instructive. Organizing and controlling parish collections, a major source of revenue, is a major internal control problem area (USCCB). The concepts involved in controlling the collection provide a model for thinking about all control areas in religious organizations. It is helpful to tackle the cash collection problem by stating in the extreme what we do not want. For example, the parish does not want to have one person taking up the Sunday collection, counting it, making out the bank deposit slip, taking the deposit to the bank, recording the contributions to the individual parishioner records, recording the receipt in the cash receipts book, posting the receipts total to the parish general ledger, receiving the monthly bank statement from the bank, and then reconciling the bank statement. This situation would be an internal control nightmare.

What *is* necessary in order to institute an internal control system is to separate each step of the process and then divide and rotate duties (USCCB 10). For example, parish internal control systems need to be established for each institutional process such as in the following nonexhaustive listing:

- Sunday Mass collection
- Payroll
- Capital expenditure authorizations
- Establishing bank accounts, including determining which individuals are authorized signatures, the number of signatures required on a check, and the dollar thresholds for signature
- Accounts payable processing
- Use of parish or agency credit cards
- Control of equipment
- Use of cars
- Investment of parish funds

To demonstrate how an internal control system might operate, the following table presents a process for a parish's Sunday collection—its most-likely internal control nightmare.

Internal Control of the Sunday Parish Collection
(Available for free download at avemariapress.com)

- Have the collection taken by parish volunteers. Have the mass assignments of the volunteers rotated often. Be especially vigilant when assigning collection staff to choir lofts and any area where the collector is out of view.

- Encourage the use of collection envelopes and checks payable to the parish. Possibly institute an alternative procedure of a weekly electronic debit to a donor's checking account or credit card. Anything that can be done to minimize the collection of cash aids in the internal control process.

- Have the collection taken to the sacristy by two or more of the volunteers. NEVER LEAVE ONE PERSON ALONE WITH THE COLLECTION. (This procedure is true even if we are talking about clergy).

- Have teams of counters open the collection envelopes and count these gifts. Assign the counting of the cash not received in envelopes to a second counting team.

- If an amount on an envelope does not agree with the amount inside, call for a supervisor to review, change the envelope, and notify the parishioner.

- Have a second team re-count the cash collection, prepare the deposit slip, and make note of the total. If there is a discrepancy in the total, have the two teams re-count until they are in agreement. Then have the two teams sign off on the total.

- Have a separate deposit prepared for the checks received. During this procedure review the checks to verify that they are properly prepared (made payable to the church, signed, etc.).

- Have the deposits brought to the bank by a third team.

- If the collection is stored in a safe prior to deposit, purchase a safe that requires the involvement of at least two individuals for the locks to open.

- In the parish office have a staff member enter the deposit total in the cash receipts journal, and compare the deposit ticket with the amount provided by the count team.

- Have a different staff member enter the individual contributions to the parishioner's contribution record book, and have this amount totaled.

- Have a third staff member reconcile the total posted from the individual record to the amounts on the Sunday envelopes.

- At month's end have the bank statement reconciled by someone not involved in posting the general ledger or any of the prior procedures.

- Require annual vacations for each of the individuals involved, including volunteers and clergy.

- Finally, regularly re-assign all tasks listed.

Many of the recording procedures may be automated, e.g., maintaining parishioner contribution records or posting ledgers, but the use of information technology (IT) does not eliminate the use of controls or the procedures outlined above. The use of IT simply creates changes in the procedures for entering and proofing of the data.

Stewardship and Reputational Risk

Based on the importance of internal controls, it is instructive to think about financial fraud and its impact on the reputation of the Church and the harm that can be caused by failure to be vigilant. The cases we are about to present (especially those involving fraudulent activity by members of the clergy) not only harm the reputation of the local parish and diocese but also undermine the trust many have in the Church as a worldwide institution. It is not prudent to assume that assets (cash, real estate, equipment, etc.) are safe when entrusted to a single person, not even a priest (Goodstein and Strom).

The *New York Times* recently carried the headline "Priest's Troubles Stun Connecticut Church: A Resignation Amid Allegations of Financial Wrongdoing." According to the *Times* article, the situation involves an allegation "that Father had been taking money from the collection plate and charging expenses to the parish credit cards totaling at least $200,000" (Stowe B-7). These expenses included $200 dinner tabs at restaurants in New York, Philadelphia, and Fort Lauderdale, along with airline tickets, limousine rides, cruises, and a $2,600 Cartier ring (Stowe). As the case unfolded and auditors were brought in to review the parish records, the amount of the fraud grew to $1,400,000. The alleged theft involved charges to parish credit cards for personal items in the amount of $829,000 and $515,000 withdrawn from parish accounts in cash or checks made payable to the pastor (Cowan, "Auditors"). The priest was eventually sent to prison for a term of thirty-seven months. However, the parish was able to recoup only between $250,000 and $300,000 (Cowan, "37-Month"), and trust suffered great damage. Subsequently, state legislation designed to wrest all financial involvement from pastors was proposed but then rescinded.

Another example shows the importance of a pastor or CEO certifying that an auditor has had access to all accounts. As part of an audit, "a priest was required to disclose all bank accounts in the parish's name. He allegedly had a previously undisclosed bank account at a local bank in the name of the parish. According to the prosecutor, when the account was discovered and reviewed, it was found that a great deal of personal expenses were paid out of that account. The prosecutor said the account was unknown to the parish bookkeeper" (Whyte 2).

While sadly the list could go on, only two more cases will be described here. The first case involved the theft of $360,000 from a parish. This was accomplished by the pastor setting up a charity account at his parish and then withdrawing more than the amount authorized by the finance committee (Wright). The second situation involved a set of altered accounting ledger books. In this case the *New York Times* report reads as follows: "The accountants wanted to see the books. . . . They immediately became concerned. First they saw a smudge on a ledger, underneath a number showing the total weekly collections from Mass. Then they saw another. Then more. All through one set of books they found eraser marks beneath new numbers, the work of an apparently determined but naïve hand. In fact, as much as $1,500 a week was unaccounted for" (Chivers). This specific fraud presented additional problems as well. An additional $100,000 had been taken from a parish mutual fund, and $2,000,000 had passed through an unauthorized parish checking account (Chivers).

Of course, this is not to say that pastors are the only individuals who may give into temptation. Recent examples have included bishops as well as lay staff members. A bishop was alleged to have covered up the theft of millions of parish money by a priest. A staff person at a Catholic Charities agency who had responsibility for dispersing checks for bill payments and staff salaries, among other responsibilities, embezzled significant amounts over an extended period (Hartocollis).

Internal Controls and the Sarbanes-Oxley Act

The importance of internal control in organizations received increased attention during the beginning years of the twenty-first century due to the scandalous financial frauds that occurred within several major U.S. companies. At the beginning of this century, series of imprudent, if not blatantly dishonest, practices caused the demise of several corporations and created global financial chaos. We have all heard the names Enron, WorldCom, Health South, Adelphia, AIG, and Lehman Brothers. Each of these cases— a number of them involving actual fraud—had a failure of the internal control system at its root cause. In the two most egregious cases, Enron and WorldCom, the failures took place because senior management overrode the control procedures. In response to these failures Congress mandated many changes in the way companies operate and the manner in which boards govern.

The Sarbanes-Oxley Act regulates how public companies are to function. The writers of the Sarbanes-Oxley Act spent many hours in planning and discussing the methods for improving internal controls and preventing fraud, and it is reasonable and prudent (although not required) to also apply these rules to the world of religious and nonprofit entities where appropriate. These rules were designed for large corporations, and some of the procedures may not be appropriate in a parish setting or small service agency where there are few paid staff and no trained fiscal managers. However, the principles remain relevant and prudent. With this constraint in mind, the list of the Sarbanes-Oxley rules that may be applied in establishing the internal control procedures in a nonprofit setting are as follows (Savich):

- Audit committees must consist solely of independent directors (persons not involved in internal operations and who have no conflicts of interest) and at least one financial expert.

- Chief executive officers (CEOs) and chief financial officers (CFOs) must certify that their financial statements fairly present the financial condition and results of their company. In a parish this responsibility would fall on the pastor, and in a service agency, on the chief administrator or financial officer.

- CEOs and CFOs must certify that they have an operational system of internal controls over financial reporting.

- A code of ethics for the executive officers and senior financial officers must be in place.

- Outside auditors must attest to and report on management's evaluation of the strength of the internal controls.

- No loans are permitted to executive officers or directors.

- There must be protections established for "whistle blowers."

The Budget as an Internal Control Mechanism

A budget may also be thought of as an internal control mechanism in that it provides future projection amounts that, when compared to actual results, highlight situations needing analysis and/or remediation. Beyond its internal control benefits, a budget provides an organization with a means to plan for the future. The budget is the road map for achieving goals. It is also a statement of an organization's value system and priorities. Budgeting allows for a systematic response to changing conditions and fidelity to mission.

As the size of the organization grows, the budget plan must, of course, become more formalized. That is, the budget process for a Catholic high school with an excess of one thousand students would be expected to be more formal than a budget for a parish outreach program that provides clothes and food in a poor neighborhood. Large organizations also require a strategic plan that sets overall goals and objectives for the organization. The strategic plan leads to long-range planning. An integral part of long-range planning is the production of forecasted financial statements for five- and ten-year periods. Obviously, the longer the range of the period covered by the forecasted statements, the less dependable they become.

Budgets should not be considered as a limit on spending. Instead, the budget should be viewed as a means to plan for the future and to assist in controlling operations by identifying deviations from the future plan. In this way the budget becomes part of the internal control process. Unfortunately, many times accountants who work with budgets become too concerned with the numbers. The better approach when preparing a budget is to have the employees who will be affected by the budget involved in its preparation. For instance, in a parish with an elementary school it is critical that the school principal understand the budget and have input in developing it. By operating in this fashion, the managers and employees who are involved in the budget process will feel more a part of the management of resources than if a budget were imposed on them. The result of the budget process is more likely to be positive and realistic, and the results more satisfactory.

Master Budget

The master budget is the analysis of the first year of the long-range plan. A nonprofit should think of its master budget as comprising at least four budgeted financial statements:

1. budgeted income statement

2. budgeted balance sheet

3. cash budget

4. capital budget

These four budget areas should be condensed into a fully integrated financial package for the organization. (Refer to the appended sample financial statements.) If these were budgeted statements based on projections for the next fiscal year, the package fits together as a coordinated financial projection. That is, the Statement of Activities (the income statement) should be projected out for the next year, and this projection should be tied into the budgeted balance sheet for the end of the following year. In our sample financial statements included in the appendix, this means that the $600,000 of "Unrestricted Net Assets" at the end of the year on the activity statement would agree with the $600,000 of "Unrestricted Net Assets" on the year-end statement of financial position (the balance sheet). Likewise, the budgeted cash flow statement for the year should relate the beginning cash balance on the opening balance sheet to the cash balance on the ending balance sheet. In other words, the ending cash balance of $1,100,000 on the year-end balance sheet is the same number found on the budgeted cash flow statement. This $1,100,000 of cash is the result of adding the cash increase for the year of $665,000 to the beginning balance of cash $435,000, as shown on the cash flow statement.

Additionally, a capital expenditure budget should be an element of the financial package. It should project the acquisitions of buildings and equipment, including major repairs to existing structures (e.g., the installation of a new heating or cooling system, purchase of additional land/building, new organ, etc.). On the financing side, the capital budget should include dollar amounts of borrowings that will be needed to finance the major projects, as well as revenues to be derived from capital campaigns. This budget should relate to the budgeted cash flow statement (in the categories of investing and financing activities) and also to the increase (or decrease) in land, buildings, equipment mortgages payable, and notes payable accounts on the budgeted balance sheet.

Conclusion

As explained in the introduction, this chapter is designed to assist administrators of religious organizations in two areas. The first is to give readers a basic understanding of accounting expertise and accounting terminology. The second purpose is to have administrators think about internal control and the related areas of fraud that are most frequently found in religious organizations. This includes viewing the budget as a means of such control.

The Catholic Church, or for that matter any nonprofit organization, cannot deliver its programs and care for its constituencies without a steady flow of financial resources, which come principally from donors. Donor faith in the organization's financial management and the controls that are in place is essential for contributions to continue. If a parish in one diocese is under media scrutiny for financial malfeasance, parishioner contributions in dioceses all over the country may be affected. It is only natural that local persons wonder how their contributions are protected and used. It is not an overstatement to say that financial support in each individual parish or Church agency is dependent on the controls found in every parish. The chain of parishioner support is only as strong as its weakest link. It is imperative then for the future well-being of the Church for pastors, bishops, and school and agency administrators to increase their financial literacy and to spend time thinking and talking to their advisors and colleagues about stewardship. Open communication and transparent reporting about financial matters instills confidence and generates continuing support.

Exercises

Read the following statements and indicate if you think the statement is *true* or *false*. The correct responses follow.

1. A balance sheet shows the results of the parish operations during the year.

2. In order to locate a parish's cash balance, one would refer to the balance sheet.

3. The total of assets on the balance sheet represents the amount that would be realized if the organization was liquidated.

4. It is permissible, as an internal control procedure, to allow the employee preparing the payroll to sign the payroll checks.

5. The excess of revenues over expenses on the activity statement will equal the amount of increase in cash on the balance sheet.

6. In designing a budget, the most important consideration is to control spending.

Answers:

1. *False.* The results of operations are identified on the statement of activities.

2. *True.* The cash balance is the first account listed as an asset on the balance sheet.

3. *False.* The balance sheet contains a mix of accounts included by different valuation bases. For example, cash is the current amount available for paying bills, but buildings are recorded at original purchase price less the total depreciation recorded since the building was purchased, not what would be received by selling the building.

4. *False.* Internal control systems are designed to protect assets. Cash is the most liquid asset and "dummy" employees may be entered into the system. The person preparing the payroll could enter the names of relatives and friends and sign payroll checks made to these friends and relatives.

5. *False.* The excess of revenues over expenses on the activity statement becomes the increase in the fund balance on the balance sheet. The change in cash is related to many factors not found on the activity statement. For example, the purchase of a building or allowing the amount of accounts payable to increase will change the cash on the balance sheet (i.e., if as

an individual you can stop paying your bills, your checking account balance will increase.)

6. *False.* The most important use of a budget is as a planning device. Budgets are best prepared when the individuals who will be affected are included in the planning process.

BIBLIOGRAPHY

Chivers, C. J., and Sarah Kershaw. "A Hole in the Collection Plate; From Smudge on Ledger to Embezzlement Inquiry." *New York Times,* October 6, 2000, Section B.

Cowan, Alison Leigh. "Bishop Offers Apology Amid Inquiry on Funds." *New York Times,* May 22, 2006, Section B.

———. "A Private Eye and the Case of a High-Living Priest." *New York Times,* May 25, 2006, Section B.

———. "Priest Spent as Diocese Grew Wary of Expenses." *New York Times,* May 29, 2006, Section B.

———. "Before the Downfall of a Connecticut Priest, A Taste of the Good life." *New York Times,* July 9, 2006.

———. "Auditors Say Priest Took $1.4 Million Before Ouster." *New York Times,* July 29, 2006, Section B.

———. "Audit Reveals Priest's Account of Spending." *New York Times,* July 30, 2006.

———. "A Whistle-Blower in a Scandal at a Church Decides to Resign." *New York Times,* August 11, 2006, Section B.

———. "37-Month Sentence for Priest Who Defrauded Parish." *New York Times,* December 5, 2007, Section B.

Cullinane, Bob. "Priest Indicted in $2M Theft." *Asbury Park Press,* June 7, 2005.

Goodstein, Laurie, and Stephanie Strom. "Survey Finds Embezzlement in Many Catholic Dioceses." *New York Times,* January 5, 2007, Section A.

Hartocollis, Anemona. "Monsignor Gets 4-Year Sentence for Large Thefts From His East Side Parish." *New York Times,* September 23, 2006, Section B.

Hawaii County Police Department. "Keaukaha Church Theft 10-30-03." Media release. October 30, 2003. www.Hawaiipolice.com/archives/archive2003/oct03/church_theft_10-3-03.htm.

Kelly, Claudia L., and Susan Anderson. "Advising Nonprofit Organizations: The CPA'S Role in Governance, Accountability and Transparency." *The CPA Journal,* August, 2006: 20–26.

Modrys, Walter F. "A Professional Approach to Parish Finances: Pastor as Financial Leader." *Church,* Summer 2006.

Nonprofit Financial and Accounting Manual. Fort Worth, TX: Practitioners Publishing Company, 2005.

Savich, Richard S. "Cherry Picking Sarbanes-Oxley: Provisions That Deserve a Second Look." *The Journal of Accountancy,* June, 2006: 71–74.

Stowe, Stacey. "Priest's Troubles Stun Connecticut Church." *New York Times,* May 19, 2006, Section B.

United States Conference of Catholic Bishops. "Diocesan Internal Controls: A Framework." Publication 5-056, 1995. www.USCCB.org/finance/internal.htm.

Whyte, Layli. "Hughes Pleads Guilty to Theft, Tax Fraud: State Seeks Five-Year Prison Term for Ex-pastor of Holy Cross Church." *Hub* (Red Bank, NJ), May 11, 2006.

Wright, Peggy. "Ex-Randolph Priest Admits He Stole Funds: Pleads Guilty to $360,000 Theft From Resurrection Parish." *Daily Record* (Morris County, NJ), October 29, 2005.

United States Conference of Catholic Bishops. *Stewardship: A Disciple's Response.* Tenth Anniversary Edition, 2002.

Glossary of Accounting Terminology

Accounting	the process of identifying, measuring, classifying, summarizing, and communicating information about economic entities that is primarily quantitative and useful for decision makers
Accounting Equation	the equation that presents the financial position of a company (Assets = Liabilities plus Fund Balance)
Accrual Accounting	the amount of revenues, expenses, and net income measured as incurred (expenses) or earned (revenues), not when cash inflows and outflows occur
Accounts Payable	amounts that will be paid in a short period of time (one to two months) and are the result of the purchase of goods or services on credit

Activity Statement	reports revenues, expenses, gains, and losses for the period. Revenues and expenses are determined by applying the accrual basis of accounting
Assets	the balance sheet list of items owned by the company
Audit	the process of gathering information about an entity in order to form an opinion on the fairness of its financial statements
Balance Sheet	(the Statement of Financial Position) – lists all the company's items of value (assets) and claims against those assets (liabilities and fund balances)
Books	the company's formal accounting records including journals and ledgers (Most often they are maintained on a computer employing a software package designed for this purpose.)
Budget	a plan that serves as a guide for future action and as a standard against which to measure future performance
Capital	money or other resources required to operate an enterprise—obtained by borrowing or by bringing additional owner investment into the business

Corporation	a legal entity viewed under the law as an artificial person having many of the rights and obligations of a real person
Contributions	an unconditional promise to transfer cash or other items of value, recorded at fair value in the period received by the not-for-profit
Depreciation	the portion of the cost of equipment or a building allocated as expense each period
Expenses	the costs a firm incurs in its day-to-day operations
Financial Statements	the end result of the accounting process; In a not-for-profit there are three financial statements: 1. The Statement of Financial Position (Balance Sheet) 2. The Statement of Activities and Changes in Fund Balance 3. The Statement of Cash Flows
Fund Balance	the amount remaining after the liabilities are subtracted from the assets of a not-for-profit (The fund balance represents the excess of revenues over expenses since the organization's inception.)
Fund Accounting	Used by not-for-profit and governmental entities for their accounting, fund accounting designates resources for a particular purpose. Separate funds are maintained to ensure that resources are used for a specific purpose.

Liabilities	the claims against the company's assets arising from its obligations and debts
Internal Control	the system of accounting safeguards that is concerned with protecting the control company's assets and producing accurate financial statements
Not-for-Profit Organizations	engage in activities that are viewed as benefiting society, including, religious, educational, and philanthropic work – funding usually comes from voluntary donations
Pledge Receivable	Pledges of support recognize unconditional promises to give as both a receivable and contribution in the period promised. The amount not yet collected at year end is reflected as a "Pledge Receivable."
Statement of Cash Flows	lists the types and amounts of cash received (inflows) and paid out (outflows) by an organization during a period of time
Surplus	an out-of-date term that is often used in financial discussions and presentations; refers to the excess of revenues over expenses for the current period (or for the cumulative excess since the date of inception of the organization)

Sample Parish Financial Statements

Statement of Financial Position
June 30, 20XX

Assets

Current Assets:

Cash and Cash Equivalents	$1,100,000
Investments in Marketable Securities	50,000
Total Current Assets	1,150,000

Non-Current Assets:

Land	350,000
Land Improvements (net of depreciation)	1,500,000
Buildings (net of depreciation)	2,500,000
Furniture and Equipment (net of depreciation)	350,000
Vehicles (net of depreciation)	100,000
Construction in Progress	400,000
Total Non-Current Assets	5,200,000
Other Assets	50,000
Total Assets	$6,400,000

Liabilities and Net Assets

Current Liabilities:

Accounts Payable	$25,000
Diocesan assessment payable	50,000
Payroll taxes payable	25,000
Current portion of Long-Term Notes payable	100,000
Total Current Liabilities	200,000

Non-Current Liabilities

Long-Term Note Payable, net of Current Portion	500,000
Mortgage Payable	2,000,000
Total Non-Current Liabilities	2,500,000
Total Liabilities	2,700,000

Net Assets

Unrestricted	600,000
Temporarily Restricted	1,000,000
Permanently Restricted	2,100,000
Total Net Assets	3,700,000
Total Liabilities and Net Assets	$6,400,000

Statement of Activities
For the year ended June 30, 20XX

Unrestricted Revenues:

Contributions	$1,500,000
Special Ministries Contributions	200,000
Tuition	1,000,000
Fundraising Special Events	400,000
Investment Revenue	5,000
Miscellaneous	25,000
Total Unrestricted Revenue	3,130,000

Expenses:

Salaries	1,500,000
Payroll Taxes	200,000
Pension Contribution	150,000
Repairs and Maintenance	80,000
Depreciation	125,000
Utilities	75,000
Insurance	75,000
Office Supplies	25,000
Fundraising Costs of Special Events	300,000
Professional Services	40,000
Diocesan assessments	250,000
Total Unrestricted Expenses	2,820,000

Changes In Temporarily Restricted Assets (e.g. Monies raised for capital expenditures disbursed this period)	50,000
Increase in net assets	360,000
Unrestricted Net Assets at the Beginning of the Year	240,000
Unrestricted Net Assets at the End of the Year	$600,000

Statement of Cash Flows
For the year ended June 30, 20XX

Cash Flows from Operating Activities

Increase in Unrestricted Net Assets	$360,000

Adjustments to reconcile increase in net
assets to net cash provided by (used in) operations

Depreciation	125,000
Decrease in Investments	5,000
Decrease in Receivables	2,500
Increase in Accounts Payable	7,500
Decrease in Diocese payable	(45,000)
Net Cash provided by (used in) operating activities	455,000

Cash Flows provided by (used in) Investing Activities

Purchase of Equipment and Furniture	(90,000)
Construction in Progress	(100,000)
Cash Flows used in Investing Activities	(190,000)

Cash Flows provided by (used in) Financing Activities

Proceeds from Note Payable	500,000
Repayment of Note Payable	(100,000)
Cash Flows provided by Financing Activities	400,000
Increase (decrease) in Cash and Cash Equivalents	665,000
Cash at the beginning of the year	435,000
Cash at the end of the year	$1,100,000

A Concise Guide to Catholic Church Management

Sample Chart of Accounts for a Catholic Parish

Receipts, Expenditures and Fund Balances		
Regular Receipts		
Account Number	**Name of Account**	**Explanation**
200	Sunday, Weekday, Holy Day & Monthly Collections	All receipts from collections taken up at various services in the parish.
201	Christmas & Easter Collections	Only those specific collections.
202	Prerequisites	Receipts the Church received for Baptism, Marriage and Funeral ceremonies.
203	Investment revenue	Funds received into the operating account from investments.
204	Catholic Charities	Special collection for this specific purpose.
Ordinary Expenditures		
301	Clergy Salaries / Stipends	Salaries for priests assigned to the parish as well as payments made to other priests for weekend work.
302	Stipend for Religious	For religious sisters and brothers working in the parish.
303	Lay Salaries	Salaries for lay employees.
304	Employers' Share of Social Security (FICA)	As required by IRS.
305	Priests' Retirement Plan	Payment amount billed by Archdiocese
306	Repairs and Maintenance	Repair of parish property and equipment and maintenance contracts
307	Utilities	Telephone, electric and heat
308	Professional Services	Cost of parish audit and legal fees
309	Diocesan Assessment	% of certain revenue accounts
Fund Balances		
701	Unrestricted Fund Balance	Accumulated Fund Balance from prior years
702	Restricted Capital Campaign Fund Balance	Balance of Parish Campaign Funds

Sample Chart of Accounts

Assets and Liabilities		
Assets		
Account Number	**Name of Account**	**Explanation**
401	Checking Account	Book (Ledger) balance of cash and cash equivalents
402	Savings Account	Book (Ledger) balance cash
403	Land	Cost of land purchased to construct church and rectory
404	Buildings	Cost of church and rectory
405	Furniture and Equipment	Cost of furniture and equipment purchase for parish use
Liabilities		
501	Accounts Payable	Amounts owed due to everyday costs (e.g. due from supplies purchases)
502	Diocesan Assessment Payable	Amounts remaining owed to the diocese
503	Mortgages Payable	Amounts owed to Diocese or other sources (e.g. Banks) arising from purchase of land, church or rectory or other parish plant

Contributing Authors

Larry W. Boone, PhD

A graduate of Lehigh University, Dr. Boone earned both his graduate degrees (MSIE and PhD) at the University of Pittsburgh. An associate professor in the Department of Management in the Tobin College of Business, Dr. Boone's primary research and teaching interests involve organization theory and behavior, creative thinking, strategic planning, and entrepreneurship. As director of the Executive-in-Residence Program, Dr. Boone supervises teams of students who work on strategic planning projects for various for-profit businesses and nonprofit organizations. He has consulted for Innodyne, Inc.; PPG Industries; Organization Design Consultants; several universities; and a variety of nonprofit groups, including the Roman Catholic Diocese of Rockville Centre. He also teaches in the Pastoral Formation Program of that diocese and has been involved with the Parish Management Programs since their inception.

Mary Ann Dantuono, JD

Prior to joining the Vincentian Center, Mrs. Dantuono served the Diocese of Rockville Centre as the director of public policy and legal affairs for Catholic Charities. Since 1996, she has held the position of associate director of the Vincentian Center for Church and Society. Additionally, she serves as an expert on women's issues for the Holy See Mission to the United Nations and holds membership on the boards of several human service organizations. For more than ten years Mrs. Dantuono served as a member of the Social Policy Committee of Catholic Charities USA, and from 1996 to 1999 as an advisor to the United States Conference of Catholic Bishops Committee on Women. From 1993 to 1996 she was a member of the New York State Catholic Conference Public Policy Committee. Mrs. Dantuono earned a Juris Doctor at St. John's University School of Law and a BA in communication arts at Fordham University.

Margaret John Kelly, D.C., PhD

Sister Kelly earned her undergraduate degree at St. Joseph College in Emmitsburg, Maryland, and her master's and doctoral degrees in English at St. John's University. She has held faculty and administrative positions at St. Joseph College, Mount St. Mary's University Laboure College in Boston, and St. John's University, where she now serves as executive director of the Vincentian Center for Church and Society. Sister Kelly has held leadership positions in her community, the Daughters of Charity, and in several professional organizations, and has also served on the boards of hospitals, health care systems, universities, social service agencies, Catholic Charities, and cultural centers. Sister Kelly has published and lectured extensively on communication, governance, leadership, religious formation, and Vincentian heritage. Pope John Paul II honored Sister Kelly for her service to the Church with the *Pro Ecclesia et Pontifice* medal.

Brenda Massetti, PhD

Dr. Massetti holds a PhD in information and management science from the Florida State University and an MBA from the University of South Florida. Dr. Massetti is currently associate professor of management in the Tobin College of Business at St. John's University. Over the past twenty years, she has taught a wide variety of management classes and has published research in a variety of scholarly journals, including *MIS Quarterly, Emergence, Complexity & Organization,* and the *Review of Business.* Her current research interest is in the area of social commerce.

James W. Thompson, EdD, CPA

Professor Thompson holds an EdD in financial administration in higher education through a joint degree program between the Teachers College and the Graduate School of Business at Columbia University. He is a licensed certified public accountant in the state of New York. Dr. Thompson, professor of accounting and taxation at St. John's University, is a chair of that department and has over twenty-five years of full-time experience as a teacher and researcher. He has authored four books, thirty-two articles in peer-reviewed journals, and two chapters in books, and he has edited a book of readings for the department's graduate capstone course. Professor Thompson has served as the controller of Marymount-Manhattan College, Mannes College of Music, and Malcolm King College, and as an independent auditor and consultant for corporations and nonprofit organizations. Since 1996 he has served on the finance board of a major religious community.